'This welcome and relevant book powerful
place of drama "at the heart of English" in
all experts in the field, consider the politica
of drama within English teaching drawing (...g theoretical framework
rooted in Vygotsky and grounded in everyday classroom pedagogies. The
book traces the complex relationship between drama and English over time,
analysing specific policy shifts which shaped perspectives about the role of
drama teaching within English. Then we move to the authors' theoretical
framing for the development of their "drama in English pedagogy".
Classrooms come to life as they share approaches and examples from their
own experience as teachers, teacher educators and researchers before closing
with a persuasive mandate for drama in English and its potential for creative,
joyful and intellectually stimulating classroom encounters between children
and the texts they read. This is a must-read book for all involved in English
teaching.'

Jo McIntyre, *Professor of Education, University of Nottingham*

'At a time when applications to study English at higher level are falling, and
students report their dissatisfaction with their experience of studying it, comes
this book to help teachers to show their students that literature is ultimately
about human experience and that drama as a pedagogy is about engaging
effectively with that experience to make it memorable and meaningful. This
helps to contextualise the problems we've encountered as a profession as
we've struggled to match the ideological demands of politicians with the very
human needs of our students. This book will help you to navigate that path
and find a mode of resistance.'

Debra Kidd, *Teacher and Author*

'There is no other book quite like this, to my knowledge: its breadth, depth
and intellectual rigour mark it out. Breadth: in its insistence on "an expanded
view of English, one that integrates English, drama and media". Depth: in its
profound understanding of the contribution drama can make to literacy and
learning, historically situated and grounded in long experience of classrooms.
Rigour: in its agile deployment of theory, and its bridge building between
dramatic play and engagement with literary narrative. It rings with the voices
of young people and teachers, and with the dramatic autobiographies of its
authors. Properly critical of a contemporary context which threatens the arts
in education, it also shows how the liberating outcomes of drama are not
antithetical to exam success. It should be required reading for all who aspire
to teach English, and to research it.'

Andrew Burn, *Professor of English, Drama and Media,*
University College London Institute of Education

DRAMA AT THE HEART OF ENGLISH

Drama at the Heart of English is unique in its exploration of drama's potential to revitalise English as a secondary school subject. It focuses specifically on the value and inclusive nature of educational drama practices in the reading of literary, dramatic and multimodal texts in the English classroom.

Examples from the authors' research show English teachers working in the drama-in-English mode with real learners as part of their everyday classroom activity. Challenging current curriculum and assessment constraints, the authors argue that drama-in-English pedagogy re-establishes English as a creative, imaginative and interactive subject. This book:

- offers a blend of theory and practice to demonstrate the powerful potential of drama-in-English
- proposes that drama is a uniquely sustainable form of learning in English when fully integrated into the daily work of classroom teachers
- highlights the intrinsic connection that exists between drama and the playful qualities of literary texts
- analyses landmark moments and key policy shifts that have shaped the development of the relationship between drama and English over time.

This resource is for all educators interested in and passionate about the field of English and Language Arts. It is a must-read for the international academic community of researchers, practitioners, teacher-educators and teachers of English, as well as student-teachers of English/Media/Drama.

Theo Bryer leads the English with Drama PGCE at UCL's Institute of Education and works on the MA English Education programme.

Maggie Pitfield is an experienced English and Drama teacher and the former Head of Educational Studies at Goldsmiths, University of London.

Jane Coles is a former Head of English and recently led the MA English Education programme at UCL's Institute of Education.

NATE

The National Association for the Teaching of English (NATE), founded in 1963, is the professional body for all teachers of English from primary to Post-16. Through its regions, committees and conferences, the association draws on the work of classroom practitioners, advisers, consultants, teacher trainers, academics and researchers to promote dynamic and progressive approaches to the subject by means of debate, training and publications. NATE is a charity reliant on membership subscriptions. If you teach English in any capacity, please visit **www.nate.org.uk** and consider joining NATE, so the association can continue its work and give teachers of English and the subject a strong voice nationally.

This series of books co-published with NATE reflects the organisation's dedication to promoting standards of excellence in the teaching of English, from early years through to university level. Titles in this series promote innovative and original ideas that have practical classroom outcomes and support teachers' own professional development.

Books in the NATE series include both pupil and classroom resources and academic research aimed at English teachers, students on PGCE/ITT courses and NQTs.

Titles in this series include:

Knowledge in English
Canon, Curriculum and Cultural Literacy
Velda Elliott

International Perspectives on English Teacher Development
From Initial Teacher Education to Highly Accomplished Professional
*Andy Goodwyn, Jacqueline Manuel, Rachel Roberts, Lisa Scherff,
Wayne Sawyer, Cal Durrant, and Don Zancanella*

Creativity in the English Curriculum
Historical Perspectives and Future Directions
Lorna Smith

Drama at the Heart of English
Transforming Practice in the Secondary Classroom
Theo Bryer, Maggie Pitfield and Jane Coles

For more information about this series, please visit: https://www.routledge.com/National-Association-for-the-Teaching-of-English-NATE/book-series/NATE

DRAMA AT THE HEART OF ENGLISH

Transforming Practice in the Secondary Classroom

Theo Bryer, Maggie Pitfield and Jane Coles

Routledge
Taylor & Francis Group

LONDON AND NEW YORK

Designed cover image: © Theo Bryer and © Getty Images

First published 2024
by Routledge
4 Park Square, Milton Park, Abingdon, Oxon OX14 4RN

and by Routledge
605 Third Avenue, New York, NY 10158

Routledge is an imprint of the Taylor & Francis Group, an informa business

British Library Cataloguing-in-Publication Data
A catalogue record for this book is available from the British Library

Library of Congress Cataloging-in-Publication Data
Names: Bryer, Theo, 1965– author. | Pitfield, Maggie, author. |
   Coles, Jane, author.
Title: Drama at the heart of English : transforming practice in the
   secondary classroom / Theo Bryer, Maggie Pitfield and Jane Coles.
Description: First edition. | New York : Routledge, 2024. |
   Series: National Association for the Teaching of English (NATE) |
   Includes bibliographical references and index.
Identifiers: LCCN 2023014205 (print) | LCCN 2023014206 (ebook) |
   ISBN 9781032269887 (hbk) | ISBN 9781032269870 (pbk) |
   ISBN 9781003290827 (ebk)
Subjects: LCSH: Drama in education. | Language arts (Secondary) |
   English language—Study and teaching (Secondary) |
   English literature—Study and teaching (Secondary)
Classification: LCC PN3171 .B79 2024 (print) | LCC PN3171 (ebook) |
   DDC 820.71/2—dc23/eng/20230621
LC record available at https://lccn.loc.gov/2023014205
LC ebook record available at https://lccn.loc.gov/2023014206

ISBN: 978-1-032-26988-7 (hbk)
ISBN: 978-1-032-26987-0 (pbk)
ISBN: 978-1-003-29082-7 (ebk)

DOI: 10.4324/9781003290827

Typeset in ITC Galliard Pro
by Apex CoVantage, LLC

CONTENTS

SERIES EDITOR FOREWORD

Recent titles in NATE's book series on the teaching of English – of which this volume is the latest – have shared a focus on fundamental concepts in English which are currently contested, and on crucial aspects of the subject which are currently in danger of marginalisation.

Velda Elliott's *Knowledge in English* (2021) explored a range of issues about the nature of the subject in the light of recent debates about the 'knowledge-rich' curriculum and the role of 'cultural capital' in relation to it. Lorna Smith's *Creativity in English* (2023) examined changing perceptions of creativity in the subject in the light of the apparent downgrading of the concept in recent manifestations of the curriculum. A future volume, currently at the writing stage, addresses the idea of 'personal growth' through English. It is anticipated that volumes on issues of race and diversity in English, on English as a socially and culturally responsive discipline and on media in English will follow.

These are now joined by this equally significant and timely addition to the series, *Drama at the Heart of English*, in which Theo Bryer, Maggie Pitfield and Jane Coles survey the history, theory and pedagogy of the integrated practice of drama-in-English, and argue for a renewal of its central role in the subject, at a time when its status in the curriculum has (along with aspects of creativity more broadly) been downgraded, and its practice as an integrated pedagogy has decreased substantially.

It is no coincidence that these significant surveys of contested aspects of curriculum and pedagogy have appeared at this time, against the background of increasingly neoliberal education policies which have begun to strip away diverse, critical-creative, student-centred approaches to English from classroom practice in favour of a set of relatively narrowly conceived, exam-oriented analytical routines which have in many cases reduced the expe-rience of the subject drastically for both students and teachers.

The commonalities between this book and the other volumes mentioned above extend, therefore, well beyond a focus on contested and/or marginal-ised aspects of English. In the foreword to *Creativity in English*, I wrote of Lorna Smith's vision of an English which 'places children's authentic voices and social relationships at its heart and sees them as creative agents in making meaning'. Such a vision is at the heart of all these books, but none more so than *this* one, concerned as it is particularly with the holistic engagement of students' imaginations, voices and bodies in meaningful learning in English through drama.

Bryer, Pitfield and Coles argue for a renewal of the longstanding tradition of drama as a central, integral strategy for English, as part of a broader practice of the development of student response to all kinds of texts and ideas through creative role-play, a mode that embraces physical drama, creative writing and media production of many types – all forms currently struggling to find ade-quate space in the curriculum. As the authors suggest, such creative role-play provides crucial opportunities for students' imaginative and critical faculties to be engaged and for their voices and ideas to be heard, supporting learning in English through the active construction of meaning.

Significantly, too, these forms of role-play are also the basis of all *literary* production: writers of fiction, non-fiction, poetry, drama, film, videogame and so on, all practise creative role-play, embodying character, voice, thought and situation and representing society in imaginative and critical ways. Indeed, dra-ma's focus on role-play as a way of understanding and responding to literary texts also echoes contemporary understandings of the *performative* nature of literature. As this book vividly demonstrates, *drama* is not the only literary form which is *dramatic*; all literature – from stories and poems to plays, films and videogames – is essentially dramatic, using characters and voices to perform narratives, shaping them in different media and using a variety of forms. Drama, then, is a singularly appropriate starting point for student response to literature.

As already suggested, the authors argue that such approaches to English also support the development of students' critical skills. Whilst there has always been a tension in English between the development of students' cre-ative and critical voices, between creative and critical responses, there has in the past perhaps been a more successful ecology in which the two are seen as interrelated, and nurtured simultaneously, in which students are seen as *creators* of texts as much as *critics* of texts, and in which readers are seen as co-constructors of meaning rather than passive recipients of knowledge. This book, then, provides a further powerful argument for a re-balancing of the English curriculum towards creativity, and a renewed understanding of English as a 'critical-creative' subject in which the *creative* is also *critical*, and the dichotomy between the two is dissolved.

Bryer, Pitfield and Coles's book comprehensively explores the particular contribution that drama can make in English, drawing fulsomely on accounts of classroom practice and research to illustrate and exemplify the ways that drama can, as they write, be 'fully integrated into the everyday practices and flow of the English lesson . . . as a sustainable and integral part of students' learning in English'.

Citing Harold Rosen's 1980 essay 'The Dramatic Mode' (Rosen 2017a), they also argue for drama as an *enjoyable* aspect of English which draws on our natural playfulness and our propensity for what Rosen calls 'dramatic behaviour'. Such behaviour, Rosen argues, is 'ordinary, pervasive and universal' (p. 315), 'intrinsic to everyday social behaviour' (p. 318), and at the same time 'available as a means of knowing and explaining our world' (p. 326). Our capacity for such 'spontaneous drama', he writes, may be seen in the way in which we dramatise experiences in our thoughts and in our everyday communications, often imitating the voices, movements and attitudes of others:

> The dramatic ends up in theatres but does not begin there . . . for as surely as we can all speak and move we can also imitate speech and movement. We can call upon this ability as a means of communicating and as a means of knowing. (p. 322)

Drama at the Heart of English authoritatively demonstrates how drama can be used powerfully in English – at the heart of the subject – in the ways that Rosen suggests: 'as a means of communicating and as a means of knowing', drawing on innate resources that are 'intrinsic to everyday social behaviour' and 'available as a means of knowing and explaining our world'.

Gary Snapper
Lecturer in English Education, University of Oxford

ACKNOWLEDGEMENTS

First and foremost, we owe a huge debt to all the teachers and learners we have been privileged to work with over our many years in education who have shaped our thinking immeasurably. Without them this book would, quite literally, have been impossible.

Special thanks to the intrepid English with Drama student-teachers (2021–22) who so readily got stuck in, trying out various drama-in-English approaches in school, and to all the other enthusiastic student-teachers who co-created with us on *Beowulf*, *Stone Cold* and many other texts.

Much work in education, whether teaching or researching, is collaborative. In particular, we thank our colleagues Anne Turvey and Gill Anderson who contributed to the sixth form *Hamlet* and *King Lear* workshops we write about; Rebecca Wilson and Michelle Cannon for their years of experimentation with digital media; and Andrew Burn for heading up the wonderfully creative *Beowulf* project. Finally, we remember Morlette Lindsay (1958–2016), friend, colleague and inspirational *Beowulf* collaborator.

We are grateful to Michael Rosen for kind permission to reprint his poem, reminding us all of the passion with which English teachers approach the teaching of our subject and what makes English memorable.

Special shout-out to Shaun Doherty who read through, and commented on, every chapter for us (almost) without complaint.

Last but not least, our long-suffering partners, Inigo, Jim and Shaun, who always recognised when we needed tea, coffee or on occasions something stronger, as the circumstances required.

PREFACE: A POEM BY MICHAEL ROSEN

What did they think they were doing
those English teachers
staying on after school
to put on plays?
I was an ant in a play about ants.
Then I was a servant
in Much Ado About Nothing.
Hours and hours rehearsing
in winter classrooms.
My father did it too,
bringing home the problem
of how to make fake blood for Julius Caesar's toga
and snakes for Cleopatra.
They got no money for it
these English teachers.
Sometimes headteachers were pleased
sometimes mildly irritated
that the hall was out of action
for their assemblies.
We left school.
They retired.
They're all gone:
Mr Jones, Mr Brown, my father.
There are one or two photos
blurred pictures of unbelievably young people
with too much make-up round the eyes;

some marked up play scripts,
the character's name underlined in red,
stage directions – 'move stage right'.
voice directions – 'urgent'.
Did they know that we would carry the memories
for decades?
60 years since 'Much Ado'.
Did they know that it'd be easier to remember
the lines and the Leichner make-up
than how to do simultaneous equations
and the correct order of the cities down the Rhine,
though I can be a red corpuscle
and describe my journey from the left ventricle
to my fingers and back
(it involves all four chambers of the heart).
Did they know that some of us
would do more and more and more
of things like saying words out loud
or writing words for others to say out loud
or just working with a few other enthusiastic people
to get something done.
Did they know that?
I once bumped into Mr Brown
on Russell Square Station.
He was in his 70s
I was in my 60s.
I had a lot to tell him.
He had a lot to tell me.
There wasn't time.
We said, 'Let's meet up'.
We didn't.
He died soon after.
He had an obituary in The Times
They asked me to add a bit.
I wanted to say that
those hours in the winter classroom
being an ant mattered then
mattered again and again
and still matter.
Well, they matter to me.
But did he know that?
Did he know that they would go on mattering?
And if he knew

where did he and Mr Jones and my father
learn that the kids in their plays
would go on thinking about
being ants and servants
for the rest of their lives?

A NOTE ABOUT TERMINOLOGY AND RESEARCH DATA

English is the name of our main secondary school subject. We use 'drama-in-English' to designate the specific form of integrated practice we describe in the book. Where we make reference to 'Drama', it is to denote the separate curriculum subject.

Many of our examples of drama-in-English practice come from our observation of learners in secondary English classrooms in and around London. In England and Wales, most secondary schools cater for learners from 11–16 or 11–18 years old, with the curriculum organised into Key Stage 3 (Years 7–9, corresponding to ages 11–14) and Key Stage 4 (Years 10–11). At the end of Year 11 (at the age of 16), students sit public examinations (General Certificate of Secondary Education, or GCSE) in a wide range of subjects (English is compulsory). Between the ages of 16 and 18, approximately 60% of the school population goes on to follow Advanced Level courses ('A' Levels) in a small number of selected subjects either in school 'sixth forms' or tertiary colleges, usually preparatory to university application.

In some instances we make reference to projects involving student-teachers undertaking a one-year Postgraduate Certificate in Education (PGCE) in English or English with Drama at three different universities in or close to London. The PGCE year is split between time in university and two substantial blocks of school-based placement.

Wherever we refer to classroom examples taken from our research, names of learners, teachers and schools have been appropriately anonymised for ethical reasons. In all cases, permissions were sought and consent obtained from participants in accordance with British Educational Research Association (BERA) ethical guidelines current at the time of conducting the various case studies.

1

INTRODUCTION

When you think back to your own school days, what kind of English lessons stand out in your memory? For everyone to whom we have posed this question it has prompted a very clear recollection, remarkably vivid even after many years. Here are our own answers to that question, formative moments from our personal and educational histories which we offer in the spirit of an 'origin story' for our joint commitment to drama within English, and as the germ of a rationale for writing this book.

> **Maggie:** I always liked English as a subject because I enjoyed writing stories, though not necessarily about the subjects set for 'composition' homework in my rather staid London suburban grammar school. I loved reading too, but again, not always the texts we were grinding through in class. Then one day near the start of the 'O' Level course, my new English teacher entered the classroom and unfurled a large painting, asking the class to look closely and discuss what we could see. So far, so unusual. Then he asked us each to select a character from the painting and write something about the scene from their perspective. There was puzzlement, surprise and no little excitement as we students set about the task: our first experience of writing-in-role! This was the same teacher who asked us to write a parody of Keats' *Ode on a Grecian Urn*, introducing us to the engaging prospect of re-creative activity in English. As if this wasn't enough, and departing from the school's tradition of staff-student productions of Gilbert and Sullivan operettas, this teacher scandalously selected Peter Terson's *Zigger Zagger* as the next school play and he cast me in a supporting role. At that moment my fate was sealed (in a good way) and I was on the path to 'A' Level English and later English and Drama at a college of education in the

DOI: 10.4324/9781003290827-1

north of England. I can honestly say that years of lecture-style English lessons have long disappeared from memory, but these experiences remain ever-fresh.

Theo: The few times that we did drama in English were the most memorable lessons for me, although they simply involved pushing back the desks to stand up and move around while we read out play texts. Otherwise my schooling in Birmingham involved two distinct types of drama. There were performances involving tedious rehearsals, inspired by the local amateur dramatics' scene, I think. I remember being told off for speeding though my lines as a narrator and not knowing how to slow down. There was another, far more enjoyable experience of running round the school hall in vest and knickers pretending to be a snowflake, probably inspired by local drama advisor Peter Slade's approach to Child Drama. It was only on my PGCE course that I became aware of drama's potential for cross-curricular learning. We did a particularly electrifying process drama based on *The Wild Man* (Crossley-Holland and Keeping), that involved exploring questions of power and oppression in the context of a story about a merman found in an 11th-century village. I played the priest and got quite concerned about the authenticity of the historical setting. I initially struggled to appreciate how our shared creation of the drama was structured around a series of questions that engendered a sense of community and helped to shape attitudes towards the strange intruder. I think of this as a pivotal moment in my learning about the significance of creating space for learners and accommodating a diversity of perspectives and ideas in developing a story together. Just like the trussed-up merman, I've been hooked ever since and monsters have continued to feature in many of my favourite schemes of work.

Jane: Even at a shiny new sixth form college, English lessons were largely more of the same from school: reading round the class, punctuated by teacher explication and a bit of desultory Q and A. Despite choosing English 'A' Level, I had always struggled to 'appreciate' Shakespeare in the way I assumed a true student of Literature should. To cap it all, I was feeling rather short-changed by what seemed to me to be my teacher's obscure and monumentally dull choice of play, *Richard II*. What radically transformed my opinion, however, was the day our *Richard II* classes were invited to a drama workshop in a little community arts centre, down a dingy Stockton-on-Tees back-street. I went along naively expecting some kind of acting class: what we got instead was collaborative and daringly exploratory. I can still picture clearly to this day, 40 or 50 of us together creating a physical 'hollow crown' within which we told 'sad stories of the death of kings' and experimented with different ways of portraying Richard's subsequent deposition through a series of tableaux. While this workshop was a one-off, it sparked in me the first inkling that literature was rather more exciting and unpredictable than I'd been led to believe. Several years later as a PGCE English student-teacher I began to realise that similar activities and approaches could be done in my own classroom, a revelation indeed! I think I've been on a mission ever since.

Of equal importance in our formation as committed drama-in-English teachers are the many young people we have encountered in our long teaching and teacher-education careers. In foregrounding here the voices of just a few of those students who have generously allowed us to interview them for our various research projects, we acknowledge that they have, in no small measure, helped us to write this book. Many learners have told us how much they have welcomed the immediacy and the level of engagement that reading texts through drama brings: 'you get more involved'; 'you understand what you're watching or reading even more, like puts you in the actual spot for it'; 'it puts you in the story'. Others have told us that 'when you're acting it out you're doing, putting across body language, facial expressions'; it helps with understanding characterisation, getting 'into another person's shoes' so that 'you understand how they seem, how they are in the text', and indeed, for some learners this process has helped with their own writing. Time and time again, a drama-based approach has helped learners 'get the point of a text'. And last but by no means least, young people have told us in no uncertain terms that they appreciate the motivating effects of embodied engagement: 'especially like, you're sitting there and the teacher's explaining, people will tend to wander off a lot, but when you're acting you're getting involved yourself, that helps a lot'.

These insights, captured as learners were stumbling towards a deeper understanding of their drama-in-English activity, raise key themes that we explore in later chapters. As such, this book represents something much more specific than the promotion of cross-curricular drama from an English perspective. Rather, guided by our own practices and those of the teachers and learners who we have had the privilege to observe and work alongside, we argue that there is a very particular, natural affinity between drama and English, which when fully exploited, enhances the experience of English for students and teachers alike. Both are creative, language-based arts subjects that promote affective and intellectual understanding of ourselves as individuals and as social beings. Both domains encourage us to draw on our own lived experiences, interrogate our present and imagine alternative futures. To borrow from Jacqueline Manuel and her Australian colleagues (2008, p. 2), 'both English and drama consider the subtle and complex idea of art imitating life, and the manifold implications of this'. Reading, writing and talk represent the bread-and-butter communicative modes of the traditional English classroom; drama expands the range available to learners, including the deployment of bodies, gestures, facial expressions and space. As the authors of a NATE[1] Position

Paper (Thomas and NATE 2020, p. 16) put it, 'Drama within English is a medium for presenting, exploring, resisting or celebrating thoughts, feelings and experiences that matter to the communicator, and matter enough to be presented to others'.

None of this, of course, is to deny Drama its place in the secondary curriculum as a separate subject with its own distinctive disciplinary history, rationale and purposes. In this book we are arguing that, *alongside* Drama as a discrete subject, a particular sustainable and embedded form of drama that we are calling 'drama-in-English' belongs at the heart of English. We are unwavering in our support for specialist secondary Drama colleagues in their claim for full, separate curricular status, particularly in England where, controversially, drama has been located statutorily as a mere adjunct of English since the National Curriculum was established in 1989.[2] Nevertheless, it is worth mentioning here that secondary Drama and English share a long and complex disciplinary legacy; we cover a little of this history in Chapter 2. Although this book is primarily targeted at an English teaching readership, we hope that it will also be of some interest to Drama practitioners and serve to encourage further cross-disciplinary dialogue and collaboration.

Curiously, drama's statutory inclusion in England's National Curriculum has always been confined to the Speaking and Listening (S&L) programme of study; indeed, in the latest iteration of the National Curriculum (DfE 2014), drama's role within English is now limited to generating occasional discussions about effective language use, while the status of S&L has itself been much reduced both in curricular and assessment terms. This is in direct contrast to the way in which drama was conceived by the original curriculum working group for English (the 'Cox Committee', DES/Welsh Office 1989), who, despite making the initial decision to locate drama primarily within S&L, reflected that it is 'not simply a subject, but also – more importantly – a method; it is both a creative art form in its own right and also a learning tool' (para 8.6). By placing drama at the centre of English, in this publication we seek not only to reclaim the possibilities of drama in the English classroom to which the Cox Committee appear to be alluding, but also to highlight the critical and creative processes involved in utilising dramatic activity, particularly in the study of literary, dramatic and multimodal texts.

What is 'drama-in-English'?

Although various publications and policy statements about educational drama are widely available, they offer confusingly contradictory descriptions about the purpose and practices of drama as part of English. To some extent, this may be explained by regional or national inflections according to the ways in which curricula have developed in different anglophone countries. More generally, however, different English teaching philosophies, competing traditions within the Drama teaching community and the interventions of policy-makers have all played their part. In England, both at secondary and tertiary level, it is entirely possible to interpret drama within English as simply the reading and analysis of plays as part of the literature curriculum, with a particular emphasis on the study of Shakespeare. It is likely to include some reading in parts, perhaps the viewing of a film adaptation or a trip to the theatre and might in some cases encompass the acting out of key scenes. Our vision for drama-in-English, however, is more creatively expansive. We regard improvisation and role-play, including writing-in-role, as being integral to the broader practices of the secondary English classroom. Such approaches provide imagined but authentic contexts in which learners are able to experiment with and develop their uses of language. Indeed, interest in drama's role in the talk-rich English classroom has a long history. For example, in a pamphlet for NATE in 1980 the internationally renowned drama educator Dorothy Heathcote wrote that 'One of the most valuable uses of the dramatic mode is the way it can provide context and purpose for talk, because talk arises out of the nature of situations' (Heathcote 1980, p. 22). But, as Myra Barrs points out in her introduction to the same NATE publication (Barrs 1980), drama is also key to the way in which knowledge about texts is co-constructed by students as they bring their own understandings and experiences to bear on their reading. She cites Heathcote's account of students engaging with Shelley's *Ozymandias* to demonstrate how drama is about 'making literature real to students . . . lifting a text off the page' so that they come 'to read it in a fuller way' (Barrs 1980, p. 2), and in doing so they shoulder an increasing degree of autonomy and responsibility for the learning that takes place. More recently the intersection between role-play and digital technologies in the study of literature (Bryer 2020; Burn 2022; Coles and Bryer 2018) has provided a new focus for the continuing discussion about the drama-English synergy, as we explore in more detail in Chapter 7.

The roots of drama-in-English are to be found in elements of 'process drama', a term attributed to Cecily O'Neill but which is often used to describe practices developed by Heathcote. Pamela Bowell (2006) helpfully suggests that process drama is 'a genre of drama applied within an educational context' (p. 28), one 'for which the audience is the people who are creating it' (p. 27) and 'the makers of the meaning are the recipients of the meaning' (p. 28). What is of most significance for English teachers is the way that process drama activates the creative, critical and analytical skills that lie at the heart of English. Throughout this book we show teachers and teacher-educators taking opportunities to explore and interpret texts alongside their students in this way. It is a pedagogy that we refer to as 'reading through drama' (Pitfield 2020), also known as 'reading with drama' (Medina et al. 2021), and it shifts the focus away from a 'toolkit' of atomised drama strategies onto the learners themselves and the ways in which they experience a text during the act of reading in the English classroom. In this approach textual investigation happens 'from the inside out' (see Coles and Pitfield 2022a), which requires more of students than simply 'interpreting the text from looking at it from the outside' (Medina et al. 2021, p. 139). Rather they are experiencing it by 'exchanging dialogue and actions *as* the characters, *with* the characters and *in* situations' (p. 139) [italics in the original], and drawing productively on their own experiences and cultural understandings to do so.

The aim of reading through drama is not to act out scenes from a text as an end in itself. Neither is it to create a theatrical product, although it is true that students' scenarios are likely to involve humour and/or tension as plays do. There will often be presentation of the work to the class to enable sharing and discussion as part of the whole meaning-making process, and when teaching dramatic literature English teachers may also use the students' presentations to initiate broader discussions about the play in performance. Teresa Grainger and her colleagues (2005, p. 90) propose that through drama 'children dig down into the substrata of the text'. For instance, students might improvise additional scenes suggested by the text, or enact what might have led up to a key event, or what might be the outcome. A scene can be replayed to facilitate closer scrutiny, or re-created from a different character's perspective, and so on. The teacher might embed a convention such as still-image (tableau), using it to freeze the action in order to prompt out-of-role discussion and evaluation. Such activities provide the space for students to spectate critically and reflexively on their work in relation to the text, and in addition, as Nicholas McGuinn (2014, p. 65) suggests, they demonstrate to students 'that language can be ambiguous, readings can be pluralistic and that narratives do not have to be constrained within a structural straitjacket of chronological plot sequencing and naturalistic or monologic telling'. It is clear, then, that the teacher's pedagogic interventions are key, as they are always looking for ways to apply different frames or perspectives to the 'what if' speculations that the text or the situation demands, and to this end may on occasion adopt a role within the drama themselves (known as 'teacher-in-role'). To approach the study of a literary text in the ways described here also 'enriches the relationship between teacher and students' (O'Toole and Dunn 2020, p. 14), as students are effectively sharing ownership of the knowledge with their teacher.

Whilst we have emphasised both the creativity and criticality involved in drama-based approaches, it is also important to highlight the everydayness of their playful nature. Harold Rosen, in an essay from 1980 entitled 'The Dramatic Mode' (Rosen 2017a), describes 'dramatic behaviour as being interwoven with all human behaviour' (p. 322), suggesting that we do not need 'to go to theatres to see and hear such things. In any children's playground the actors will be at work' (p. 314). Enjoyment is an important aspect of dramatic play, and there cannot be many English teachers who would wish to deny the proposition that enjoyment should be a foundational element of literary study, especially at the stage when young people are developing their reading practices and habits. Certainly, in the English context enjoyment is conspicuously absent from the reading specifications in the current National Curriculum for secondary English (DfE 2014), and it is dispiriting that the so-called vision of policy-makers is limited to a demand for the nation's 14–16-year-olds to be 'taught' to 'appreciate' great works from the English literary canon including Shakespeare. It is also concerning that the level of students' 'appreciation' is assessed solely by means of a terminal written examination that privileges narrow forms of textual analysis along with memorisation of quotations as markers of success.

Nevertheless, in this book we argue strongly that drama activity and examination success are by no means antithetical, and we press for drama-based activities, fully integrated into the everyday practices and flow of the English lesson, to become a regular part of teachers' pedagogical repertoires. This is not the 'special event' form of drama that requires full-on, workshop-style lessons, a large space and particular theatrical expertise on the part of the teacher. Rather, as our examples from research and practice demonstrate, this is drama as a sustainable and integral part of students' learning in English across the entire secondary age range, including examination classes at GCSE and Advanced Level.

The background to this book

Despite the wealth of scholarship, practical guidance and research about the value of drama-based pedagogies in learning across the curriculum, only a relatively limited range of published material deals specifically with the common ground that drama and English share. As we illustrate in Chapter 8, the majority of English teacher handbooks aimed at a UK-based trainee teacher readership include some advice about teaching drama, but they vary considerably in the ways they interpret the scope and purpose of this statutory obligation. When it comes to other publications about secondary English the picture tends to be one of drama's absence (unless specifically dealing with Shakespeare), particularly over the past 40 years in the UK. For example, in an anthology of articles from the pioneering *English Magazine* (renamed *The English & Media Magazine*) between 1979 and 1996 (Simons 1996), out of 39 articles selected to 'give a flavour of some of the key issues and moments in English teaching over the past two decades' (p. v), only one is explicitly about English and drama. In stark contrast a whole section (11 articles) is devoted to English and media/new technologies. Meanwhile, in a more recent volume entitled *Debates in English Teaching* (Davison and Daly 2020), the editors allocate two whole chapters explicitly to media, while drama is reduced to a couple of passing references. Likewise, Marshall et al.'s (2019) comparative overview of English teaching in England, Scotland and Canada pays disappointingly scant attention to the presence or otherwise of drama-based pedagogy across the three jurisdictions. Even the names of prominent professional development institutions such as The English and Media Centre in London appear to signal the irrelevance of drama in English; similarly, we note the symbolic erasure of drama from the title of NATE's professional magazine in 2013 when it converted from *English Drama Media* to simply *Teaching English*.

It is possible that drama's association with play and educational progressivism is one reason for this apparent lack of interest when it comes to English. The 'messing around' connotations of play and the lack of coherence in some progressive approaches present convenient but unfair caricatures. But as we point out in Chapter 2, although new pedagogic ideas involving drama within English have emerged sporadically over the years, they have rarely become embedded or widespread in day-to-day classroom practice. This is not a situation unique to England. Even in Australia, which appears to have had a more consistent record of publication and project work in this area, Manuel and her colleagues noted in 2008 that major developments have not always been reflected in the work of English classrooms. Interestingly, these writers identify a very accessible British text from the 1980s as 'the last major book on the topic of drama in English' (Manuel et al. 2008, p. 7). This is Ken Byron's *Drama in the English Classroom* (1986) which did indeed represent a step forward. Byron offered English teachers a philosophical rationale, tackled concerns head on, dealt with the purposes and evaluation of drama right across the English curriculum, and illustrated this way of working with sample schemes of work. The publication of *Drama in the English Classroom*, part of a series on the teaching of secondary English, received an enthusiastic welcome in the *Times Educational Supplement*,[3] the reviewer citing the timely, practical and inspirational nature of the series' content. It is curious, therefore, that Byron's book has not continued to enjoy the same degree of influence with English and drama practitioners in the UK as it has in the Australian context, and it is currently out of print. Yet, when published, its prescient perspectives on drama within English were very much in line with the key concerns of English teaching at that time, and we can only assume that interest in it was superseded by the imposition of the National Curriculum for English (DES/Welsh Office 1989) and the ensuing political fallout. Whilst there is an acknowledgement by Michael Anderson, John Hughes and Jacqueline Manuel (2008) of the significance of Byron's book, their own edited publication takes a different approach, assembling a group of expert drama and English educators, each describing how drama activity can be applied to a particular aspect of the English curriculum. These accounts are framed by an introduction which gives an overarching rationale and reaffirms some of the key arguments regarding the importance of drama to learning in English.

Julie Dunn and Adrianne Jones (2022) suggest that things have moved on since 2008 and, in Australia at least, they detect growing interest in drama-based pedagogies. They highlight a more recent text by John O'Toole and Julie Dunn (2020) which focuses on dramatic engagements with literary texts and offers detailed accounts of schemes of work, as well as an 'instruction manual' (p. 19) for teachers to develop their own schemes. However, a surprising omission from Dunn and Jones' overview of relevant texts is Nicholas McGuinn's *The English Teacher's Drama Handbook* (2014), and it is difficult to explain their apparent lack of interest in a text which sits firmly within the purview of drama as part of the English curriculum. Perhaps the reason lies with McGuinn's account of the post-Second World War (WW2) development of drama within English which almost exclusively focuses on the British context. However, he offers some important insights, despite some glaring gaps in his own historical account (such as the influences of Ken Byron, Myra Barrs and the American academic James Moffett, all of whom we discuss in Chapters 2 and 3). While McGuinn's suggestions for actual classroom practice differ from our own in key respects (see Chapter 2), his text deserves more attention, particularly for the way he brings together the heated debates that took place over curriculum content and pedagogical approach in both the Drama and English subject areas. He also synthesises ideas from an eclectic range of references, and summarises the implications of key policy interventions, all of which are likely to resonate to some degree with the experiences of readers beyond these shores.

Dunn and Jones (2022) note that, in general, teaching handbooks such as these are important in providing advocacy for drama-based learning in English, but are also clear that other measures are necessary to support a more widespread uptake of practices. In their summary of the effects on learning and student engagement in English of the drama-based pedagogies employed during the Brisbane-based *Y Connect Project*,[4] these writers highlight the need for sustained teacher involvement in professional learning projects of this kind. They also make the case for drawing directly on students' experience of the learning to ensure that an important pedagogic perspective is not lost to the discussion, and thus they foreground student voice in their report.

As well as the texts summarised above, there is a growing body of international research from other anglophone systems, particularly the USA, that has relevance for English teachers. For example, in their research reviews Edmiston and Enciso (2002), Medina et al. (2021), and two meta analyses of studies from roughly the last 30 years compiled by Lee, Patall and Steingut (2015) and Lee, Enciso and Brown (2020), all point to the wide range of literacy benefits, often focusing on primary (or elementary) education, that can be attributed to drama-based practices. There are also broader outcomes, some of which are to do with the interplay between the affective and critical in learning, whilst others demonstrate how drama-based pedagogies promote learner agency and support students' navigation of meaning-making in the English classroom. Findings that relate to the relationship between drama and reading are of particular importance, because, as Andrew Goodwyn (2010) highlights, surveys spanning a number of years have continued to indicate that literature retains a very significant place in the hearts of English teachers, and a central role in the curriculum. This is borne out by the prevalence of literature-based work that we have observed through our own research, aspects of which provide the examples that we draw upon for this book. Such a situation strongly suggests that the National Curriculum for English (DfE 2014) would better serve teachers if it properly reflected how drama can be employed to engage learners in the study of literary texts, rather than reducing drama to a brief mention in the spoken English section. According to Goodwyn (2010, p. 21), teachers in England 'show a strong willingness to revitalise literature teaching but also a stark recognition that much externally driven, current practice has a very negative effect on current teaching'. If this was the case in 2010, it is even more marked now in 2023 given that policy-driven institutional pressures increasingly encourage English teachers to 'teach to the test'. We argue that drama-in-English pedagogy not only revitalises literary learning but can be regarded as foundational to it.

It is our belief, therefore, that it is time to reinvigorate the case for drama at the heart of English. In this book we: define its purpose, rooting it within a clear theoretical framework; identify key developmental moments, past and present; and, most importantly, offer examples of drama-in-English lessons and projects undertaken by English teachers and teacher-educators with real learners as part of their everyday classroom activity. We recognise, however, that advocacy needs to be accompanied by action, which is why this book draws on our wider engagement in the field of education in English over many years. This includes our historical participation in key national projects; involvement with professional subject associations such as NATE, LATE, NATD and London Drama;[5] contributions to magazines and journals read by English and Drama teachers; the dissemination of our expertise at teachers' conferences through academic papers and practical workshops; and last but by no means least, our active, campaigning membership of education trade unions.

Working in the current context: Systems of schooling

In promoting a pedagogy that regards classrooms as social, dialogic spaces where meanings are made rather than merely transmitted, we are, to some extent, placing ourselves at odds with the direction of educational reform promoted by successive neoliberal administrations in the UK, the USA and Australia. Drama-in-English represents a critical-creative pedagogical approach that is attentive to the social and cultural lives of learners and which acknowledges, rather than denies, difference. In contrast, systems of state-funded schooling in the UK and other anglophone jurisdictions have become progressively standardised, prone to imposition from above and subject to tight political control. In the UK, the Conservative government's 1988 Education Reform Act heralded the introduction of an increasingly regulated, outcomes-focused educational landscape, marked by low levels of professional trust and policed by means of a punitive inspection regime (Ofsted)[6] along with the competitive ranking of schools according to league tables of examination results. Twenty years later even the UK Parliament's own Children, Schools and Families Committee (House of Commons 2009) had concluded that a 'scaling down' of curricular prescription was urgently required, along with a rebalancing of professional trust in order to facilitate greater 'ownership' by teachers. An earlier parliamentary report (House of Commons 2008) had already raised critical questions about the testing burden imposed on teachers and students, concluding that:

> Tests, however, can only test a limited range of the skills and activities which are properly part of a rounded education, so that a focus on improving test results compromises teachers' creativity in the classroom and children's access to a balanced curriculum.

However, little change came about as a result: a few years later Merryn Hutchings (2015) likened English schools to 'exam factories' in a research report commissioned by the largest teaching union in the UK. She observed that:

> . . . [whilst] accountability measures have achieved government aims of bringing about an increased focus on English/literacy . . ., this has been achieved at the cost of narrowing the curriculum that pupils experience. The narrowing of the curriculum is greater for year groups taking tests/ exams, pupils with low attainment, disadvantaged pupils and those with special needs. (p. 5)

Given this scenario, it is perhaps unsurprising that the OECD Programme for International Student Assessment (PISA) 2018 results indicate that, although reading scores for students in England are close to the OECD average, our young people are more likely to hold negative attitudes to reading (OECD 2018). UK research suggests that performative pressure on teachers results in a narrowed range of pedagogic practices and a reduction in professional autonomy (Hutchings 2015; Perryman et al. 2011). Gunther Kress et al. (2005) argue that this amounts to a 're-agenting' (p. 14) of schools, where professional attention has shifted away from teachers as curriculum innovators and intellectual workers onto teachers as deliverers of universal curriculum content. Indeed, the current Westminster government's controversial decision to fund a 'strategically aligned' curriculum quango, Oak National Academy, to produce 'off-the-shelf' (Mansell 2022) sets of 'knowledge-rich' lesson plans for the nation's schools represents the logical conclusion to that de-professionalising shift.

Prescriptive policies and standards-based reform in the USA (for example, No Child Left Behind, introduced in 2002) appear to have impacted practice in broadly similar ways to the UK. Researchers point to the negative effect of state-mandated testing on students' well-being and motivation (Clarke et al. 2003; Jones and Egley 2004), and on teachers' morale (Pedulla et al. 2003). Teachers are more likely to feel under pressure to limit their pedagogical range (Pedulla et al. 2003), and teach to the test (Pedulla et al. 2003; Rothstein et al. 2008). One study of high school English teachers found that policy discourses served to reduce their 'abilities to work as autonomous professionals', leading to 'scripted, text-based lessons' (Stewart 2012, p. 377).

Within a hyper-accountable system, the essentially collaborative and situational nature of process drama may appear to present the English teacher with too much of a risk. And yet, recent research into effective teaching methods conducted by academics from Bristol, Oxford and Harvard for the Nuffield Foundation (Burgess et al. 2022, p. 4) supports a more collaborative, interactional approach specifically in English, even when preparing for formal assessments: 'For English exams . . . more time working with classmates predicts higher scores'. It lends support to numerous small-scale classroom-based accounts by secondary English practitioners and researchers (see, for example, Doecke and McClenaghan 2011; Yandell 2014) which promote socio-cultural understandings of learning in English, yet are ignored by the anonymous authors of Ofsted's so-called 'Curriculum Research Review' for English (2022).[7] Doecke and McClenaghan remind us that 'peer interaction is just as important as the exchange between a teacher and a pupil in creating a sense of expectation and possibility, of experimentation and play' (2011, p. 91).

In later chapters we provide examples from our own research and that of others where teachers – often working in unpromising circumstances – have succeeded in opening up opportunities for adolescent learners to explore areas of the English curriculum through drama-based approaches (also see Coles and Pitfield 2022b). We are, however, acutely aware that the examples of drama-in-English practice presented in the following chapters reflect a narrowly canon-heavy range of literary texts (a key exception being Salman Rushdie's *Haroun and the Sea of Stories*, see Chapter 7). Regrettably, this represents a realistic snapshot of the texts we have observed being taught in contemporary London classrooms, and indeed chimes with recent survey data (Smith 2023) suggestive of a constricted literary diet on offer in English departments throughout England and Wales, even at KS3 where a degree of curricular flexibility is possible. Curricular arguments around literature, identity and representation are complex (Coles 2020; Guillory 1993), but a foundational principle of any English curriculum should be that all young people have the right to see themselves reflected positively in some of the texts they encounter at school (Bishop 2012; Chetty 2017). Lesley Nelson-Addy (2020, p. 35) concludes that the current English curriculum, as amended in 2014, amounts to 'a violent political statement' that does not even acknowledge its 'erasure of the Black presence and experience in Britain'. We salute grassroots campaigns to decolonise the English curriculum not only in terms of text choice, but also in adopting new ways of talking and thinking about texts. At the same time, a key argument of this book is that drama-based approaches are ideally suited to prising open texts so as to enable critical re-tellings in a range of voices, in ways that challenge conventional perspectives and address 'the danger of a single story' (Adichie 2009). It is a pedagogy equally applicable to canonical or non-canonical literary texts.

Working in the current context: Knowledge in English

Current debates around 'powerful knowledge' (Young 2008) and the 'knowledge-rich curriculum' (e.g., Gibb 2017) have been prompted in part by the work of US educationalist E. D. Hirsch (1987, 2007). According to Hirsch, there exist universally agreed sets of 'essential' canonical knowledge, acquaintance with which all young people are entitled in the name of empowerment and social justice – what Hirsch calls 'cultural literacy'. Nick Gibb, British Schools Minister and self-confessed Hirsch enthusiast (see Gibb 2017), is generally regarded as a key architect of current schools policy in England. For him, knowledge is conceived of as a stable and self-explanatory commodity that can be exchanged in a straightforward one-way classroom transaction between the knowledgeable and the knowledge-less:

> Education is about the transfer of knowledge from one generation to the next . . . The rich language of Shakespeare should be the common property of us all. The great figures of literature that still populate the conversations of all those who regard themselves as well-educated should be known to all . . . And they must be taught to everyone. (Gibb 2010)

Misappropriating French sociologist Pierre Bourdieu's term 'cultural capital'[8] to describe this process of acquisition, ministers have now embedded it within Ofsted's Education Inspection Framework[9] as a criterion against which judgements are made about the 'quality of education' offered by individual schools. Cultural capital is defined – perversely – by Ofsted as 'the essential knowledge that pupils need to be educated citizens, introducing them to the best that has been thought and said . . .', a culturally authoritarian notion that owes far more to Victorian poet, critic and school inspector Matthew Arnold[10] than to Bourdieu. While Bourdieu proposed his theory of cultural capital to expose one of the key ways in which social and educational inequalities are systemically reproduced (see Bourdieu and Passeron 1990), UK politicians have, instead, further entrenched privileged forms of cultural capital in the school system.

This concept of education as the passing-on of pre-packaged canonised knowledge is particularly problematic when applied to English, a discipline, after all, that values interpretation and personal response especially in relation to the study of texts (Elliott 2021). Our own experiences both as readers and as teachers indicate that the acquisition of meaningful literary knowledge involves a rather more complex process of engagement than is generally suggested by promoters of a 'knowledge-rich' English curriculum and its recommended pedagogies. As Robert Eaglestone (2020) notes, literature is about values, beliefs and feelings: 'Subjectivity is part of the subject, because we humans are the subject of the humanities' (n.p.). In respect of the acquisition of literary knowledge he adds that, rather than being a simple matter of knowledge transmission, 'disciplinary consciousness' in English 'is made by all the people in the classroom together as they develop their own "ideas and emotions"' (n.p.). Eaglestone is highly critical of Michael Young's (2008) insistence that objective forms of 'powerful knowledge' should be separated out from context and personal experience (an idea derived, as Eaglestone points out, from studies of Maths and Science education). It is an approach to learning that in practice, whether intended by Young or not, tends to place an emphasis on memorisation rather than experience. Surely, as Eaglestone argues, literary knowledge *'begins* in the experience of seeing or reading it. Teaching grows this knowledge in dialogue by helping the student articulate, reflect on, adapt and mature their view' (n.p.) [italics in the original]. Eaglestone concludes that any attempt to teach a work of literature that does not start with students' own lives and beliefs 'betrays both the discipline and the point of literature', a conviction that underpins our drama-in-English pedagogy.

The structure of this book

In Chapter 2 we offer a historical perspective on the complex relationship between English and drama, charting a drama-in-English timeline by means of various landmark reports that have sought to shape the functions and forms of drama within English over the past century. Later in this chapter we consider the influence of three practitioners who are often cited as early pioneers, then take a closer look at some key themes emerging from this history. In Chapter 3 we outline the theoretical frameworks that underpin our concept of drama-in-English, building on a Vygotskyan understanding of the learning process. Our socio-cultural perspective of the English classroom synthesises the work of literacy and drama specialists such as Myra Barrs, Dorothy Heathcote and Cecily O'Neill with Louise Rosenblatt's reader response theory to develop an understanding of reading and writing essentially as forms of enactment. We also explore how the reading of a literary text through drama might be regarded as a transformative or 're-creative' process, one that involves learners drawing on multimodal resources to engage in the creative and critical processes of meaning-making. Across Chapters 4 to 8 we apply our theoretical stance to rich accounts of classroom practice, a number of the examples having been gathered from our many years of research in London secondary schools. So, in Chapter 4 we focus on the affordances of role-taking as a key facet of drama-in-English; in Chapter 5 we explore the productive relationship between drama and writing; in Chapter 6 we apply a critical lens to the teaching of Shakespeare, the one area of the English curriculum which has traditionally been linked to drama-based pedagogies; while in Chapter 7 we argue for an expanded view of English, one that integrates English, drama and media. Specifically, we consider what media production has to offer students learning about texts through drama. We press the case for a flexible, forward-looking English curriculum that reflects the contemporary context of rapid social, cultural and technological change and meets the needs of 21st-century learners. In Chapter 8 we turn our attention to how English-and-drama teacher identities are made; in doing so we raise questions about teacher education, teacher agency and the ways in which the professional confidence of early career English teachers can be supported. In our concluding chapter we return to the thorny question of why drama is not more frequently considered by English teachers as an appropriate pedagogical choice when students engage with texts. We draw attention to the radical potential of a differently inflected version of English, one that recognises the centrality of drama to the creative practices and social contexts by and in which young people learn. Importantly, we emphasise the significance of enjoyment to memorable learning in English. Pleasure in reading is central to the practices we describe.

Notes

1   The National Association for the Teaching of English, the main subject association in the UK for English teachers.
2   Until 1998 education legislation authorised by the UK government in Westminster applied only to England and Wales. Thereafter, Wales having gained further devolved powers (and in 2020 published a separate Welsh National Curriculum), it applies only to England. On the occasions when we are discussing more general political/cultural issues rather than specific education policies, we refer to Britain or the UK.
3   The *TES* is a national educational publication, issued weekly in the UK.
4   *Y Connect* was an in-depth project (2016–18), undertaken in a Brisbane secondary school with a very diverse student intake. It employed arts-based pedagogies across the curriculum, and involved senior leaders, teachers, creative artists, arts organisations and researchers from Griffith University.
5   The National Association for the Teaching of English; the London Association for the Teaching of English; the National Association for the Teaching of Drama.
6   The Office for Standards in Education (established 1992) is the UK government department responsible for inspecting schools and other services for children.
7   The English and Media Centre, a well-respected London-based educational charity, has produced a highly critical analysis of this document, available at: www.english andmedia.co.uk/blog/review-of-ofsted-curriculum-research-review-english

8 Bourdieu conceived of cultural capital as the habits and tastes associated with a person's social background/environment and the cultural practices that go with it. One of Bourdieu's concerns was that in a class-based society these cultural goods are regarded as of unequal value, only certain of which can be exchanged for educational and social advantage.

9 The revised version published in 2022. See www.gov.uk/government/publica tions/education-inspection-framework/education-inspection-framework

10 See Chapter 2, footnote 2.

2

DRAMA IN ENGLISH

A historical perspective

It is by no means a simple matter to pinpoint the beginnings of the English–Drama relationship, nor to chart the ways in which drama-based pedagogy has contributed to English since its inception as a school subject in the early 20th century. It is often assumed that Drama is the 'younger' of the two subjects, yet Drama historians (largely drawing on the Graeco-Roman theatrical and literary tradition) highlight its role in education stretching back centuries prior to the introduction of curriculum English. David Male (1973, p. 38) cites the training of Elizabethan boys in 'oratory, an activity very close to acting'. Peter Cunningham and Yoko Yamasaki (2018) point to the staging of classical and religious plays, the former in elite British schools from the 12th century onwards, the latter in the Jesuit schools of Europe from around the 16th century. They also discern an educational impetus to the street theatre and storytelling traditions of medieval times. Gavin Bolton (1998) chooses to shift attention away from Drama's performance-orientated origins, focusing instead on its inception as a curriculum subject. In all these accounts, however, the roots of more contemporary understandings of educational drama and its relevance to English are detectable, including: drama as a powerful means of communication; the study of plays for performance; the history and traditions of theatre; and social, cultural and embodied storytelling.

Our historical approach focuses more specifically on the emerging relationship between English and drama following the inclusion of English as part of the school curriculum in England. We begin by mapping out a timeline by means of various landmark reports that have sought to define and shape the functions and forms of drama within English over the past century. Next, we consider the influence of three practitioners who are often cited as early pioneers of educational drama, Harriet Finlay-Johnson, Henry Caldwell

DOI: 10.4324/9781003290827-2

Cook and Marjorie Hourd, examining their legacy in relation to drama within English. From there we take a closer look at some of the key themes that seem to us to be important in terms of our investigation into the progress of drama-in-English practices over time. Although our account draws primarily on examples from the British educational system, wherever appropriate we make comparisons with other anglophone jurisdictions, in the expectation that the insights and issues discussed will be of interest to readers in a wide range of contexts.

Landmark reports

The Newbolt Report (1921)[1]

The first UK government-commissioned policy document that offers a developed rationale for the inclusion of English as a school subject is the Newbolt Report, officially titled *The Teaching of English in England*. Its publication is described by Australian academic Brenton Doecke as marking a defining moment 'in the emergence of English as a cultural praxis' (2017, p. 231). The particular socio-political context of its production in the aftermath of the First World War (WW1) is reflected in the report's uneasy blend of 'nationalist sentiments' and 'progressive proposals' (Doecke 2017, p. 239). It is unsurprising, therefore, that the Newbolt Report's educational purpose is described in consciously Arnoldian[2] terms, promoting the induction of young people into accepted and acceptably civilising forms of aesthetic appreciation as a means to effect social and personal transformation. Literature, in particular Shakespeare, is central to the study of English, and the tensions between progressive and traditional forces that Doecke (2017) alludes to above are nowhere more apparent than in the report's recommendations for Shakespeare study. While advocating the development of students' aesthetic sensibilities through dramatisation of his plays, the authors also pursue a moral mission, evident in their endorsement of recitation and verse-speaking practices as valuable tools in the 'fight against the powerful influence of evil habits of speech contracted in home and street' (Newbolt 1921, p. 59). Consequently, dramatising Shakespeare is not simply conceived of as an aesthetic experience, it is also regarded as an important corrective weapon to be deployed in working class schools. According to Bolton (1998), this was one reason why, in the years following publication of the report, drama within English proceeded along a somewhat narrow path of elocution and speech training.

At its most progressive, the Newbolt Report promotes play-making, whether through action or writing, as a productive activity, 'in the fullest sense, practical English composition' (p. 312). The authors also refer positively to the ways in which drama facilitates collaborative learning experiences in the English classroom; they praise a particular type of teacher–student interaction arising out of the collective composition of a play for which the teacher acts as scribe. However, such moments are comparatively rare. More typically, the teacher is invoked as the one cultural and elocutionary expert in the classroom, and traditionally authoritative ideas about the teacher–student relationship are woven throughout the report.

Despite these caveats, it is fair to say that the Newbolt Report is foundational in offering an embryonic definition of drama as both content and method in English, and demonstrates that, at a key moment in its development as a school subject, certain forms of practical dramatic activity are recognised as inherently a part of English.

Dartmouth Seminar reports (1966 onwards)

The month-long Anglo-American Dartmouth conference signalled another landmark moment in the evolution of English as a school subject. Jointly sponsored by the US-based National Council of Teachers of English (NCTE) and its UK sister organisation NATE, it brought together prominent educators at Dartmouth College in New Hampshire. Amongst the British organisers and attendees were Douglas Barnes and James Britton, both inspirational figures in LATE and what has become known as London English,[3] and the American contingent included the innovative practitioner and academic James Moffett. Both Barnes and Moffett were members of the Dartmouth Seminar Study Group on Drama.

It is noteworthy that drama as part of English features substantially in two out of the six post-conference reports, Barnes' (1968) *Drama in the English Classroom* and Moffett's (1967) *What Is Happening: The Use of Dramatic Activities in the Teaching of English*. In his preface Barnes unequivocally positions 'drama and dramatic experiences within an overall conception of the activities of the English classroom' (1968, n.p.) and as part of a democratic and inclusive educational tradition. The purpose of dramatic activity is primarily to draw on and extend the rich communicative resources of young people, 'whether they are using their own words or those of the dramatist' (Barnes 1968, p. 47), a far cry from any notion of drama as elocution and speech training. As a highly respected expert on language development, but a self-confessed non-expert in drama practices, Barnes shares his own drama-based classroom experiments with a refreshing degree of honesty that is in keeping with the collaborative approach he adopted as an innovative Head of English at Minchenden Grammar School in the late 1950s (see Medway et al. 2014). Yet, intriguingly, the report makes no mention of earlier drama-English pioneers (who we discuss below), and so lacks clarity as to whether Barnes and the Study Group were even aware of this legacy.

Moffett's monograph sets out a theory of discourse which places drama, particularly improvisation, at the heart of both literacy and literary learning. For Moffett the immediacy of a play 'has fundamentally the same impact on the spectator as real-life events' (1967, p. 1), and this makes a script highly suitable for exploration through improvisation, which is 'a learning process that can be exploited for many discursive purposes' (p. 27). When dealing with narrative texts, 'improvisation renders a special service: it translates *what happened* back to *what is happening*' (p. 27) [italics in the original], and thus 'the abstraction of a story' is returned 'to present actuality' (p. 27). This concern with improvisation may not be a new phenomenon – for example, Hourd (1949) explores ideas about the purpose of improvisatory activity in English – but Moffett's account represents a step forward in that he makes a properly theorised case for its contribution to all aspects of learning in English.

Whilst Barnes' and Moffett's reports are by no means contradictory, there is little sense of cross-fertilisation in the process of their production. This may partially reflect Dartmouth's ultimate failure to reach an overarching consensus about learning in English (see Gibbons 2017). In fact, Moffett's report is based on a pre-existing monograph for NCTE, so it is unlikely he is summing up an agreed approach to drama within English on behalf of the Study Group. The Foreword, written by the Secondary Section Chairman of NCTE, refers to Moffett having 'pursued singly' his ideas, which NCTE regard as 'intriguing' rather than '"correct"' (Maxwell 1967, p. v), hardly a ringing endorsement by Moffett's American peers who, Gibbons (2017, p. 23) notes, generally favoured a more 'structured skills-based curriculum'. It would seem that Moffett had more in common with the 'personal growth, English-as-language, model' (Gibbons 2017, p. 20) espoused by many of the English contingent.

This is not to imply that the delegations to the Dartmouth Seminar were unable to reach consensus on any important principles or that its outcomes lacked impact. Indeed, in terms of drama within English one of its key recommendations, 'not only that drama activities be part of all English teaching, but that all English teaching approach the condition of drama' (Barnes 1968, p. 52), provides the epigraph for O'Toole and Dunn's (2020) recent handbook on literature teaching through drama. It is, however, more difficult to judge whether and to what extent this recommendation influenced policy-makers and practising English teachers at the time. Issues of NCTE's *English Journal* from this period provide little evidence of any particular interest in Dartmouth's discussions around drama as part of English. It was not until 1976, when NCTE's Standing Committee on Teacher Preparation and Certification published *A Statement on the Preparation of Teachers of English* (Larson et al. 1976), that changes in thinking about English, including the need to recognise a place for 'improvisation' and 'enactment' (p. 197), were beginning to permeate US teacher education programmes (see Chapter 8). By contrast, the third issue of the newly established NATE journal, *English in Education*, published in 1969, is entirely devoted to different types of drama activity, perhaps another indication that Dartmouth was more in tune with the discussions about English teaching that were already taking place in England. This lends some credence to McGuinn's (2014, p. 56) claim that, post-Dartmouth, 'English pedagogy was beginning to adopt some of the most cherished principles of drama', although he identifies our next landmark report, *A Language for Life* (DES 1975), as markedly unhelpful in maintaining this momentum.

The Bullock Report (1975)

Before examining McGuinn's criticisms, it is worth noting that *A Language for Life*, also known as the Bullock Report, represents to this day a highly influential, ground-breaking contribution to the contentious debate about the purpose of English, what its content should be and how it should be taught. It puts the focus on language development in context rather than decontextualised grammar exercises and emphasises the importance of oracy. Bullock also promotes language learning across the curriculum and the need for every school to implement a language policy; further, in recognition of the increasing diversity of school populations in the UK, it requires schools to engage positively with the language and culture of the home. The authors consider reading to be an important part of language development, as literature 'brings the child into an encounter with language in its most complex and varied forms and is a valuable source of imaginative insight', and they warn against allowing the demands of examinations 'to distort the experience of literature' (DES 1975, p. 525). Given the principled lead that Bullock is prepared to take in such controversial matters, the report's equivocation about drama within English is genuinely surprising. In what McGuinn (2014, p. 44) describes as 'a meagre five pages' out of over 600, the Bullock Report poses some 'fundamental questions' (DES 1975, p. 160) about the role of drama in English teaching, but provides no answers. Even Bullock's positive move to engage English teachers in the debate is immediately undermined by the statement that some might not have the 'temperament to handle improvised drama' (DES 1975, p. 224). Mixed messaging such as this only serves to encourage teachers to think of drama activity within English simply as a matter of individual choice, a position which we argue has had a lasting, detrimental effect on establishing it as part of the curriculum, as we note in Chapter 1 and develop further in Chapter 8.

The National Curriculum and beyond (1988 onwards)

To prepare the ground for the 1988 Education Reform Act and the imposition of a National Curriculum, a series of discussion documents was published by Her Majesty's Inspectorate (HMI) of which *English from 5 to 16: Curriculum Matters 1* (DES 1986) was the first. It proposes drama activity as a means of 'extending the pupil's language repertoire' (p. 15), and although its account is not particularly well-developed, crucially it describes drama as 'essential' in English. This is a perspective shared by the authors of the inaugural version of the National Curriculum for English (the Cox Report, DES/Welsh Office 1989) who give a reasonably expansive description of drama's contribution to English, subsequently attributed by Brian Cox (1991a) to the advocacy of two drama experts on the committee. Nevertheless, the Cox Report confines drama to the Programme of Study for S&L, as we have noted in Chapter 1, but on the plus side it advises that plays, including Shakespeare, should be studied through the dramatic medium and that role-play is useful in exploring a range of both literary and non-fiction texts. In addition, the accompanying (non-statutory) guidance compiled by the National Curriculum Council (DES 1990) acknowledges the opportunities that drama provides for learning across the English curriculum, offering advice to teachers under such headings as 'Drama as a Method', 'Drama as Communication' and 'Drama as Text' (section D11, paras. 3.2–3.8).

While it was the intention of Margaret Thatcher's right-wing Conservative government to use the National Curriculum to dictate subject content, Tony Blair's New Labour government (1997–2007) not only retained the idea of a national curriculum, but also sought to intervene in matters of pedagogy by means of its National Literacy Strategy (NLS). The *Key Stage 3 Framework for Teaching English* (DfEE 2001) was non-statutory in name only as its objectives-led model, incorporating a set of teaching routines and a formulaic lesson structure, was supported by specially appointed Local Authority literacy consultants and policed nationally by Ofsted. The model was disseminated to teachers via top-down, compulsory training and an accompanying plethora of teaching materials, including a *Drama Objectives Bank* (DfES 2003). Despite its skills orientation and a tick-box approach to the development of schemes of work, the *KS3 Framework* at least paid reasonable attention to drama within English – there were 14 drama objectives across Years 7, 8 and 9 relating to textual study and spoken language development. In a largely useful account of drama activity as a part of S&L teaching and assessment, Andy Kempe and Jan Holroyd (2004) draw on this *Framework* model, although their recommended practices inevitably come up against its constraints, a prime example being its atomised approach to language development. This is particularly marked in Kempe and Holroyd's use of decontextualised extracts from scripted plays solely to teach specific modes of speech. In addition, and as we have argued elsewhere (see Pitfield 2006 and 2020), the *Framework* is overly reliant on a set of pick-and-mix drama conventions, not helped by an alphabetised glossary of strategies appended to the *Drama Objectives Bank*. We look at a more integrated approach to the application of drama conventions in Chapter 4.

During the most recent National Curriculum revision exercise (DfE 2014), Michael Gove's[4] low opinion of drama is inherent in his ultimately unsuccessful attempt to exclude it both as an optional GCSE subject and as part of the National Curriculum for English. Although both were saved, the tightly restricted language-related role that drama within English is now afforded has much in common with Newbolt's notion of drama as speech training, a stubbornly recurrent theme in policy over the past century.

The centralising impetus of politicians in England (and Wales until 1989) may well resonate with readers from other anglophone jurisdictions. For instance, when Doecke and McClenaghan (2011) describe schooling in Australia as progressively marked by the imposition of standardised testing, curricular constraints and accountability procedures, they could just as easily be describing current educational systems in England and the USA. In this context any agreement about educational drama's inclusion in the secondary curriculum, whether as part of English or a discrete subject in its own right, can never be considered as settled. Gove's reforms clearly demonstrate this, as do struggles in New Zealand (O'Connor 2016) and Australia (Freebody 2020; Stinson and Saunders 2016). Nevertheless, it is important to remember that top-down policies never fully reflect what is actually happening in English classrooms, and with that in mind, we now turn to an examination of the experimental classroom practices of three early pioneers.

Early pioneers of English through drama (1911–49)

Harriet Finlay-Johnson, Henry Caldwell Cook and Marjorie Hourd all wrote first-hand accounts of their distinctive teaching methods, published in 1911, 1919 and 1949 respectively, thus ensuring their ideas reached a wider audience. Caldwell Cook's approach to English teaching was referenced approvingly by the authors of the Newbolt Report. Although Finlay-Johnson was not singled out by Newbolt in the same way, her work was promoted by the reputedly progressive Chief Inspector of Schools, Edmond Holmes, who was himself quoted by both Newbolt and Caldwell Cook. Helen Nicholson (2011) notes that Finlay-Johnson's work 'became well-known internationally and, within months of the publication of her book, she was cited by scholars across the Atlantic' (p. 46). Caldwell Cook also found an international audience; this is apparent from an enthusiastic account published in the NCTE journal (Lester 1926), and according to Bolton (2007), his methods had an influence on aspects of teacher training in some areas of the USA. Hourd, a key advocate for drama as part of the English curriculum, was in 1940 writing for the international audience of *The New Era* journal, a publication produced by and for educationalists and practitioners, part of a much wider educational movement for peace following WW1. Articles about drama in a number of *The New Era* issues published from the late 1920s onwards are indicative of the fierce debates concerning 'New Methods' in English teaching.

Caldwell Cook's practice at the Perse School in Cambridge signalled a new direction for early 20th century educational progressivism. Through collaborative dramatic activity he promoted the development of 'a long-term, collective [group] identity' (Bolton 1998, p. 33) amongst his students, whereas progressive principles had previously held fast to the individualism of the child and freedom of personal expression unrestrained by teacher intervention. In the Mummery, a specially adapted theatre space for the drama activity he pursued as part of his English lessons, Caldwell Cook eschewed the more traditional method of teaching literature, favouring instead the cooperative endeavour of physically staging a Shakespeare play as if for the Elizabethan theatre. His students were expected to assume the identity of a company of players and it was this that shaped their encounters with the texts studied.

It is difficult to gauge to what extent Caldwell Cook's methods had an impact on English teaching practice more generally. Christopher Parry (1969), who as a student and then teacher at the Perse School benefitted from and writes approvingly of Caldwell Cook's legacy, nevertheless suggests that the effect of his book, *The Play Way* (1919) 'was much less powerful than it might have been' (Parry 1969, p. 139). This, he claims, was because of Caldwell Cook's overly sentimental style of writing. Like Parry, we fully acknowledge Caldwell Cook as an innovator who broke new ground in terms of his practice, such as the role-within-role approach to the study of script described above, but there are aspects of his book that deserve critical scrutiny. Perhaps inevitably, some of Caldwell Cook's commentary makes for uncomfortable reading in more contemporary times when issues of diversity and inclusivity are rightly at the forefront of educational discourse. We have in mind his condescending judgements about women – their poor vocabulary choices seem to attract particular criticism (1919, p. 92) – and about students' 'ability', for example, when describing what might be achieved if there are not too many 'stupids' (p. 32) in a class. Colonial inflections in his writing are in tune with the very specific context of the independent (fee-paying) Perse School, with its notions of 'the gentlemanly, "fair play" of the cricket pitch or colonial battlefield' (Kitchen 2018, p. 71). Thus, his methods of promoting student self-governance and 'individual responsibility in learning' (Caldwell Cook 1919, p. 72), usually highlighted as signs of his progressivism, may also reflect the school's underlying mission to prepare the sons of 'the elite' for their future leadership roles.

Harriet Finlay-Johnson was the headteacher of a rural state elementary school, a far cry from the exclusive setting of the Perse School. Dramatisation was at the core of her interdisciplinary methodology and this meant that it was afforded substantial curriculum time. Although she was not solely an English teacher and her approach to educational drama was very much cross-curricular, she 'had a particular interest in the ways in which drama principles and strategies might enhance the teaching of English' (McGuinn 2014, p. 17). This interest, which is implicit in her description of students engaged in dramatising a Shakespeare play, was focused more on the learning potential of their dramatisations than on performance. In this sense her practice was closer to Hourd's (1949), for whom 'the experience of dramatising is far more important than the result' (p. 43), although as McGuinn suggests, Hourd's explicitly political interpretations of the plays in the post-WW2 context set her apart from both of her predecessors. Finlay-Johnson also encouraged her students to invent plays, an activity which had an improvisatory feel, and these served as a stimulus for other classroom activities such as writing or research. Doing drama was therefore intended to arouse her students' '*desire to know*' (Finlay-Johnson 1911, p. 20) [italics in the original], giving them ownership of the learning inspired by their dramatisations. The rest of the class were encouraged to act more as 'critical "spectators"' (Bolton 1998, p. 18) than passive audience, an approach rooted in the belief that young people should be allowed to share their knowledge and learn from each other. Most importantly, the students' drama activity constituted 'a creative and collaborative act of selecting from a body of knowledge and finding their own dramatic form for its presentation' (Bolton 1998, p. 21) and, as far as Nicholson (2011) and Michael Anderson (2012) are concerned, she was the first to properly theorise drama practices.

The writing of Marjorie Hourd, an English teacher at a selective girls' school, also shows 'a determination to find a theoretical basis for understanding literature through Drama' (Bolton 1998, p. 95). In both her article for Volume 21 of *The New Era* journal (1940) and her book (1949) she rejects the narrow interpretation of drama within English encouraged by the Newbolt Report's adherence to 'correct' forms of speech. The article recommends the teaching of epic stories through classroom dramatisation with students between the ages of eight and eleven, and uses this example to set out the developmental process involved in reading literature, drawing a strong link between early enjoyment and future appreciation. She quotes directly from students' reflections on the work, as well as from an example of one student choosing to write in role during a test, all of which gives a genuine insight into the drama-in-English teaching and learning processes of her classroom.

Hourd suggests that a feeling for literature is generated when students improvise and compose their own versions of what are considered to be 'great' works. Whilst Hourd trusts in the powerful effect of the literature she selects for study, she does not require her students to be deferential. They are 'free to rebel and dislike' (1949, p. 128) the text, and the teacher's role is not to dictate 'what it is you ought to say' but rather to make 'it safe to say what you really want to say' (p. 129). The choice of literature is therefore very important and Hourd takes the ballad as her starting point, with dramatisation in the form of 'The Ballad Mime' (1949, p. 31) offering a way for students to begin to grapple with a literary work. This is a process by which Hourd's students, with a degree of spontaneity and trial and error, mime in response to hearing the poem read aloud several times. Caldwell Cook (1919) also writes about the use of mime in the study of balladry, but for him rehearsing a 'vocabulary' (p. 232) of mime, its gestures, signs and conventions, and applying this to mimed performances of ballads, is of greater importance. Hourd is more attentive to the way that the poem is transformed into action via expressive embodiment, each iteration putting 'the child into direct contact with the meaning of the ballad' (1949, p. 31). Although the resources of the body are crucial to the meaning-making process, in contrast to Caldwell Cook, Hourd's practice does not require a special space. She paints a picture of her classroom in which 'A few desks at the front can be pushed backwards' (p. 35), and students are 'sitting on desks and in window sills and sometimes on the floor' (p. 36) to watch each other work.

Hourd's ideas for group play-making around a text such as *The Iliad* include a complex mix of improvisation, scripting and students' written reflections on the characters they would like to play, which enables them to offer more sophisticated interpretations than those reliant on a traditional teacher-led question-and-answer approach. Hourd also demonstrates that, when a student acts as playwright rather than critic, they become 'the active participant in a creative process rather than the passive recipient of meanings interpreted directly by the teacher' (Hourd 1949, p. 62). It is worth noting that some 25 years after Hourd was writing, the findings from Robert Witkin's (1974) wide-ranging classroom-based research echo her concerns about focusing too closely on what Witkin refers to as the 'stylised analysis' of '"critic talk"' (1974, p. 66) or 'exam talk' (p. 67), a process that is antithetical to the stimulation of creative and expressive responses to literature.

There were nuanced differences in the practices of Finlay-Johnson, Caldwell Cook and Hourd, not least in their approach to teaching Shakespearean drama and in the degree of teacher intervention that they favoured. However, all three were concerned with the ways in which dramatic activity encourages student self-direction and enables embodied and imaginative engagement with stories and plays 'from inside the action', to utilise Bolton's (1998, p. 34) phrase. This presupposes a particular approach towards teacher–student and student–student relationships in the classroom and establishes two important principles, familiar to us today but far less so when these practitioners were writing: that students should develop and interrogate textual understandings collaboratively; and that the learning prompted by this sharing of perspectives can be significant. For these pioneers drama also had a part to play in supporting language development, and whilst they did not favour a narrow drama-as-speech-training approach, certain elements of Caldwell Cook's 'Littleman Lectures' come uncomfortably close (see Caldwell Cook 1919, pp. 93–96). Clearly Finlay-Johnson, Caldwell Cook and Hourd were innovators of some significance, each working in their particular contexts towards a concept of drama as central to the various elements of English, and as such they have left a rich legacy. We now go on to explore two controversial themes associated with their practices which have continued to reverberate in English teaching to the present day.

Progressivism and play

i. Progressivism

The work of the early pioneers, along with the later London School group of practitioners, brought new perspectives to educational progressivism that are particularly pertinent to drama-in-English practices. However, the post-WW2 progressive educational 'orthodoxies' that emerged were particularly vulnerable to attack from the right, as Ken Jones (1983) argues, precisely because they lacked a fully articulated programme or coherent manifesto. A concerted 'right-wing counter-offensive' (Jones 1983, p. 2) reached a head in the latter half of the 20th century, mostly succeeding in its aim to tarnish non-traditional educational practices as lacking in purpose or 'rigour' in the public consciousness. The infamous 'Black Papers' (Cox and Dyson 1969) provided the ideological springboard for this assault, followed by a series of curricular and pedagogical interventions by successive policy-makers reasserting the primacy of canonical texts, direct instruction and examination preparation (most recently, for example, Gibb 2017; Gove 2013b).

Criticism of progressive practice has not been confined to politicians, however. David Hornbrook (1989, 1998) is prominent amongst Drama practitioners for his controversial rejection of child-centred educational drama that purports to be 'a therapeutic or pedagogic process' (Hornbrook 1998, p. 14), preferring instead a model which foregrounds subject knowledge in terms of theatre arts and theatrical craft skills. For Hornbrook (1998, p. 14) '*cultural induction*' [italics in the original] is 'in some significant part' a key component of drama education. Nevertheless, Mike Fleming (2011), writing about creative arts in the curriculum, sees a place for both approaches. He characterises the latter as '*learning in*' (p. 177) [italics in the original], because it focuses on the art form itself and, following Hornbrook's model, on the culture(s) to which it belongs. The other approach, which looks outwards to 'a more inclusive, democratic and contemporary approach more suited to recognising the place of arts in education' (p. 181), is described by Fleming (p. 177) as '*learning through*' [italics in the original]. In finding connections between *learning in* and *learning through*, he concludes that educational drama can comfortably exist as both an art form and a medium for self-expression and creativity. Fleming (2011) is also supportive of drama as a means 'to enrich learning experiences in other subjects' (p. 180), a stance reflected in NATE's, 'Position Paper' on Drama (Bunyan et al. 1998).[5] Unsurprisingly, Hornbrook (1998, p. 14) is unconvinced by a more expansive account of drama education, citing English teachers who have 'slipped across' to Drama teaching as being at least in part responsible for a dangerous dilution of its subject knowledge base.

ii. Play

Play has often been a casualty of the negative connotations ascribed to progressive educational thinking, and with the exception of play in Early Years education, playing and learning are often – unfairly – regarded as antithetical in Western culture (Holzman 2010).

The importance Caldwell Cook places on play is implicit in the title of his book, *The Play Way* (1919), although this is somewhat ambiguous since its content is also about working with plays. He associates play with learning-by-doing, but he also notes its importance in stimulating the imagination. He posits that the common ground between play and art is identification with people and situations, and hints that play can act as a rehearsal for the dramas of life. Early 20th-century practitioners continued to explore links between play and learning, particularly in English, as evidenced by several articles in Volume 12 of *The New Era* journal. For example, Wyatt Rawson (1931, p. 75) points out that 'Every child play acts and would continue to do so in a more and more adult fashion up to the end of its school life, did we not almost completely neglect this universal means of cultural education'. Erica Inman (1931, p. 96) finds the origins of play-making with eight-to-twelve-year-olds in the '"let's pretend" spirit of nursery days', and suggests that this type of imaginative engagement is an essential feature of both play and drama. She highlights how young people express themselves not just in words but through their bodies, which prefigures much later ideas about the 'bodiliness' (Franks et al. 2014, p. 172) of drama and its importance in 'embodied reading' activities (Yandell 2014, p. 108). Inman also persuasively argues that young people who play together are learning to work together, and as a result what happens in the classroom becomes more student-directed and less teacher-focused. Hourd's (1949) ideas about the connection between play and reading are also relevant. She proposes that the fantasy life of the dramatic play experienced by students in nursery and Early Years educational settings supports their later, more complex engagements with the imaginative world of books.

It is Myra Barrs (1987) who, with the benefit of access to Vygotskyan theory, mounts the most significant argument for play as part of the learning process in adolescence, decisively demonstrating the ways in which drama-in-English practices draw productively on the dramatic features of play. In Chapter 3 we offer a detailed examination of the social constructivist framework that underpins her approach.

The contribution of drama to language and literature learning

The ways in which drama activity relates to the different aspects of curriculum English continued to develop across the latter half of the 20th century. In terms of language development, Moffett (1967) argues that drama provides 'motivated discourse' and 'realistic contexts' (p. 16). And Barnes (1968) sums up the rationale for drama activity in English that emerged from the Dartmouth discussions in this way: 'to help our pupils to use language to explore and develop the world they live in . . . we should subordinate all other considerations to furthering that exploration and development' (p. 47).

Both, moreover, suggest that drama is a methodology capable of integrating all aspects of English. Moffett (1967, p. 27), for example, highlights the important connection between students' dramatic improvisations and their reading of plays: 'the 'power to bring a script alive in his [sic] mind is constantly recharged by his continued experience in inventing dramas'. When Barnes was Head of English (from 1959) improvisation was also a feature of practice at Minchenden School – one of three case study English departments identified by Peter Medway et al. (2014) as innovative at that time. An English teacher in his department recalls that students' writing, particularly personal writing, '"always arose out of some activity, it could have been some free drama, it could have been a book we'd read"' (Medway et al. 2014, p. 134).

The use of improvisation may not have been widespread but it was gaining ground as an approach. A glimpse at the English syllabus written by Harold Rosen when Head of English (1956–58) at Walworth School – another of Medway et al.'s innovative English departments – shows how spoken language and student experience formed the philosophical centre of the department's English work. Yet, the section on drama recommends a more standard diet of 'dramatic study' of plays and 'floor reading[s]' to stimulate the students' 'dramatic imagination' (Rosen 2017c, pp. 212–213). Soon, though, Rosen's successors, John Dixon and later Alex McLeod (as Heads of English between 1959 and 1965), were introducing improvisation, albeit in what seems to have been an ad hoc fashion, as part of the students' language-rich experience (see Medway et al. 2014). Rosen and Dixon were key figures in LATE, and it is worth noting that by 1980, in an essay on 'The Dramatic Mode', Rosen (2017a) demonstrates how both his own and wider thinking about classroom drama had moved on. At this point the role of improvisation as instrumental in both literature and language learning had received a degree of 'official' sanction in the Bullock Report (DES 1975), and Rosen, by then an academic at the Institute of Education in London, was exploring a more improvisatory approach. He was also developing ideas around the notion of 'dramatic behaviour' as 'ordinary, pervasive and universal' (Rosen 2017a, p. 314), echoing the work of Moffett (1967), and covering similar philosophical ground to Raymond Williams (1983).

It is these types of integrated approaches that were at the core of London English and which laid the foundations for projects with a wider reach such as the National Oracy Project (1987–93) and the Language in the National Curriculum (LINC) project (1989–92). Both focused on working with teachers at a grassroots level to create resources and influence classroom practices, and they provided a sympathetic context for drama activity in English. The extent of the government's hostility to the LINC approach to language teaching is indicated by the project's enforced, premature closure in 1991, the rejection of its report and suppression of its teaching resources.[6] Yet the draft resources were clandestinely circulated via English teaching networks and so the practices they espoused inevitably found their way into some English classrooms. The English Centre, funded by the Inner London Education Authority (ILEA, 1965–90), produced resources such as 'The Island' project (The English Centre 1985) and 'School Under Siege' (Nash et al. 1979), which required sustained engagement in an imagined situation and, *inter alia*, stimulated writing-in-role.[7] The popularity of these publications is indicative of the types of drama-friendly practices found in many English departments at this time, certainly across London, and possibly further afield. Also worthy of note is Beverley Naidoo's account of her classroom-based research (1992) exploring students' attitudes to issues of racism and other forms of injustice encountered in the literary texts they are reading together. Drama-based approaches form an integral part of her methodology, particularly role-play and the hot-seating of teachers and other adults in role. Naidoo reflects that 'A teacher who can move in and out of role her or himself – at times to further the internal drama or to halt it for external reflection – may be in the best position to enable students to face up to difficult challenges at an emotional as well as intellectual level' (pp. 116–117).

None of this is to suggest that ideas about the purpose of drama within English routinely meet with widespread agreement. For example, tensions between residual and emerging practices resurfaced at intervals throughout the 1970s, epitomised by the contrasting positions of John Seely and Christopher Parry. Seely (1976) is unequivocal in his belief that 'The development of pupils' language is the central concern of the English teacher' (p. 3), and so his primary focus is on the ways in which improvised drama, which may or may not lead to scripting, offers students opportunities to explore 'Situations and social interactions' (p. 3) that develop their facility for language use. When Seely very briefly discusses text work, improvisation remains his focus, his preference being to use a snippet from a short script as a stimulus 'to improvise away from or towards it' (p. 134). There is a sense that the playscript is secondary because it is utilised as a vehicle to 'psychologically and linguistically' enrich students' 'improvised situations' (p. 137). Although Seely proposes that students learn about a play through 'the relationship between their own view of life expressed in their improvisations and that of a playwright expressed in a scripted scene' (p. 137), this is an underdeveloped part of his argument. He does, however, seem to be working towards the notion that drama, and particularly improvisation, facilitates opportunities for students to bring their own experiences to bear on their understanding of the dramatic texts studied.

It is unsurprising, therefore, that Seely criticises Parry (1972) for an account of drama within English that harks back to an earlier tradition, one that was inherited from Parry's English teacher, Douglas Brown, who himself was a pupil of Caldwell Cook. Seely (1976) disapproves of Parry's practices, describing them as 'old-fashioned "dramatics"' associated with the 'old-fashioned English teaching' of the 'highly selective school' environment (p. 148), and rebukes him for saying 'nothing about the close linguistic relationship between "English", the pupils' own language, and improvised drama' (p. 148).

Male's (1973) account of drama activity in English also struggles to escape from past practices, particularly in respect of speech training, despite his stated awareness of recent innovations in the study of linguistics. When it comes to teaching dramatic literature, he is adamant that it should not 'be directed towards producing recruits for the acting profession' (p. 46), yet his description of the 'basic requirements for good speech' (p. 46) still comes close to promoting 'actorly' speech training as a way of doing justice to the script and ensuring that the 'sounds that issue forth . . . project the intended meaning' (p. 47). Significantly, he goes on to suggest that there is 'an acceptable meaning' which equates with 'the author's intention' (p. 47). It is therefore unclear what the students might bring to this type of drama activity in terms of their own interpretations and experiences, or what the learning gain might be if performing is seen as an end in itself simply because 'plays are written for performance' (p. 38).

Drama or drama-in-English: A continuing debate

i. Drama as a discrete subject

As is apparent from the 'fundamental questions' (DES 1975, p. 160) about drama posed by the Bullock Report (DES 1975), the 1970s also saw the debate about the place of Drama as a discrete subject in the secondary curriculum gain momentum. Parry (1972) sees 'drama – by which I mean enactment that brings to life the word' as 'the proper medium for *English*; the right way of tackling the subject' (pp. 222–223) [italics in the original], but this view is out-of-step with those such as Lynn McGregor and her colleagues (1977) who strongly advocate for Drama as separate to English. *Learning through Drama* (McGregor et al. 1977), which emerged from a three-year Schools Council Drama Teaching Project, 1974–77, is largely concerned with presenting this case. The authors suggest that practices in English offer only a limited account of drama, criticising a tendency 'to think of plays in terms of literature rather than in terms of performance' (1977, p. 153), and they argue that Drama not only requires separate provision but also specialist teaching. In a brief, two-page section on 'Drama and the English Teacher' they acknowledge some overlap between the two subjects, citing a mutual concern for communication and 'the appropriateness and effectiveness of language usage in varying situations' (p. 153). As far as the teaching of literary texts is concerned, they apportion to drama within English only the responsibility for 'deepening the child's appreciation of, and sensitivity to' (p. 154) literature without mentioning its rich potential for collaborative meaning-making around texts.

ii. Drama and drama-in-English

In many ways the debate about Drama versus drama-in-English represents a false binary. The potential for their co-existence and cross-fertilisation are clear in NATE's Drama 'Position Paper' (Bunyan et al. 1998). Significantly, some of Drama's most internationally renowned practitioners, theorists and researchers, Dorothy Heathcote, Cecily O'Neill and Jonothan Neelands, have been reluctant to take a divisive approach. Heathcote, who advocates for drama as the basis of all learning, has written for English teachers via NATE (see, for example, 1980) and has influenced the thinking of English specialists (see Barrs 1987). Over many years O'Neill has run workshops for English and Drama teachers, both separately and together. She acknowledges that her role-play activities around literary and dramatic texts 'occupy an area between English and Drama which is sometimes viewed with unease from both sides' (O'Neill 1983, p. 20). However, her use of drama methodology to '"pry open"' literary texts so that students can 'enter, experience and explore the imagined world' (O'Neill and Rogers 1994, p. 48) is of real significance to English teachers. In a number of articles for NATE's *English Drama Media* magazine, Neelands also identifies significant synergies between English and Drama, not least that both are committed to a process of social transformation and are situated within a 'pro-human' (Neelands 2004, p. 12) educational tradition. He also reminds us that 'there would be no drama in our secondary schools if English hadn't given time for it in the first place' (2010b, p. 70).

iii. The centrality of drama to English

Looking back at some of the key texts highlighted in Chapter 1, it is interesting to explore where they stand in relation to the ongoing debate about drama's purpose in the English curriculum. As a general rule, their publication dates offer some insight into their stance. For example, *Drama in the English Classroom* (Byron 1986) was published just a year prior to Barrs' (1987) seminal article on role in reading and writing and was not yet bound by the strictures of the National Curriculum. Thus, Byron builds on Moffett's ideas: 'operating in a drama mode allows us to elaborate narrative and to expand our apprehensions of the entire pattern of events, attitudes, behaviours and interactions which the narrative represents selectively' (Byron 1986, p. 75). This is not drama as a means 'merely to *animate text*' (p. 66) [italics in the original]; rather, in a nod towards reader response theory, Byron exemplifies how drama activity draws productively on 'what might be described as a dialogue between reader and text' (p. 68). He makes the important point that drama supports inexperienced and experienced readers alike by mirroring and making explicit key aspects of the reading process, such as '"read[ing] between the lines"', and 'elaboration', by which he means the student '"remaking" the novel in his or her own head' (p. 75). He roots these ideas in schemes of work which are discussed during (fictional) conversations between two English teachers. 'Mike' is insecure about his attempts to introduce drama into his English lessons, and 'Maggie' is his supportive, more experienced drama-in-English colleague. Their discussions mirror the type of professional dialogue that many English teachers find useful in developing practice.

Since the publication of Byron's (1986) handbook much has happened to alter the landscape for English teachers in England, and consequently for drama within English. The introduction of the National Curriculum for English (1989), the NLS in secondary schools (2001) and the latest revision of the National Curriculum (DfE 2014) that makes barely a mention of drama have had a significant impact on curriculum and practice. One constant since 1989 has been the prominent place afforded to Shakespeare. The development of 'active Shakespeare' pedagogies, including high-profile theatre-inflected education initiatives such as led by the Royal Shakespeare Company (RSC) and the Globe Theatre, have served to single out Shakespeare as the aspect of English best suited to drama-based approaches (which we say more about in Chapter 6). The 2011 special drama edition of NATE's journal *English in Education* reflects this tendency: in a rare opportunity to showcase drama's unique contributions to English, the majority of the articles focus on the teaching of Shakespeare's plays.

Shakespeare also makes an appearance in one of McGuinn's (2014, p. 94) proposed 'activity sequences' described in the second part of his handbook. Although work around poetry is also included, on the whole literary texts are not the focus, and his sequences generally serve as a vehicle to investigate language use. Clearly influenced by the terminology of the NLS *KS3 Framework* (DfEE 2001), sequences are organised into text, word and sentence, and whole text level work. One, entitled 'From phoneme to word level' (p. 110), draws on the levels of a relatively little-known writing schema developed by Richard Andrews (2001), which offers a somewhat atomised approach to language study. In McGuinn's sequence (pp. 111–118), this leads to a set of stand-alone drama activities, some of which appear to be little more than speech and vocal exercises.

Certainly, McGuinn's proposed practices do not chime with those academics and practitioners writing in the Australian context, whose concern is more to do with drama activity integrated within the broader study of literature. This is apparent in *Drama and English Teaching* (Anderson et al. 2008), and more recently in *Stand Up for Literature: Dramatic Approaches in the Secondary English Classroom* (O'Toole and Dunn 2020). It is worth noting that the latter was published when the terms of reference for a significant review of the Australian National Curriculum for English were being agreed, and that the focus on language is very prominent in the revised curriculum that was subsequently implemented. 'Language' and 'Literacy' feature as two out of the three strands, and references to drama are largely absent, except in terms of the reading of plays and one mention of role-play as a way to adjust language teaching to meet diverse student needs. Additionally, in the accompanying 'Scope and Sequence' document, role-play and performance make only a very brief appearance as part of the 'Literature' strand. In the Foreword to *Stand Up for Literature* Peter Freebody (2020, p. ix) proposes that the book offers a challenge to rigid curriculum and assessment regimes that constrain 'teachers' readiness to respond in innovative ways to the more important, durable goals of the English curriculum, and in ways that might better respond to the diverse needs of their students'.[8]

Bringing us right up to date, O'Toole and Dunn's (2020) perspective is rooted in process drama practices, and theirs is very much a 'how to' book – the authors use the term 'DIY manual' (p. 33). It contains many exemplars for ways of working with particular texts through drama. The authors also provide useful definitions of a range of different approaches as well as advice on managing drama activity in the classroom. It is likely that a section on 'The Elements of Drama' (pp. 9–11), which includes tension and framing and how these are applied during the dramatic exploration of a text, will be of particular interest to English teachers. However, as Kempe (2021) suggests in his review for NATE's *Teaching English* magazine, it is problematic that the literary texts cited tend to serve the purposes of the drama activities rather than the other way round, which calls into question 'the extent to which it [the book's approach] provides insights into the text itself as a piece of literature' (Kempe 2021, p. 81). Kempe concludes that, despite the wealth of practical detail, the book 'demand[s] a good deal from the teacher' (p. 81), and this may well prove a risk too far for those English teachers who lack confidence or experience in working with texts through drama.

Continuing challenges

Confidence can certainly be an issue for English teachers inexperienced in planning for and managing drama-in-English activity, a situation made worse when government policies (and, as we see in Chapter 8, even teacher handbooks) emphasise the 'difficulties' rather than the affordances of pursuing drama as part of the English curriculum. In England, the suggestion of optionality that we have discussed above in relation to the Bullock Report and the limiting reference in the current National Curriculum serve to undermine the significance of drama-in-English. Another issue, and in our experience the one that English teachers are most likely to cite, is the lack of time in a packed curriculum and the accompanying pressures of preparing students for high-stakes examinations. These legitimate concerns will no doubt have a resonance for colleagues in other anglophone jurisdictions. However, it does not have to be like this, and it is possible for assessment to validate drama-in-English approaches, as was the case, for example, in England and Wales between 1986 and 1994, when drama-based criteria were built into GCSE English coursework assessment. We are not suggesting, however, that drama-in-English can only survive in a coursework-assessed curriculum. Students interviewed more recently as part of our case study research have articulated the value of drama activity in preparing them even for the rigours of terminal examinations (see Chapter 5).

This necessarily brief and selective history of landmark moments, movements and trends demonstrates that the impetus for drama as part of English has, over time and despite setbacks, remained persistent and strong, although not always reflected in official policy documents. In the chapters that follow we explain the theoretical framework that underpins our drama-in-English approach, and then go on to illustrate our argument with examples from classroom practice.

Notes

1   Reports commissioned by the UK government are referred to by the last name of the committee chairperson, in this case, Sir Henry Newbolt.
2   Matthew Arnold (1822–88), played an important role in the promotion of English Literature as a school subject. His writings about the civilising potential of literature, particularly for working-class children, have left a problematic legacy, most recently invoked by Secretary of State for Education, Michael Gove (2010–14), in the run-up to the 2014 curriculum review. Ironically, whilst Gove has overseen curriculum revisions which strip English of much of its creative potential, Arnold was a passionate advocate for creativity in education and a staunch critic of rote-learning.
3   As Simon Gibbons (2013) reports, London English – alternatively the London School – grew out of endeavours by post-war practitioners based in and around the capital to adopt a more inclusive, essentially classroom- and child-focused approach to English teaching, particularly attentive to language in use.
4   The Secretary of State for Education, 2010–14, in the Conservative-led Coalition Government.
5   Subsequently updated in 2006 in the context of the Literacy Strategy.
6   In a contemporaneously written article, Alastair West (1996, p. 75) records: 'Not only has the government now refused to publish the material and refused to waive Crown copyright to enable its commercial publication by any one of the international publishers who have expressed strong interest in doing so, but it has also denied publication to a report by Her Majesty's Inspectorate (HMI) which comments very favourably upon the LINC project work'.
7   For a discussion about the pedagogical assumptions underpinning 'The Island', see Gillian Anderson (2013).
8   Interestingly, the new Education Wales/Addysg Cymru curriculum (2020, implemented in 2022) adopts a more creative and inclusive approach to language study and literature choices.

3

DRAMA-IN-ENGLISH FRAMEWORKS

This chapter outlines the theoretical frameworks which have shaped our thinking about drama-in-English and which underpin our interpretations of what happens in the social context of real-world classrooms. We begin by exploring the interrelationship between language and learning, and its implication for understanding processes by which we acquire knowledge. We then consider the key role of play and imagination in the conceptual and emotional development of young people, moving on to highlight the centrality of role-play in drama-in-English classrooms, particularly its function in respect of literary study. Importantly, we draw attention to the inclusive and culturally responsive nature of this way of working.

Learning and knowledge acquisition in English

Our social constructivist model of drama-inflected English practice draws substantially on the work of Soviet psychologist Lev Vygotsky, whose early 20th century writings have been influential in Western educational thinking since they were first translated into English in the 1960s. At the heart of Vygotsky's theory of cognitive development is the understanding that learning arises out of interaction between the learner and others in their social, cultural and material contexts. Crucially, language mediates these experiences. In *Thought and Language* (1986), Vygotsky pays particular attention to the dual function of language as both a social and a psychological tool, arguing that we not only use language to communicate existing knowledge and experiences to others, but also to develop new knowledge and (re-)organise our individual thoughts accordingly. These functions operate in an ongoing dynamic interrelationship. While children's early language development is shaped by the particular community they are born into, as they grow up they are naturally

DOI: 10.4324/9781003290827-3

engaged in an internal psychological process of adaptation and reinterpretation prompted by fresh experiences and new contexts:

> In that process, the relation of thought to word undergoes changes that themselves may be regarded as development in the functional sense. Thought is not merely expressed in words; it comes into existence through them. Every thought tends to connect something with something else, to establish a relation between things. Every thought moves, grows and develops, fulfils a function, solves a problem. (1986, p. 218)

The pedagogical implications of this insight are profound, not least the necessity of providing a talk-rich classroom environment designed to acknowledge, and build upon, the diverse social and linguistic backgrounds of the learners. It is an understanding of learning and language development that runs counter to the so-called 'knowledge-rich' (Gibb 2017) and 'word poor' (Quigley 2018) orthodoxies currently promoted by neoliberal administrations in the UK and, to some extent, in the US.[1] Vygotsky argues that on its own the 'direct teaching of concepts' – what we might today describe as 'transmission model' teaching – merely leads to 'parrotlike repetition' and 'empty verbalism' (1986, p. 150) on the part of the learners. By way of illustration, Vygotsky quotes from Leo Tolstoy's own account of attempting to teach children literary language: 'any teacher will confirm' that the teaching of specific words 'is not difficult to comprehend, but [it is] the concept denoted by this word, which the child does not understand' (1986, pp. 150–151). Instead, Vygotsky states that the development of 'mature concepts' relies upon a dynamic interplay between the abstract, disciplinary knowledge taught in school (what Vygotsky calls 'scientific concepts') and learners' existing, everyday knowledge accumulated from real life experiences ('spontaneous concepts'). This is by no means a straightforwardly one-directional cognitive process. So, while scientific concepts take on a more concrete, graspable form as they interact with a learner's store of everyday knowledge, at the same time spontaneous concepts become more systematised and abstract.

It is difficult to overstate the significance of this proposition in relation to debates about the nature of knowledge acquisition in education. It is fundamentally inclusive in orientation; as John Yandell (2014, p. 16) argues, it means that 'the everyday knowledge that the students bring may also transform and reorganise the curricularised knowledge of schooling'. This echoes Douglas Barnes' (1976, p. 14) proposition that, in order to be rendered meaningful, a curriculum must be 'enacted by pupils as well as teachers . . . embodied in the communicative life of an institution, the talk and gestures by which pupils and teachers exchange meanings . . .'. In other words, the study of English (or, indeed, any other school subject) is not reducible to the simple 'delivery' of pre-ordained curriculum content in classrooms. By way of illustration, Yandell and Brady (2016) compare the teaching of *Romeo and Juliet* and the discussions it raises about familial relationships in two differently situated classrooms, one just outside of London, the other in Ramallah, Palestine. They argue that reading experiences – the way readers make sense of texts – can never be divorced from the social and cultural dimensions of students' lives experienced outside the classroom.

More recently, Robert Eaglestone (2020) adopts a similar position in his philosophical discussion about the formation of literary knowledge. He conceives of disciplinary knowledge as porous rather than being fixed and rigidly bound, a process he compares to an ongoing conversation. Literary knowledge, he argues, '*begins* in the experience of seeing or reading it. Teaching grows this knowledge in dialogue by helping the student articulate, reflect on, adapt and mature their view' (n.p.) [italics in the original]. He adds that any attempt to teach a work of literature that does not start with students' own lives and beliefs 'betrays both the discipline and the point of literature' (n.p.). This collective approach to knowledge production might be regarded as a 'characteristic pedagogy' of the English classroom (Elliott 2021, p. 11).

Scaffolding learning through drama and role-play

Importantly, Vygotsky's writings also begin to provide us with a theoretical paradigm for understanding the pedagogical value of drama and role-play in education. Many readers will be familiar with the concept of the 'Zone of Proximal Development' (or ZPD), probably the best-known – but not necessarily the best understood – area of Vygotsky's research. Here Vygotsky directs his attention to the ways in which learners make progress and how teachers might help them reach their full potential. He proposes a forward-looking form of supportive pedagogy that anticipates what a child might achieve with assistance but would not yet be able to achieve independently. In *Mind and Society* (1978, p. 86) he describes the ZPD as:

> . . . the distance between the actual development level as determined by independent problem solving and the level of potential development as determined through problem solving under adult guidance or in collaboration with more capable peers.

This is an understanding of children's capacity to learn that is contingent upon the creation of a nurturing and collaborative learning environment – a far cry from the discourse of individualised deficit in popular currency. Indeed, Vygotsky invites us to regard a learner's cognitive functions not yet matured as 'buds' or 'flowers' waiting to become the 'fruits' of development (1978, p. 86). The less flowery metaphor of 'scaffolding' (Wood, Bruner and Ross 1976) has more recently been adopted by educationalists, particularly in the UK and USA, in their attempts to develop practical applications of the ZPD for classrooms. Many of these popularised versions of the ZPD, however, have tended to instrumentalise Vygotsky's original concept by neglecting its social and reciprocal dimensions.

We want to approach the concept of scaffolding from a different direction. Of significant interest to drama-in-English practitioners are Vygotsky's insights into the potential of play and role-play for creating a supportive framework for learning. From his observations of young children, Vygotsky (2016) concludes that play represents a leading factor in development through which children develop the capacity to imagine situations outside of their immediate context and experiences. As Vygotsky notes, the moment a child at play is, for example, able to pretend a stick is a horse, 'one of the basic psychological structures determining the child's relationship to reality is radically altered' (p. 13). Vygotsky also draws attention to the roles children assume within their games, such as spontaneously adopting the familiar role of sister or mother. In order to enact this role, the child must play according to the culturally defined rules that guide behaviour in their specific social context. Importantly, since this play requires a *re-working* of what has been observed in real life, it expands the child's horizons by going beyond the merely imitative. Thus, Vygotsky proposes that play serves to create a specialised form of ZPD by making new intellectual, behavioural and emotional demands on the learner:

> In play a child is always above his [sic] average age, above his daily behaviour; in play it is as though he were a head taller than himself. (2016, p. 18)

Taking this proposition a stage further, a number of English and Drama practitioners have argued that educational drama can foster a particular form of collaborative ZPD. For example, secondary Drama teacher Maggie Hulson (2006, p. 7) demonstrates by means of examples from her own practice the ways in which: 'The children can participate at their own level in the company of their peers who are participating at their levels, and with their teacher as a guide . . ., leading them, challenging them, structuring their work individually and collectively'.

Making, learning and 'serious play'

There is, according to Gavin Bolton (1998) little, if any, difference between improvised, make-believe playing and the drama activity of the classroom since both require young people to actively engage in composing and creating. He refers to this as 'making', which involves a combination of dramatist, spectator, participant and directorial functions (p. 267), including the creation and critical review of the learners' own drama 'texts'. This process, whilst seemingly complex, has an everyday quality, drawing on the child's 'normal capacity for playing and imagining' (Barrs 1987, p. 11). When applied to drama in the classroom, 'making' has the following features: it is part of a larger 'collective enterprise, culturally determined in language and action' (Bolton 1998, p. 271); it enables learners to try out a range of identities within the framework of the imaginary context; and it provides opportunities for learner reflection during and after the event.

With this in mind, how might play be viewed specifically in relation to the study of English at secondary level? An understanding that is key to Barrs' (1987) exploration of role-taking and enactment in English is that all creative play involves the adoption of roles. Furthermore, she argues (p. 11):

> Enactment is both *action* and *symbolization*. It is thus a pivotal symbolic category and learning mode, drawing on *both* the individual's powers of social action *and* on the normal capacity for playing and imagining. [italics in the original]

Because role-play and enactment 'draw on a fundamental mode of learning' (Barrs 1987, p. 11) whilst simultaneously allowing learners, through play, 'to use powers that they naturally possess' (p. 11), this is a winning combination as far as English is concerned. Andrew Burn (2022), for example, points to the essentially playful qualities of any piece of literature. In terms of Burn's particular area of interest, digital games, he speculates that all texts, including novels, can be re-imagined through 'playful reading' (p. 1), a process that Margaret Mackey (2007) refers to as 'playing the text'. His argument, that play is central to both the creative act of producing a literary text and the types of adaptation that occur when learners engage with it through re-creative activities such as drama, is very relevant to the English classroom.

Vygotsky suggests that in adolescent play 'young people become conscious of their feelings and motives' (Barrs 2022, p. 127), which means that imaginative 'serious play' (Vygotsky 1978, p. 104) should not be dismissed as only appropriate in early years or primary settings. Immersion in a '*what if* world' [italics in the original] (Lee et al. 2017, p. 159) is common to both imaginative play and the reading of literature. Furthermore, learners' understanding is inevitably filtered through their own real-life experiences, the fiction-making of their drama activity acting as 'a mirror in which one might glimpse oneself' (Bolton 1998, p. 266). Their experiences permeate and inflect their dramatic engagements with a text, helping them to position themselves in relation to it. Lee et al. (2017, p. 159) seek to sum up this process by describing the 'incremental, collaborative practice' of drama and the way in which it brings the '*what if* world' of the literary text into view, opening it up to both affective engagement and critical interpretation. O'Neill and Rogers (1994, pp. 47–48) describe this way of working as 'Prying open the text', and they highlight the 'direct access' that such an approach affords, contrasting it to an over-reliance on teacher-subscribed and -directed question-and-answer routines, which, at worst, distance learners from the world of the text whilst delineating their responses to it.

How, then, can the English teacher utilise play to incentivise students' learning and intervene in the process so that their learning is extended 'beyond what they already know' (O'Neill et al. 1976, p. 7)? Geoff Gillham's (1974) identification of 'play for them' and 'play for teacher' is useful here: 'play for them' refers to the way in which learners might initially be encouraged to play with an idea free from too much teacher direction; and 'play for teacher' alludes to the negotiations that enable teachers to deepen the drama by questioning and challenging those involved. The 'play for them' draws the learners in, builds their investment, and is an important stage in creating a connection with the 'play for teacher'. Montgomerie and Ferguson (1999, p. 18) explain this in Vygotskyan terms, offering a practical example of how, during process drama activity, there are pivotal moments on which the teacher capitalises to move the learners' experience of a text 'from spontaneous play into the realm of the scientific'.

Education and imagination

Also of significance for teachers of English are the connections Vygotsky makes between children's play and the internalised development of imagination (or 'fantasy') in adolescents (and, indeed, in adulthood when responding to and enjoying various forms of art and literature). Vygotsky asserts that after puberty the imagination becomes a subjective form of thinking, or 'play without action' (1978, p. 93), borne out of inner desires and the drive for creative expression. It enables 'higher syntheses of personality and world view' (1931, p. 23), at once an intellectual and an affective psychological development. As Barrs (2022, p. 133) summarises: 'imaginative thinking has the capacity to greatly enrich realistic thinking by liberating it from too close a dependence on immediate perception and reality, and enabling it to achieve a freer and more speculative character'. Anton Franks (1997, p. 138) suggests that in providing space for creative production in classrooms, we enable adolescents to 'play through' their imaginings, albeit within the confines of institutional boundaries, and subject to peer observation and interpretation. He observes a group of Year 8 boys in a London classroom expertly creating a physical representation of a Harley Davidson motorbike (a material 'object of desire' for boys of this age), using just their bodies and voices. Franks notes that 'desire energised the work of the group' (p. 140) in a 'socially oriented' way (p. 141), operating at both an individual and collective level. As is the case in make-believe play, the physical nature of dramatic activity fulfils 'the drive for action, for embodiment, for realization that is present in the very process of imagination' (Vygotsky 2004, p. 70). Indeed, Vygotsky is explicit in his promotion of acting, playwriting and dramatisation as potentially transformative educational experiences, involving a complex interaction between language, semiotic tools and artefacts:

> Drama, more than any other form of creation, is closely and directly linked to play, which is the root of all creativity in children. Thus, drama is the most syncretic mode of creation, that is, it contains elements of the most diverse forms of creativity. (p. 71)

For Vygotsky, imagination is of the very highest social and cultural importance, and indeed, drives all progress in society:

> But in actuality, imagination, as the basis of all creative activity, is an important component of absolutely all aspects of cultural life, enabling artistic, scientific, and technical creation alike. In this sense . . . the entire world of human culture, as distinct from the world of nature, all this is the product of human imagination and of creation based on this imagination. (pp. 9–10)

English represents a crucial curricular space within which opportunities to develop learners' imagination can be fostered. Because works of literature – a core element of our subject – provide rich material for what Vygotsky refers to as learners' 'accumulation of experience' (2004, p. 15), drama activity offers the English teacher a significant means of approaching texts in an appropriately experiential way.

The centrality of role in the English classroom

As we have seen, Barrs (1987) persuasively argues that so much of what happens in English is about enactment, making use of young people's strengths and the powers they already naturally possess. Essentially, Barrs proposes that reading is drama in the head, writing is drama on paper and physicalised role-play is a crucial part of the whole-class reading experience, one which recognises the body as a key interpretive resource. Barrs' (1987) approach is based on a Vygotksyan view of learning, draws on aspects of Heathcote's drama practice, and nods towards the influential work of literary theorist Louise Rosenblatt, which we consider in more detail later in this chapter.

It is important to note how activities in the drama-in-English classroom both relate to and draw from the wider cultural context. Just as Barrs highlights the everyday qualities of enactment, Raymond Williams (1983), the renowned literary and cultural commentator, finds value in the very ordinariness of culture being made and re-made daily in our 'dramatized society' (p. 11). He argues that drama forms part of 'the rhythms of everyday life' (p. 12); it therefore has 'direct cultural continuity' (p. 14) with our own lives, in very much the same way that drama in the English classroom strives for cultural continuity with the lives and experiences of the learners. Williams' analysis focuses on the televised drama of his day, but, if anything, the notion of a dramatised society is even more applicable today, particularly in terms of the role-based cultural activities that young people practise on digital platforms (Burn 2022). Williams' thinking is also very relevant as far as the use of a drama-based pedagogy to explore literary texts is concerned. His description of texts as works of art that are 'in one sense explicit and finished forms' but also waiting to be completed, to be made 'present, in specifically active "readings"' (1977, p. 129) is foundational to our concept of drama-in-English. As he suggests, the making and remaking of art 'is never itself in the past tense. It is always a formative process, within a specific present' (p. 129), and this seems to us to sum up succinctly what happens when students engage with texts through role-play, remaking culture in the English classroom.

The ordinariness of role-play is also emphasised in the work of sociologist Erving Goffman (1959), who employs a performance paradigm to describe the social interactions of everyday life. His theories provide an understanding of how human interactions, particularly the social roles we adopt, shift according to the context in which we are operating. Role as a state of being (Goffman) and role as it is utilised in the classroom to examine how we live (e.g., Barrs) are different but connected concepts. Heathcote (2015b) takes inspiration from another of Goffman's (1974) core concepts, 'frame', to recognise the significance of the perspective from which students enter the fictional world. This is a strategy that readily lends itself to the English classroom. The class may assume roles that are suggestive of some kind of shared interest, as members of a residents' association, say (see Chapter 4 for an example within a *Frankenstein* sequence of learning); of reporters providing a removed account of the actions of the protagonists; or of archaeologists making sense of scraps of text. Introducing some distance from an emotional or dramatic event is a way of ensuring that those involved are better placed to evaluate what is happening. Role-taking in English is therefore not primarily concerned with developing characterisation in an actorly sense; rather it can be indicative of attitude or concern captured in dramatic action (Wagner 1999). Barrs (1987, p. 11) recognises the significance of this approach in her reflections on the critical power of writing-in-role: 'Role is another way of focusing – of taking up an attitude to your material'. We discuss this further in Chapter 5.

Both everyday playfulness and classroom drama activity involve degrees of make-believe and mimetic activity. To enter into a fiction as part of the English lesson, students draw on their experience, garnered from play, of mentally inhabiting two worlds at the same time, their own and that of the fiction. This provides an important starting point for drama-in-English. The fictional world is in large part delineated by the source text which in itself is a literary interpretation of a 'lifeworld as lived' (Glover 2018, p. 68). Illuminating it but not identical to it is the world created by the students' role-plays and enactments based on the text. The final world is the students' own, which infiltrates and inflects these other two (see O'Neill and Rogers 1994). The fictional context of the drama activity heightens students' awareness of the choices they are making. Moment-by-moment they are thinking about what they need to do and say next, and are observing themselves doing and saying it. This is the process known as self-spectatorship, which, as Bolton (1998, p. 266) puts it, requires 'being an audience to one's own creation and being an audience to *oneself*'. Students are therefore both '*engaged* and *detached*' (Bolton 1998, p. 200) [italics in the original], which again highlights the productive interplay between their affective and critical responses when they engage dramatically with texts. The collaborative nature of drama activity also shields learners from direct exposure to the sometimes challenging emotional aspects of the roles and contexts being explored, because students share in and experience these collectively – and, crucially, because they are not playing themselves.

Neelands (2011, p. 174) identifies role-play as particularly powerful because 'role-taking allows young people to work as, rather than learn about'. We suggest that in English there are many productive opportunities for students to engage in this manner, ranging from whole-class role-play to fleeting moments when individuals take on a role to embody a moment of insight about a text that they are studying (Bryer and Coles 2022). As well as drawing from students' naturally occurring resources, this type of work acts as a prompt to the imagination, which enters a particularly intense phase during adolescence (see Vygotsky 2004). Neelands (2011, pp. 170–171) suggests that role-play invites students 'to imagine themselves in new ways', and by acting on the (imagined) world from this new perspective, they are developing the confidence and insight to 'change themselves and the world in actuality'. In later chapters we go on to explore in more detail some of the ways in which learners, from both our own research and that of others, use drama activity to make sense of and engage creatively with the texts that they are studying.

Reading through drama

According to Rosenblatt (1994, p. viii), the act of reading involves a 'dynamic interfusion of both reader and text', and although her approach is essentially reader-centred, it is important to note that she does not 'deny the importance of the author's text' (1994, p. 15). This has relevance for what happens in a drama-in-English classroom when students collectively and willingly submit to what O'Neill and Rogers (1994) refer to as manipulation by the author's fiction. Students' responses are guided and shaped by the world that the text creates to a greater extent than might be the case in the type of Drama lesson which uses the text primarily as a jumping-off point. Thus, the teacher in a drama-in-English classroom is continually shifting the focus between the text itself and the students' responses to it. This process draws from Rosenblatt's notion of efferent and aesthetic reading, the former describing the ideas, concepts and actions that readers are left with after the reading, the latter what they undergo during the reading event. Indeed, when Rosenblatt casts literary reading as dynamic, 'lived through in our own persons' and likely to expand 'the boundaries of our own temperaments and worlds' (1994, p. 68), she might just as easily be describing the reading through drama experience. It is therefore no surprise to find drama terminology threaded throughout Rosenblatt's account of literary reading. For example, she uses the analogy of an actor preparing to play a part, proposing that the reader hears the sounds and rhythms of the words internally. This echoes Barrs' (1987, p. 8–9) description of the ways in which a text 'lives *through us*' whenever we tune 'our own voice to its demands' [italics in the original]. Rosenblatt's analogy of a theatre director 'who has to supply the tempo, the gestures, the actions' for 'the whole cast' (p. 13) evokes the way in which readers manage the bigger picture of the text whilst their reading of it progresses.

Rosenblatt's concept of a lived through reading experience is actualised in drama, not least because, as Heathcote says, 'The thing to be taught must be discovered via human beings in action' (1984, p. 48). Living through in drama is a creative process but it also places critical demands on the learner who has 'to think from *inside* the responsibility of a situation rather than to think it over and about it' (Heathcote 1980, p. 9) [italics in the original]. Thus, dramatic engagement with a text does not require the learner to be subsumed uncritically into the life of a character or situation; rather they are trying on a role, or donning a mantle in Heathcote's terms, for a period of time. In this way the learner gains both immediate experience of the text and conscious insight into the distinction between the 'reality' of the fiction and the actuality of the 'real world'.

The connection that readers draw between fictional and actual reality is also explored in the work of reception theorist Wolfgang Iser. He suggests that the illusionary world of the text signals to the reader that it 'is to be viewed not as reality but as if it *were* reality' (Iser 1989, p. 251) [italics in the original]. Reading relies on the creativity, imagination and playfulness of this 'as if' mode of thinking, features of which are also the bedrock of dramatic activity. The potential for 'as if' is built into the 'structured blanks', gaps and indeterminacies of the text, and these 'prompt acts of ideation on the reader's part' (Iser 1980, pp. 111–112) such that readers taking part in collaborative drama-in-English activity can, in a very real sense, inhabit the gaps. Burn's (2022, p. 1) concept of 'playful reading' in some respects echoes Iser's (1989) identification of the textual gaps as 'play-spaces' (p. 253), and 'the text is the playground' (p. 250) in which the author and reader share a game of the imagination. The reward of this game is to be found in the richness of the meaning-making experience.

For its relevance to a reading-through-drama approach, it is worth mentioning Jerome Bruner's writing about the narrative mode of thought as a way of interpreting reality. Although not a reception theorist, and more famous for his work as an educational psychologist, there are some parallels between Iser's and Bruner's theories, particularly Bruner's concern with the verisimilitude of literary texts. He also borrows from Iser's concept of the virtual text when he describes the reader–text interaction as an evolving journey, for which readers' encounters with other stories and experiences provide something akin to a route map. Unlike Iser, though, Bruner focuses as much on the text as on the reader, and he is particularly interested in the 'processes that are loosed by the text in the reader's mind' (Bruner 1986, p. 7). For Bruner, 'stories with literary merit' (p. 24), which presumably encompass those read in English classrooms, have very particular qualities. These are texts that create uncertain worlds, evoke a range of possibilities and allow play for the learner's imagination to construct a virtual text which 'changes almost moment to moment in the act of reading' (Bruner 1986, p. 7), whilst the actual text remains unchanged. By way of illustration Bruner notes how readers, when asked to '"tell back"' (p. 6) a story, do so in different ways and with different conceptions of the kind of story being re-created. It is this susceptibility to polysemy (the co-existence of many possible meanings), that makes dramatic telling back such a powerful tool to employ in the English classroom. Learners are in 'the subjunctive mode' (p. 26), to utilise Bruner's terminology, when engaging dramatically with narratives which render aspects of the familiar world strange in the sense that they might be seen from a new or different angle. This finds resonance with Heathcote's conception of distancing in process drama, whereby a situation, event or issue is explored in 'the *now* time of drama' (2015b, p. 72) [italics in the original], but with opportunities to freeze the drama in order to step back, re-awaken learners' attention to the situation and prompt them to reflect on it afresh. Through this 'inside/outside reflective dialectic' (Davis 1998, p. XI), a balance is maintained 'between engagement and detachment that protects the students from uncritical absorption in the emotional elements of the work' (O'Neill 2015b, p. 39).

When it comes to the social processes of reading in the drama-in-English classroom, some aspects of reader response and reception theories are problematic. These include the assumption that readers are culturally homogenous with similar levels of competence. Another issue is a failure to recognise the collective nature of the reading that takes place in English lessons. As Yandell's (2014) socially oriented model demonstrates, reading encompasses and benefits from a complex web of interactions, including those between readers. Drama activity affords learners the opportunity to explore each other's literary and lived experiences in relation to the text, or as Neelands puts it, to tell their own stories in relation to the stories of others (see O'Connor 2010). Although Rosenblatt is critiqued by Yandell (2014) for her emphasis on the individual reader, she too notes that 'Learning what others have made of a text can greatly increase such insight into one's own relationship with it' (1994, p. 146). This is borne out when learners from our research discuss the ways in which drama activity has, over time, supported them to develop and write about their own interpretations of literary texts (see Chapter 5).

Drama as a form of 're-creative' activity

As we have already observed, central to reader response theory is the notion that a text is, to some degree, re-made every time it is read. The pedagogical concept of 're-creativity' (McCallum 2012) further develops this idea. It involves the intentional manipulation of a source text to create something new, for instance by shifting the narrative perspective, or recasting the piece in a different genre. Such activities, according to Knights and Thurgar-Dawson (2008), position learners not only as active, engaged readers but also as cultural producers, and serve to highlight the connection between the critical and the creative aspects of the reading process. Additionally, they carry echoes of the creative processes that produced the original work itself. As McCallum's (2012) work in this area indicates, to engage learners in re-creative activity in response to reading a literary text has long been a staple of English lessons in secondary schools, however it has been most commonly achieved through written tasks, either composed collaboratively or individually. Our proposition is that drama provides an ideal medium for re-creative activities in the literature classroom.

The relationship between the source and re-creative text is an intertextual one: all texts are written and read in the light of the other texts to which they implicitly and explicitly refer within the historical and cultural contexts of both their production and their reading. Thus the study of literary texts in drama-in-English lessons draws on a network of textual experiences from both within and beyond the classroom context as other texts are 'folded into' (Burnett and Merchant 2016, p. 273) the storying-through-drama which takes place. In this model, meaning-generation is a dynamic process. As McCallum (2012) points out, as with learning itself, this process involves the application of existing sets of knowledge to new material in order to bring about fresh insights.

As the learners re-create aspects of the literary texts through drama, 'the result is a complex interpenetration of alternate worlds' (O'Neill and Rogers 1994, p. 50). The first is circumscribed by the source text which is itself a symbolic form, a literary interpretation of real life. Illuminating this but not identical to it is the drama world. The final world is the learners' own which infiltrates and inflects these other two (O'Neill and Rogers 1994). Reading the ways that their peers have interpreted the text with words and bodies is a prompt for students to recognise the relationship between the physical and the metaphorical, a phenomenon we explore further in Chapter 7.

Crucially, in re-creating the source text through dramatic interactions between self, group and text, learners are encouraged to position themselves alongside the author. This amounts to a process of co-authoring which reaches beyond the boundaries of reader response theory and the transaction between author and reader, because the learners in the English classroom share responsibility for the ways in which texts are read and interpreted not only with the author but with the teacher and with each other.

Importantly, McCallum (2012) reminds us that acts of textual re-imagining, however radical and playfully experimental, do not compromise the materiality of the source text, since 'The words on the page remain the same' (p. 57). Instead, re-creativity 'cultivates careful thought about source material and encourages a direct comparison between an original and what it inspires' (p. 54).

Adaptation

Adaptation takes the notion of 're-creativity' a stage further. Here, productive, dramatic engagement with literary texts involves conscious adaptation of a source text, achieved, for example, by devising creative enactments of specific episodes from alternative viewpoints, or improvising 'missing scenes'. In Chapter 7 we explore the generative relationship between English, drama and media production, and the rich forms of literacy resulting from working with transmedia adaptations of literary texts such as *Beowulf*. Of course, film, television and graphic adaptations of classic literary texts have over many years become a well-established feature of the English classroom in support of textual study. Elliott and Olive's (2021) recent survey of secondary English teachers in England, for instance, indicates that availability of film versions remains a factor in determining specific choice of Shakespeare plays for study. Undoubtedly, comparing clips from adapted versions and the ways in which they differ from the source text has the potential to open up the printed texts for richly interpretive exploration (e.g., Bousted and Ozturk 2004), although it is important to deal with what Burn (2022, p. 16) terms 'the fidelity problem', whereby the 'original' is *de facto* regarded as the correct version, and typically judged to be of greater cultural worth (a phenomenon, it must be said, perpetuated by examination systems that narrowly focus on close analysis of the 'original' printed text). What is of particular interest to us is what happens when students take on the mantle of adaptors themselves, and as educators how we conceive of both process and product within this dynamic pedagogy.

Adaptation theorist Linda Hutcheon (2013) concedes that all literary texts are, in a Bakhtinian sense, adaptations of previously existing stories and texts, but she argues that what distinguishes 'adaptation' as a specific concept is the degree of interpretive intentionality required on the part of the adaptor. Hutcheon contends that adaptations should be valued as texts or works of art in their own right, framed as 'intertextual webs or signifying fields, rather than simplistic one-way lines of influence from source to adaptation' (2013, p. 24). This 'de-hierarchizing' (p. xiv) of the relationship between adaptations and their precursors both at the point of creation and reception has the potential to open up classroom textual explorations in ways that democratise creative processes and help break down conventional lines of demarcation between canonical and popular culture, as we illustrate in later chapters with reference to our own classroom research.

Drama-in-English as inclusive and culturally responsive pedagogy

As Heathcote (2015b, p. 71) reminds us, drama's particular capacity to combine multiple communicative modes (the spoken, the visual and the physical) renders it especially suited to the development of literacy for a range of learners:

> Students deserve the best systems of communication we can give them. I wonder if we would have fewer 'slow learners' if we used a more meticulously selective and complete signing system as our means of communication with such students. Individuals read signs very differently, and therefore decipher the code more easily if it is rich, full and highly selective for its present purpose.

It is a sentiment echoed more recently in a NATE Position Paper (Thomas and NATE 2020, p. 15) in which the authors caution that the current dominance of 'literacy' as the medium of creativity in English 'may be an inhibitor for the hesitantly or reluctantly literate'. Our contention that drama-in-English represents an inherently inclusive pedagogy, capable of supporting all learners, is evidenced not only by our own classroom experiences and observations (some of which we draw on in subsequent chapters) but also by a growing body of international research. Bridget Kiger Lee et al.'s (2020, p. 22) meta-analysis of 30 years' worth of accumulated research into drama-based pedagogy (DBP) concludes that 'DBP does have a significant effect on literacy related outcomes for K-12 students, especially when led by a classroom teacher over many hours of instruction'.[2] Importantly, Lee et al. also conclude that the meaningful use of drama pedagogies in the classroom not only raises students' academic achievement but also improves attitudes. To cite one specific example from this substantial body of research, DeMichele's (2015, p. 1) action research study in US high schools shows how improvisatory approaches help students 'overcome their reluctance or inability to engage in the writing process' and serve to boost written outcomes for learners with special needs, both in terms of text length and written fluency.

Similarly, findings emerging from the Sydney-based School Drama Programme (2009 onwards) suggest that drama 'has the potential to nurture every aspect of learning to be literate', and is equally supportive of those who find learning difficult as of high achievers (Saunders and Ewing 2022, p. 433). In the UK, Yandell (2014) offers persuasive case study accounts of drama-inflected classroom practice which supports and enriches literacy development for a range of learners, including those who perform least successfully in formal written exams. For instance, he highlights the way in which 'semiotically rich' (p. 171) short improvisations and in-role activities scaffold Year 9 students' understanding of *Richard III* incrementally over the period of study. In the class teacher's own words, role-play offers her mixed attainment inner-London class the opportunity to 'put themselves into a story', to 'bring their own world knowledge, their own context to that story' and to 'work with peers to construct their own interpretations' (cited in Yandell 2014, p. 177).

As we argue in Chapter 1, questions about identity, culture and representation are inevitably raised in any meaningful study of English. Helen Nicholson's (2005, p. 13) description of drama's essential properties suggests that in this respect the two subjects are well-matched:

> Applied drama is intimately tied to contemporary questions about the politics of context, place and space, and this means that working in drama often brings into focus questions of allegiance, identity and belonging.

Role-play, in particular, presents an effective medium through which issues around social justice can be raised and matters of cultural diversity explored in the English classroom (e.g., Hulson 2006; Kana and Aitken 2007; Naidoo 1992). By imagining alternative identities and perspectives, and given the space to inhabit these 'other possible selves, other possible worlds' (Yandell 2014, p. 171), students naturally dip into diverse funds of knowledge (Moll et al. 1992) brought into the classroom from their lives outside of school. Working with acting students in the multi-ethnic context of Singapore, Charlene Rajendran (2014) uses the affordances of in-role activities to raise postcolonial questions about the dominance of the Western canon and the primacy of English as the medium of instruction. By inviting students to create character-based improvisations drawn directly from their everyday lives and observations, Rajendran and her class create 'a space to participate in the reimagining of cultural norms' (p. 169).

Burcu Yaman Ntelioglou's (2011) research with a linguistically and culturally diverse group of adult migrants learning English in Toronto highlights the importance of enabling learners, no matter what their age, to draw on their personal and cultural experiences. The drama work that Ntelioglou's students produce in their new language 'often symbolised, explicitly and implicitly, critical issues at stake in their lives. These issues were representative of political, social, and economic life conditions' (p. 602). Although the group of students in this study were initially resistant to drama-based learning, Ntelioglou notes that by the end of the project 'the process of creating performance-based identity texts engaged students creatively, emotionally, physically and cognitively' (p. 610). Approaching a similar topic ('exploring the experiences of those of us who become refugees') with adolescents in a multi-ethnic London classroom, Maggie Hulson (2006, p. 41) illustrates how process drama, including teacher-in-role, can be employed to construct a necessary 'protective fiction' through which the potentially controversial theme of immigration can be explored sensitively with younger learners.

Drama is the ideal vehicle for creating a learning environment in which bilingual students' first languages and their own diverse sets of cultural knowledge are celebrated and valued. This sharing of knowledge can enrich the cultural capital of all participants. In our own research we have observed GCSE students of South Asian heritage drawing on their knowledge of popular Indian film in their analysis of *Macbeth*, deftly working across genres and cultural codes, an educative process for all concerned including the teacher (Coles 2020). Fellowes' (2001, p. 4) practitioner account of middle school students inhabiting Shakespeare's plays through their home languages and cultures indicates that a cross-cultural drama-based approach is one which 'enables bilingual pupils to understand [Shakespeare's works] better at their own level of personal experience' and 'provides them with the scope for blending eastern and western traditions'. As Fellowes comments, 'Bilingual pupils are consummate code-switchers. For children who regularly switch from everyday English into Panjabi, back into English and then possibly into Urdu, Elizabethan English becomes another language to move to and from' (p. 98). He adds that there are also benefits for monolingual children in the same class who are encouraged to become less self-conscious about switching into Shakespeare's language.

Use of drama as a vehicle specifically for ESOL (English for Speakers of Other Languages) development represents an area of increasing international interest; such research typically adopts a Vygotskyan framework within which language learning is regarded as both 'dialogic' and embodied (Stinson and Piazzoli 2013, p. 209). Process drama, particularly the adoption of role, replaces the more conventional scripted conversation practice that will be familiar to many ESOL practitioners. Role-play has been found to provide a meaningful context for language use (Stinson 2008), support the introduction of new vocabulary (Bundy et al. 2016), and reduce learners' anxiety in voicing the new language aloud (Bundy et al. 2016; Piazzoli 2011; Stinson 2008). Bundy et al.'s (2016) research in Brisbane with refugee children aged 9–13 years concludes that drama-based approaches offer ESOL learners ways to communicate that are not normally available to them through other pedagogies. The collaborative nature of classroom activity means that learners 'draw on their collective potential' (p. 155), and because the drama is set up to support students' own experiences, 'language is authentically embodied and emotional connections and new opportunities for critical and imaginative thinking are made possible' (p. 167). Learner agency is an important factor which aids motivation and metacognitive awareness. For example, when students in Stinson and Piazzoli's research (2013) are invited to reflect upon their learning experiences, they show recognition that they have been building on each other's ideas within the drama to the benefit of their individual linguistic progress.

In the UK's multi-ethnic context (as, indeed, in other anglophone countries), ensuring successful outcomes for 'EAL' (English as an Additional Language) learners in mainstream classrooms represents an area of significant concern for secondary school English teachers. We are proposing that this growing body of international ESOL research offers valuable insights into drama's potential for any English teacher working in classrooms that include developing bilingual (and multilingual) learners, and we suggest that this is an area ripe for further research particularly in the context of the climate crisis and the prospect of increased global migration.

The importance of art and literature in education

We end this chapter by highlighting one aspect of Vygotsky's work that has until recently attracted less attention: his writing about the place of art and literature in education. As Barrs (2022, p. xv) comments, 'Vygotsky's strong focus on the arts and on play, creativity and imagination, the emotions, and their role in thinking, is a central component of his psychological theory that still needs more emphasis in Vygotskyan studies, and in practice'. Vygotsky remained a keen theatre-goer throughout his adult years, and indeed his doctoral thesis included an analysis of *Hamlet*, reportedly influenced by Konstantin Stanislavski and Gordon Craig's 1912 production on the Moscow stage (Barrs 2022). Vygotsky was convinced that the arts, especially literature, should form a central component of the state education system. In one of Vygotsky's earliest publications, *The Psychology of Art* (1971, p. 249), he draws attention to the social and affective impact that art and literature can have on young people's emotional development: 'Art is the social technique of emotions, a tool of society which brings the most intimate and personal aspects of our being into the circle of social life'. Significantly, Vygotsky believed that this is not just to the benefit of the individual learner, but of society itself, and should be one of the main objectives of education. The literary education he had in mind, however, was very different to the dry, instructional approach he had observed in Russian classrooms of his day where, as he puts it, '"pupils are beaten with sticks to learn Pushkin as if they were cattle herded to the watering place"' (cited in Barrs 2022, p. 28). No doubt this description will strike a chord for many an English teacher today involved in the preparation of adolescents for literature examinations.

Vygotsky believed that children's emotional and creative development are as important as the cognitive. His concern that the affective aspects of learning are too easily overlooked by educators is one we share.

Notes

1 For a critique of deficit-based language learning pedagogies, see Ian Cushing (2022).
2 K-12, i.e., Kindergarten to 12th grade, used to designate the full age range of schooling in the US.

4
READING AND ROLE

This chapter deals with the possibilities afforded by engagement with forms of role-play and includes practical examples of how drama has been used to shape learning in English classrooms. We build on the theoretical understandings of role and role-play outlined in Chapter 3 to explain how we have applied our approach to reading through drama-in-English. Our conception of this form of drama does not necessarily make demands on students to respond in performative ways that are markedly different from their responses to reading with texts in hand – role-play can happen at desks and involve talking to a neighbouring student, for example. But we recognise that the invitation to imagine or enter a fiction marks a significant change in terms of the ways that learners interact with each other, in-role, and potentially with their teacher also in-role.

Heathcote explains the power of 'role at its simplest. *I talk as if I'm there*' (2015b, p. 72) [italics in the original]. This switch into a fiction can happen momentarily, spontaneously and with little fanfare and yet yield surprising responses, offering learners opportunities for engaged and memorable shifts in perspective that draw on the full range of their communicative and expressive resources. Assuming a role provides a platform for critical exploration of texts and a heightened awareness of aspects of narrative, character, genre, mood, tone, register and the visual dimension of texts.

We refer to two research projects in some detail to exemplify these possibilities: a project developed in 2022 with a group of student-teachers experimenting with drama-in-English towards the end of their PGCE in English with Drama, and a two-day workshop about *Beowulf*, conducted in 2015 with a group of PGCE English and English with Drama student-teachers, part of a large-scale funded research project.[1] Throughout both projects the student-teachers involved were positioned primarily as learners and readers, and

DOI: 10.4324/9781003290827-4

subsequently invited to reflect on the possibilities for learning opened up by working in-role in their English classrooms.

Understanding role and role-play

The theatrical origins of the term role come from an obsolete French word, referring to the roll of paper on which an actor's part was written. Over the course of the 20th century the term was increasingly used to explain the ways that we behave according to socially defined categories (Goffman 1959, 1974) and drama was seen to offer possibilities for an interrogation of human behaviour through an amplified or selective reflection of particular social interactions. Our interest lies in the processes of generating a role and role-play through improvisation rather than acting a character based on a set script. The Western obsession with Naturalism and Stanislavskian-inspired acting or 'getting into character' may be relevant in a rehearsal room but rarely in a classroom context. Heathcote (2015b, p. 78) suggests that what distinguishes all in-role interactions from everyday life, whether they be momentary or theatrical, are that they are '*totally* based in sign' [italics in the original], ushering in a heightened awareness of forms of communication that draw on the resources of bodies and material objects as well as words. In this chapter we explore a range of opportunities for learning and prompts to the imagination generated by the sign-making associated with working in-role and with 'story-dwelling as much as story-telling' (Cannon 2018, p. 144).

Heathcote's understanding of role as attitude or frame rather than character is a significant aspect of the way that she conceptualises dramatic interaction in a learning context. In McGuinn's (2014, p. 62) analysis of Bolton and Heathcote's role-play, he notes the ways in which they devise tasks that appear to be on the margins of the make-believe, making maps or addressing an empty chair that stands in for a character, for example. These pedagogical choices relate to the way a dramatic event is framed, shaping the interest and perspective of learners entering the dramatic scenario or confronted with a fictional problem. The process of focusing on a particular concern is intended to generate engagement and tension and to open up a space for reflection. For Heathcote an affordance of role-play is the opportunity it offers to explore a feeling such as anger, rather than to immerse oneself in it (Bolton 1998, p. 199), as we explain in Chapter 3.

Working in-role is an immensely flexible approach, that can take a range of forms in the classroom. This range may include a collective role that the whole class assumes as one character exploring a decision or individual roles, perhaps as participants at a meeting that is important to a fictional situation. It may involve improvisation as characters reflecting on an incident, developing some future or back-story or exploring the tension on the cusp of a climax or of some violent action. Role may assume a more expressive inflection in the form of a still or moving-image. In our own research (Bryer and Coles 2022) we have identified more informal moments when individuals take on one or more roles to embody, explain or communicate a moment of insight about a text. Roberta Taylor (2016) describes the process involved when two students assume a series of roles as they work together to transpose a scene from *Macbeth* into a modern context. She identifies how their roles, briefly realised in the form of gestures, posture and tone of voice, give the students access to intertextual references that they both recognise, generating empathy and rapport that feeds into their writing. This rich account is suggestive of the many affordances of role that are applicable to English.

Role-play has the potential to heighten awareness of the visual and intertextual dimensions of texts, supporting inclusive communication through the creation and reception of signs (Bryer 2020). This form of enactment also opens up opportunities for learners to bring aspects of their identities and experience to the processes of critical enquiry in English, meaning that, as Franks (1996, p. 113) asserts, forms of classroom drama are 'always bound to be reflexive, possibly critical and perhaps even transgressive or subversive of "cultural norms"'. Yandell (2014) and Brady (2014) outline the possibilities for the exploration of narrative perspectives and the motivations and challenges to convention that emerge through the process. Brady (2014), for example, analyses how role-play related to Steinbeck's *Of Mice and Men* enables learners to navigate complex questions associated with their gender and the constraints of living under occupation in a Palestinian context. Kana and Aitken (2007) explain how process drama offers student-teachers the opportunity to explore the experience of cultural exclusion in classrooms in New Zealand.

A sequence of learning involving a pre-text

As part of our research project with a group of English with Drama student-teachers (2022), we worked through a short scheme of work that is characteristic of our drama-in-English approach, originally developed to support learning about *Frankenstein* and the Gothic genre. In presenting this example we aim to explain a sequence of drama activities, rather than focusing on isolated instances of the use of particular drama strategies. The emphasis is on the ways that a text taught in English becomes a 'pre-text', as O'Neill (1995) describes it, or stimulus for dramatic action that provides a class with an insight into its themes, genre and tone. Engaging in this practical drama together offered the student-teachers a platform to consider why and how they might deploy the different approaches to role in English lessons.

The introductory activities were designed to offer manageable shifts into a dramatic scenario. The drama began with a question: *What does it feel like to be an outsider?* Initially the learners were framed by a role suggestive of some kind of shared interest or responsibility. Individuals were not asked to take on characters, in an actorly or performative way. The learners were told that they all lived in a block of flats together and they determined the name of the block. A subtle shift into role happened when the tutor asked them, as residents, what kind of things '*you*' might hear and smell at dusk on a November evening. The tutor, in narrator mode, introduced a twist suggesting that recently residents had noticed unusual noises and smells that bothered them, offering the group a particular perspective on the unfolding dramatic action. This shift from the everyday to something odd or uncanny provided a hook into the drama – a mystery and a shared concern – that became the focus of a meeting managed by the tutor-in-role as chair of the residents' association. The tutor-in-role dropped hints in the meeting that the disturbance seemed to be something to do with their shared neighbour, a doctor, who appeared to be up to something in an old boiler room.

The next sequence in the drama involved learners moving into small groups of four or five and assuming a still or frozen pose, representing individual residents positioned as if they lived together, each group in a separate flat. They were simply asked to demonstrate a particular attitude – to show that they had had a bad night's sleep after the revelations of the meeting. The tutor commented on how the learners manifested their tiredness and disquiet and then instructed everyone to start talking to each other in their small groups about a dream that they imagined having and gradually to realise that everyone else in their group/flat had shared the same dream.[2] They were asked to make the dream up and develop it through this improvised dialogue. The subsequent creation of still-images from these shared dreams provided rich material for an audience of their peers to consider. The audience gave some of the still-images resonant titles. Other groups brought their images to life for a moment. This gave rise to a discussion of Gothic elements, including intense emotion and gestures; strange figures; clawed creatures; and other spectral subjects.

The tutor narrated the learners into the next moment, suggesting that as residents, haunted by these dreams, they felt particularly compelled to find out what the doctor was doing in the old boiler room late the following night. She then read the first paragraph of Chapter 5 from *Frankenstein* and discussed its implications with the group, including some reflections on the ways that the iconic moment of the creature coming to life has been realised in different media and popular cultural forms. In pairs the learners assumed new roles in the creation of their own short enactments of this moment, one person playing Dr Frankenstein, the other the creature. There was no dialogue and the short pieces of movement ended with a freeze. As audience to these moments, performed to sinister music one after the other, learners were asked to identify what told them that each creature was now alive (the signs of an intake of breath or eyes opening, or of a hand reaching out, for example). The emphasis was not on performance skills, nor on the generic 'what went well' or 'even better if', but on these precise acts of interpretation. This part of the drama ended with the whole group returning to their role as residents, reacting in slow motion to one of the learners in-role as the creature, in his first moments of life. The tutor directed the residents to try to make eye contact with the creature. Most chose to express horror and disgust at what they were witness to. We then returned to the question that framed the drama about how it feels to be an outsider and concluded with some writing-in-role as the creature recalling their 'birth' (see Chapter 5).

In reflecting on the relevance of this sequence to the teaching of the novel and of Gothic literature in general, one student-teacher noted that framing the activities with a question provided a helpful focus, so that 'you have a question in your head before you do the work because then you know what to look out for . . . the concept of the outsider'. Barrs and Cork (2001, p. 212) similarly see the value in 'the delaying of the introduction of the text itself until some aspect of the fictional world had been prefigured through drama'. In this drama the questions that led the learners through the action, including the significance of the uncanny disturbances, the dream sequences and creation of a strange being, were intended to serve as a map of the literary terrain (Bolton and Heathcote 1997), bringing elements of the Gothic into focus.

We discussed the way that the student-teachers felt they listened differently to the second reading of the excerpt from Chapter 5, once made aware that they were going on to re-create that moment. One identified that she became more alert to the sensory impact of Shelley's language, focusing on particular words that they were to embody. As she began to visualise the action, she was prompted to consider what resources were available that she could use to create an appropriate mood, the lighting, for example. She identified key dramatic moments so that for her the text was transformed into something that was, as she put it, 'ready to go'. In this expression she captured the impetus implied in the invitation to dramatise. Thus, the excerpt became a pre-text for drama prefigured as 'a design for action' (O'Neill and Rogers 1994, p. 49).

Role conventions

Since the experience of teaching online or with students sitting in rows deliberately distanced from each other, as a consequence of the global Covid-19 pandemic (2020–2023), we have been thinking further about ways that role-play might be integrated within English in the most constrained of circumstances.

Those familiar with what happens in Drama lessons will be aware of the influence of Jonothan Neelands and Tony Goode's (2015) *Structuring Drama Work* on the development of what has become known as the 'conventions approach' (Neelands 2010a, p. xvii) in classrooms across the world. Neelands and Goode's (2015) catalogue or toolkit of a hundred different ways of working (like still-image and cross-cutting) has been critiqued for being too atomised and lending itself to reductive forms of assessment (Cziboly, Lyngstad and Zheng 2022). Many of the examples the authors offer are based on an exploration of significant content, often related to literary texts. However, an orientation towards some kind of performance requiring resources such as space implies a significant commitment that may be off-putting for English teachers. We have found Heathcote's role conventions more relevant for our purposes, a list of suggestions that she added to and exemplified throughout her career in her *Notes on Signs and Portents* (2015a, pp. 79–87). Neelands (2010a, p. xviii) acknowledges the influence of Heathcote's conventions on his work but crucially notes that he and Heathcote part ways because her emphasis is on learning rather than drama. We argue that Heathcote's focus on role, rather than drama strategies or techniques, means that her approach is particularly applicable to English teaching because of its orientation towards reflection, exploration and learning. This explains our emphasis on role in this chapter. It was through these 33 conventions that she developed practical ideas about how to examine a situation, event or issue from a new or different perspective. We also find Brecht's notion of 'making strange' (see Eriksson 2011) relevant to the ways that role-play can provide unexpected insights in the analysis of a moment from the text. Heathcote's (2015a) ideas about the form or medium in which a role might be presented to a class do not imply a performative outcome but the opening up of a platform for motivated exploration and reflection.

Heathcote's (2015a, p. 79) interest in encouraging a class to focus on the interpretation of meaning is evident in the first two conventions:

1. The role actually present, naturalistic, yet significantly behaving, giving and accepting responses[3]
2. The same, except framed as film . . . 'Film' can be stopped and restarted, or rerun.

Over the years we have observed many English teachers using props and objects in the ways that some of the conventions suggest. These conventions include: 'The clothing of a person cast off in disarray' (p. 82); 'Objects to represent a person's interest' (p. 83); a letter, read to the class in different ways, 'in the voice of the writer' or 'without feeling. For example, as evidence' (p. 85); reports of various kinds, including 'of a conversation' (p. 86); and 'The finding of a cryptic code message' (p. 87). They offer engaging introductions to a character or aspect of a narrative that involve pre-prepared resources and learners responding to what they see, in or out of role, without necessarily having to move from their seats. Heathcote's notes include detailed reflections on a range of 'implications for learning' and practicalities such as 'Teacher must foresee the implications in the chosen objects' (p. 83), anticipating how the narrative might develop further in the form of drama or writing-in-role. In relation to the stimulus of the cast-off clothing she explains how learners may be involved in 'Making sense out of apparent chaos', especially if 'framed as "detectives" with a puzzle to solve' (p. 83). The role of detective is one that lends itself well to interpreting these kinds of evidence in English classrooms.

Creating and responding to dramatic resources

The student-teachers involved in the research project (2022) discussed Heathcote's (2015a) conventions and then adapted some of the ideas in their English classrooms while on school placement. Several reported that they found creating resources offered opportunities to engage students in imagining the specific contexts or settings of the texts they were studying, providing further stimulus for focused dramatic interaction. Some of these re-creative activities relate to Heathcote's (2015a, p. 81) conventions numbered 8–15, including 'the role depicted in picture . . . made by the class'. They represent a form of edging into role, implying the material creation of a fictional world and suggesting an imagined audience of characters from the text. The student-teachers reflected on how ascribing a role for the class to interpret the resources (like the detective role), offers distinctive possibilities for a critical engagement, providing a platform for debate and active interpretation. Below we share specific examples from the student-teachers' classrooms.

Erin and Rachel asked their students to create Wanted posters for Fagin (*Oliver Twist*) and Magwitch (*Great Expectations*) that involved drawing the characters and explaining their crimes. Creating posters prompted students to refer to Dickens' text to find evidence of the characters' wrongdoing and to develop an informed imaginative response in their framing of the characters as criminals in the Victorian era. Asha asked her students to create posters convincing young men to sign up for WW1, salient to the experience of the protagonists in Michael Morpurgo's *Private Peaceful*. Penny's creation of Wanted posters for some of the characters in *Romeo and Juliet* provided a stimulus for more interactive role-play. She hung them up around the classroom and then told her students that they needed to gain information to survive in their home town of Verona. She left clues on the posters including blanked out words, necessitating some reference to the text that she noticed students discussing with each other, in-role as fellow citizens. Drawing on Heathcote's (2015a, p. 85) conventions 22–24, based on letters, Asha copied Wilfred Owen's handwritten draft of his poem 'Mental Cases' and presented it to her class to decipher, with a view to speculating on the poet's state of mind when he wrote it. In reflecting on the ways that she introduced this resource she saw potential in enrolling the learners as doctors at the military hospital (Craiglockhart) where Owen had been staying, providing a more motivated engagement with the 'evidence' and opportunities to reflect on the significance of shell shock that is at the heart of the poem.

Hot-seating

Heathcote (2015b, p. 75) explains that all her conventions offer possibilities to '*slow down time* and enable classes to get a grip on decisions and on their own thinking about the issues they are dealing with' [italics in the original].

Several student-teachers reported using hot-seating in their English class-rooms with varying degrees of success, in terms of student engagement and opportunities for learning. Heathcote presents this convention as the first in her long list (see above for her description), and she is clear it has to be managed carefully to avoid everything happening too swiftly for 'classes to become absorbed in and committed to' it (p. 75). The most successful of the hot-seating interactions that the student-teachers reported on involved the teacher taking on a role. Erin assumed the role of Fagin, managing her class's shift into a dramatic engagement with the character through a carefully staged process. She distributed worksheets that asked individuals to draw Fagin and to list his personality traits and how he is described, including a prompt to consider what questions they might ask him, *if* they ever met him. Students then advised her how she should stand and speak as Fagin, taking responsibility for remembering the details of all that they had read, viewed, drawn and written about the character. Once the questioning started, Erin was struck by the opportunities that the process offered for an exploration of Fagin's implied motivations, 'things that aren't clearly written in the book', she reflected, 'So, with Fagin, it was like the idea of why does he collect all these kids? You know, does he have a conscience? Does he worry about ruin-ing their lives?' Facilitating the role-play in this way ensured that there was time and space for the 11- and 12-year-olds to ask questions about aspects of the novel and its context that they found troubling, confusing and intrigu-ing. As before, we reflected on how planning a role for the class might offer more meaningful opportunities to critique the text and explore its histori-cal context. Questioning Fagin, either as police officers, the children who work for him, or even as historians, implies different categories of question, providing 'a range of interpretations through . . . changing perspectives' (O'Neill and Rogers 1994, p. 50).

Lisa frequently found role useful for exemplifying complex ideas. She was pleased that she was able to demonstrate how Shakespeare satirises actors in *A Midsummer Night's Dream* by asking students to write Bottom's accept-ance speech for a Golden Raspberry Award (traditionally given to honour the worst cinematic achievements). Some of the students then performed their speeches in-role as Bottom, as if he believed that he had actually won an Oscar, capturing the way that the character is positioned and how Shakespeare parodies his actorly pretensions. For Lisa, a playful, improvisational approach is a significant tool in her pedagogy but the activities that she initiated were not designed simply for her students to enjoy themselves; these were carefully planned and structured to help them to make sense of aspects of the English curriculum. Although she did not do drama in all her English lessons, Lisa's students were aware that on occasion something dramatic *might* happen. As Hope put it, 'it's the *might* that keeps them hooked'. The student-teach-ers noted how introducing a dramatic frame meant that they had to make it really clear to their classes what the narrative implications were of particular moments from texts. Penny realised that although the class had read and discussed *Romeo and Juliet* together, it was only when she asked students to assume the collective role of Juliet to work out how to resolve her parents' demand that she marry Paris (Act 3, scene 5), that the full force of the character's situation seemed to come into focus. All of the student-teachers reflected on how inclusive these processes were, yielding surprising responses from learners who were not always engaged. Bethan talked of a student motivated to speak for the first time in one of her classes, in response to a role-play activity.

Reading through role: *Beowulf*

The *Frankenstein* drama is designed to happen at an early stage of a class's study of a novel or literary genre. Here we offer a second extended account of a sequence of learning, exemplifying how in-role work can support the ongoing reading of a text, in this case the Old English epic poem, *Beowulf*. This sequence included the use of small group role-play in different iterations, narration-in-role and teacher-in-role.

Beowulf has many features that we were drawn to in our choice of text for this project as 'a profoundly unstable text of unknown origins and precarious existence' (Coles and Bryer 2018, p. 55), based on oral versions or adaptations belonging to an earlier century. We also saw particular opportunities to challenge gender expectations within the heroic genre. While we introduced the student-teachers to some aspects of Old English language and verse form, we mainly worked with excerpts from Seamus Heaney's (2000) version of the poem. We also considered versions of *Beowulf* in popular media and children's books, and subsequently encouraged the learners to regard their own adaptations as of equal value.

The introduction to the text involved learners working in groups to create moving-images based on specific quotations, including some assumption of the protagonist roles and some voicing of lines, ending in a freeze. Although, ideally, this group work requires working in a desk-free space, this is not an activity that is complicated to set up or to explain, relying on the provision of pre-prepared and self-explanatory resources (a set of quotations). We asked each group to share their images, one after the other, without stopping. One tutor signed that this was a moment of theatre with an announcement that we were creating 'The story of *Beowulf*', in an epic tone underlined by a flourish of an arm, followed by three beats on a drum to cue in each group, in turn. Although framing this as a deliberately performative assumption of role was faithful to the poem's roots in oral culture, our focus was on making sense of the text through a collaborative and embodied approach that was designed to familiarise the learners with Heaney's (2000) language and the text's narrative arc – bringing their bodies into play in capturing key moments. For these purposes the learners were not performing characters but were in-role as dramatic interpreters of the text, sharing their impressions with an audience of their peers. We made this clear by explaining that the outcome was a whole-class reading of *Beowulf*, rather than inviting the audience to judge aspects of their peers' performances. There was potential for further reflective activity in finding a role for audience members as 'historians, archaeologists and art-historians' to frame the sharing of the images (Neelands 1984, p. 12).

We are always concerned that those making drama should not feel self-conscious, recognising, like Heathcote (2015b, p. 72), that they have not necessarily given permission to be stared at as they work (even within a research context). Yet, we cannot know what shapes or meanings our body, or bodies, evoke until they are received by others, any more than we can judge the impact of our ideas until they are voiced. Asking those watching: 'What do you see? How do you know? What does it remind you of?'[4] encourages the audience to read the signs that their peers are making, bringing this sharing of insights and ideas into tighter focus and acknowledging the ways that the work is situated within a particular cultural realm. The quotations from Heaney's (2000) translation that the learners enacted were full of violent action, leading the learners-as-audience to reflect on the tone of the text and generating a sense of the warrior world conjured up through their embodied action.

Through our research we recognise that learners' conceptions of a drama task, in whatever context, depend on their prior experiences and the cultural knowledge they bring to the activity, and that these are the resources they draw on to make meaning, a process that is key to reading through drama. Thus, we were interested in the variety of ways that individuals responded to a brief transformation into role. Some appeared to recognise different possibilities in the task, depending on their familiarity with particular modes or ways of working. Sophie was an experienced dancer and explained that she was accustomed to using her body as 'a tool'. Not all the learners felt comfortable using their bodies for these culturally specific, dramatic purposes and Sumaya reflected that she found striking a violent pose quite exposing. However, in the creation of a nightmare sequence later on, Sumaya's haunting singing in a minor key provided powerful context for an enactment of a warrior being snatched up by an invisible force. Sumaya reported that she felt more comfortable in making this aesthetic choice. Our emphasis on an exploration of the community's fears through the creation of a nightmare scene also signalled a shift in focus from performing the role of a protagonist. The teacher's responsibility is to create possibilities for different engagements with the text through these forms of role-play, so that all students are offered opportunities to make meaning and share their contributions with their peers. A flexibility in terms of outcomes is not always on offer in classrooms – most students are expected to respond in writing to tasks set in English and this can feel as exposing and indeed performative for some as striking a pose. This is particularly the case with a canonical text that some students may have more familiarity with than others; obviously white, male warriors and heteronorma-tive content do not have a universal appeal.

With this concern in mind, the next episode focused explicitly on the female monster, Grendel's Mother, and her fight with Beowulf. The focus was on a storytelling mode with brief in-role interactions, designed to draw students into the fictional world, with less emphasis on the representation of warriors. Through these drama activities we modelled the ways in which working-in-role offers opportunities for learners to pry open a relatively unfamiliar text.

At the outset our priority was to foreground what was at stake for those involved in the particular moment that we had chosen to dwell in. We started with narration to frame the learners into a particular communal role, as a mix of Beowulf and King Hrothgar's warriors, signalling to them what our concerns as a community were so that we might build the narrative together, taking our cue from the tone and language of Heaney's (2000) text. As a hook, we aimed to generate a sense of the supernatural and fear of the unknown alluded to in Hrothgar's description of the monster's lair, where 'At night there, something uncanny happens'. We switched from reading the text to a form of narration in-role, to help build an atmosphere and to find a focus for the dramatic action. Echoing Heaney's (2000) language, the tutor announced:

> All those years we sensed their evil presence. The shadow-stalkers, the misbegotten spirits . . . I know the smell of them, like a stagnant pool. What about you? What have you seen or sensed, heard or smelt, out on the moorland, in the twilight?

This appeal to the senses was intended to situate the group in a particular imagined time and place, with reference to what had happened (Grendel's fight with Beowulf and Grendel's Mother's reaction) and some indication of the threat that the community continued to face. These events became our overriding concern, one that defined our collective role. In-role the tutor leant forwards, using her gaze and a circling gesture to bring everyone close, and then indicated that she anticipated a response from each learner in turn. Although this was quite directed, she offered individuals choice about what they imagined they had witnessed, edging them into role through the pro-cess. Private exchanges in pairs might have felt less exposing but the ritual of speaking, one after the other, also offered a certain predictability and was designed to heighten awareness of the choices of tone, register and vocab-ulary that played their part in summoning up a particular context, accord-ing to the group's evolving sense of the fictional world. Through our initial question, we aimed to focus the group on the language and sensory elements of the landscape that are integral to the narrative, to generate a sense of foreboding.

One self-avowed *Beowulf* enthusiast amongst our student-teachers explained this section of the drama, in a post-project interview:

We were describing what we felt, what was going on – the eyes in the mist – constantly watching, feeling his breath and it was how we as a community felt about that.

He recognised how the learners talked their way into the narrative through the articulation of imagined memories and feelings, generating a sense of a group identity through the process.

Teacher-in-role

Inviting the learners into the story through this process is referred to as teacher-in-role. Heathcote (2015b) proposes that the function of the teacher-in-role is to address and question the participants in the drama, to draw them into the action. Through the process, roles are sketched out for those involved that imply a particular attitude to the significant events of the text. Teacher-in-role can be used in focused ways in English, to model an approach and to pose questions. Betty Jane Wagner (1999, p. 132) describes this as working in the realm of a twilight or 'shadowy role' rather than acting or taking on a character. She defines this as assuming 'an interest, an attitude appropriate for the situation' (p. 132) and communicating it clearly. It involves a continual process of framing or finding a focus for the dramatic action, similar to the responsibility that an English teacher takes for shaping a classroom discussion. Thus, while taking on the role of a fellow warrior, the tutor was simultaneously giving a clear indication to the group that the situation was fearful and that individuals were expected to provide an example, in turn, about what they imagined they had seen, sensed, heard or smelt. A sense of audience helped learners to shape their contributions but our orientation was towards the weaving of a fiction that they dipped into, rather than moments of performance. Theatrical expectations did not intrude – there was no clapping after each person spoke, for example. It is worth emphasising that from the point of view of the tutor and learners' capacities or experience of acting, focusing on a shared concern is also a helpful distraction from performance anxiety. The point is to open up space for a class discussion, in-role.

During the course of an earlier iteration of the project (Coles, Bryer and Ferreira 2021), the tutor took on a role with echoes of the character called 'Unferth the boaster' in Heaney's (2000) translation. She drew on O'Neill's (2006, p. 144) use of dramatic irony as a provocation, modelling an attitude of fear and scepticism, in-role. O'Neill and Lambert (1982) identify the ways that hinting at a teacher-in-role's dubious motives can encourage a class to pose questions. The tutor-in-role suggested that it was not necessarily everyone's duty to follow Beowulf into danger. Some of the learners picked up on the signals that they might assume this contrary point of view in a way that generated tension. Engaging with a character who introduces a problem that requires attention, or a point of view that needs teasing out, can provide a compelling way of shifting into dramatic action.

One of the ways of addressing the group that we initiated in the next stage of the drama is indicative of a particular affordance of role that we became more aware of when doing drama with bilingual learners. In this instance learners seemed to respond more readily, when the teacher adopted a narrator 'register' (O'Neill 2015a, p. 18) to explain the next sequence of dramatic action in-role, rather than breaking the spell of the narrative to issue further instructions. Thus, using a storytelling tone to explain that the warriors slept in small groups and that as they slept, 'images came to them in their dreams', the tutor simultaneously indicated to the learners that they should create moving images, and modelled something of the atmosphere that we anticipated. Franks (2014, p. 8) explains the processes of transformation involved in 'Shifts in modes, from verbal utterance, through imagistic physical work in tableaux and then movement in space to the creation of the scene'. Assuming a narrator-role appeared to smooth the transition; to maintain the atmosphere and to give purpose to activities within the imaginative realm or over-arching narrative frame. Modelling, albeit briefly like this, also offered opportunities to heighten the group's aesthetic awareness of the language and tone that we were attempting to build through our interactions.

O'Neill (1995, p. 146) commends the creation of moving images from dreams or nightmares in the anticipation of 'a disturbing event', offering opportunities for symbolism in the exploration of a dramatic premonition. It also has the advantage of making imaginative physical demands on the learners, if, as in our project, that seems appropriate. At this stage we asked learners to create short pieces of action reflecting the community's fears of an attack by Grendel's Mother. This might also be a point at which a class is asked to write in-role about their concerns. Being flexible about the medium in which learners assume a particular role offers opportunities for drama, whatever the constraints of the classroom context. In Chapter 5, we explain the possibilities of drama on paper (Barrs 1987) in more detail.

Learning through role

The question of what the participants learnt through generating these different readings of the text through role-play is key. After the sharing of their nightmare fight scenes, the student-teachers reflected on some of the tensions in Grendel's Mother's mode of attack, that it was 'calculated', 'predatory', 'personal' and yet 'desperate'. Even though only a few of them inhabited the role of Grendel's Mother briefly (for the length of a cry, in one instance), they were able to derive insights into the community's fear as well as recognising the monster's motivations and how the violence she engages in relates to her identity and the ways she is represented in the poem as a female monster.

Heathcote's (2015b, p. 74) claim that when working with students 'Role helps them *do*, and the teacher helps them *see*' [italics in the original] is suggestive of the possibilities of working-in-role in an English classroom in a reflective and carefully managed way that facilitates discussion, debate and reflection. There is much to recommend using role conventions that encourage a class to look closely, question, interpret and develop 'a quite specific relationship with the action' (p. 77) through dramatic interaction. The examples offered here are suggestive of the inclusive way that role-play can offer learners opportunities to make sense of texts that they are studying through their engagement in 'the best systems of communication we can give them' (p. 71). Framing learners into a position of shared concern and legitimising an open and dialogic response (as in the whole-class meetings) has the potential to initiate a range of productive engagements with texts like *Beowulf*. In the examples offered here, the participants generated readings that were pertinent to their own enthusiasms, experiences, criticality and cultural insights. Modelling and clear expectations supported the creative process but learners also needed some freedom to make choices, in order for them to make meaning through role-play. In the *Beowulf* project, offering space for the student-teachers to assume responsibility for developing the dramatic fiction in different ways prompted them to draw on individual interests and skills that involved varied and vivid embodiments of the text. When working with texts that do not reflect aspects of readers' identities or experience, taking on roles can become an inclusive endeavour, particularly if those involved are offered a range of modes to adapt and interpret what they are presented with. In terms of their responsibilities, when creating a role for themselves in this kind of classroom drama, learners are 'fiction-making' (Bolton 1998, p. 278) – authoring their own dramatic readings or sharing authority with the authors of the texts they are studying – in memorable ways.

Notes

1 Funded by the Arts and Humanities Research Council, 'Playing Beowulf' involved university English, Drama and Education departments in London and Sydney, the British Library and five London schools (https://darecollaborative. net/2015/03/11/playing-beowulf-gaming-the-library/).

2 This particular idea comes from a drama developed by Franks (from O'Neill). Another aspect is discussed in Franks and Bryer (2019). There have been many iterations of this drama, including an adapted version by Bryer and Pitfield for a workshop at a London Drama conference (2017).

3 Heathcote does not call this hot-seating but it fits the description of this familiar strategy.

4 We are indebted to Franks for the phrasing of these questions.

5

DRAMA AND WRITING

The capacity of drama to enrich writing activities in the English classroom is well-documented, and is one of the key reasons why we propose that drama should be at the heart of English. From a pedagogical perspective the links between drama activity and writing are significant. Drama-in-English relies upon creative collaboration with others, which is crucial when generating and shaping ideas in all aspects of literacy learning, including imaginative writing (see Saunders and Ewing 2022). The processes of drama and writing mirror and enhance each other as both 'are acts of composition. All of the elements of re-ordering, referring, re-using, and editing can be found in each' (Neelands et al. 1993, p. 9). Furthermore, drama activity enhances creative writing, not only because it rehearses the kinds of language use that can be transformed into the written form, but also because it evokes positive, affective engagement with content (Dunn and Jones 2022). Allying drama and writing sharpens awareness of audiences and purposes in both modes (Dunn et al. 2013).

Whilst the above offers a persuasive rationale, a drama-in-English approach to writing might appear at first glance to be incompatible with current curricular and examination writing routines. Nancy Rankie Shelton and Morna McDermott (2010, p. 124), writing from the American standpoint, suggest that a constrained curriculum and onerous accountability measures, which silence teachers and learners alike, leave 'little room . . . to work in a way that invites creativity and critical thinking'. Nowhere is this more apparent than in those assessment approaches which cast writing as a formulaic activity. Bridget Kiger Lee and her colleagues (2017) describe the extreme effects of US state and federal tests on students' writing practices and attitudes to writing. The observation that 'students learn that writing is drudgery' provides the context

DOI: 10.4324/9781003290827-5

and impetus for their Literacy to Life project, an '8-week story-writing and improvisational drama intervention' (2017, p. 3) in elementary schools in an urban district of Texas, a project involving teachers, academics and 'teaching artists'. In England too, the turn towards a highly instrumental model of writing has restricted rather than expanded the potential of students' language use. In part, this can be attributed to the legacy of New Labour's objectives-led Literacy Strategy, imposed first in primary (1997) then later in secondary schools (the 'Key Stage 3 Strategy', 2001), and more recently to the Conservative Government's decision to return to 100% terminal examinations at GCSE, removing any remaining element of coursework assessment. Although we do not deny the pressures of curriculum and assessment demands, we are keen to dispel a pervasive perception that drama-in-English is in any way detrimental to examination performance; rather we suggest the opposite.

Types of writing

So what does writing in the English classroom generally look like? Genres that are routinely explored include fictional narratives as well as persuasive and informative writing. Many writing tasks come about as a response to reading literary texts and fall broadly into one of two categories: a critical or a creative response. In England, when drama activity is utilised, it is more often in support of the latter, although we argue that it has relevance for both, whether at KS3, GCSE or 'A' Level, and that, in any case, the critical and creative should not be regarded as markedly distinct processes. The capacity to analyse texts critically is only one amongst many components of literacy learning (see Saunders and Ewing 2022), although 'A' Level specialist Kate Bomford (2022, p. 2) notes that the 'unhappily close relationship' between critical analysis and high stakes assessment has afforded it undue primacy in the curriculum. Bomford questions the prevailing notion that the critical essay provides an intellectually more rigorous response to literature. She explores the limitations and contradictions of its current assessment-dominated form whilst making a strong case that writing-in-role provides students with opportunities to express critical insights. The intellectual properties of a re-creative response include the 'capacity to project oneself into the world of a literary text and the experiences it communicates', and 'the powerful and sophisticated manipulation of language' (p. 14). Developmentally, the knock-on effects as far as reading is concerned are also significant, as Barrs (2000, p. 59) suggests: 'readers who are aware of what is involved in structuring a narrative experience for others are likely to read more critically and responsively'.

Writing-in-role fosters what Bomford (2022, p. 13) refers to as 'imaginative projection', and she draws on Barrs' (1987) analysis of the processes involved to justify role-based responses to reading literary texts. An 'A' Level *King Lear* workshop we ran at a local sixth form college perfectly illustrates Bomford's point that in-role activity is effective in supporting advanced literary study. As part of our overarching exploration of power, status and patriarchy in the play (based on an 'A' Level examination question), we showed a clip of Lear cursing Goneril to her face (Act 1, scene 4) from the austere Peter Brook (1971) film version. This production draws particular attention to the cruelty of his words ('Into her womb convey sterility . . .', lines 230–244) and the immediate effect they have, as reflected on the stricken face of his daughter. We then moved on to the much later scene in which Lear mounts a mock trial of Goneril (Act 3, scene 6, from the 1608 quarto), with his absent daughter represented by 'a joint stool'. We invited students to 'write back' in role as the silenced Goneril. A range of perspectives emerged from the students' writing-in-role, reflecting a complex understanding of the ways in which Goneril is represented as a daughter. These were communicated especially powerfully when four volunteers read back what they had written in tandem with a performance of the short scene. In this example, the writing-in-role developed out of performance-based activity (a film clip and the initial enactment of the trial) and was then fed back into it, with the final presentation enhanced by the written accounts.

We are interested in the ways that drama can provide both a stimulus for focused in-role writing and a means to develop further the narratives and reflective accounts of learners. Even the briefest moment of role-play can inform learners' writing, as suggested by Cathy Burnett's (2015) account of a boy playfully assuming the role of a zombie while his teacher's back is turned, prior to the class embarking on writing mystery stories. Burnett (2015, p. 203) explains how intertextual references are realised through this fleeting and unplanned embodiment of role, and that the boy's playful action 'reworks and recontextualises his knowledge of the genre'. She suggests that his zombie mime, instantly recognisable to his classmates, goes on to inform the children's narrative compositions. Karen Daniels' (2014) research in an Early Years setting identifies the ways in which the children's dramatic role-play, based around their 'collective interest in aliens', not only 'fuelled the direction of the play' (p. 109) but also built a bridge between the cognitive demands of 'the stable and structured written form' and 'the syneasthetic literacy practices with which most children engage in with ease' (p. 105). These researchers are not alone in drawing attention to the significance of playfulness. In the teacher-instigated dramas that are central to the Literacy to Life project (Lee et al. 2017, p. 20), 'playful improvisation' is regularly factored in as part of the drama work, to both stimulate ideas and shape learners' developing narratives. Lee et al. emphasise the benefits of this approach in terms of developing the quality of the learners' writing, particularly but not exclusively in those schools which have a Title 1 designation.[1]

From play to writing

In our own research we have observed English lessons which draw on 'zestful imaginative play' (Bruner 1986, p. 4) as the wellspring of cultural production, manifested in both physical drama and written forms. One teacher, reading Morpurgo's novel *War Horse* with her Year 7 class of 11–12-year-olds in an inner city boys school, designed a lesson sequence which culminated in the students exploring, through their own writing-in-role, the literary trope of anthropomorphism that is central to the novel. There is a sound, subject-related basis for experimenting with this genre of writing. Kimberley Reynolds (2011) notes that, culturally and historically, animals feature prominently in young adult fiction, because 'giving animals human speech and rationality holds up the mirror to our own behaviour, enabling young readers to comprehend forms such as satire or to recognize political critique' (2011, p. 82). The teacher wanted her students to access the affective and sensory aspects of the anthropomorphic literary tropes, and so from the outset she harnessed the power of play, providing opportunities for learners to spontaneously embody an array of animals, joining in herself on occasion. In a further lesson, as the class continued to share the reading of the novel, the students used tableaux and stylised movement to explore what it might be like to be the horse, Joey, trapped on his own in no man's land during a scene of trench warfare in WW1. She also introduced other resources, such as toy and cartoon representations of horses and a poem with an anthropomorphic theme, to stimulate role-play activity. Finally students were asked to write imaginatively in the voice of an animal of their choice.

In the following extracts from the writing of three students, the desire to create a compelling narrative is discernable in both the structural and lexical choices that they make. Their writing also points to the way in which the teacher's use of drama has set up a productive interplay between reading and writing, and has provided the students with a motivation to write. This, as Vygotsky (2004) notes, is so important in developing the 'individuality and vitality' (p. 45) of learners' writing and their 'literary creativity' (p. 46). In each case the transcription preserves the spelling and punctuation of the original.

Ricky, writing as a snow wolf, sets the scene in the build-up to a hunt:

> Being a Snow Wolf is hardly ever easy. Hunting is all I care about. The feeling when my sharp, white teeth dig into the innocent flesh of another animal is just exhilerating. I was looking forward to this kill particularly. The last hunt had only ended with a small penguin to feed fourteen hungry Snow Wolves.

Here he achieves a 'balance of retrospection and anticipation' (Glover 2018, p. 69), the characteristic of reader response engagement that is indicative of a 'clear narrative construct' (p. 69).

Like Ricky, Sammy, another student, writes about his chosen animal in the context of a hunt. He is a young lion about to prove himself to the pride. His writing captures the immediacy and visceral nature of the action, successfully retaining something of the physicality of the drama work:

> Lions, Lionesses and Antelopes were darting in different directions, an Antelope ran right in front of me and I shot out at it with my jaws chomping. Snap! I grabed the Antelope by the neck snaping it and puncturing its windpipe. I let go, it ran a few more steps then fell to the ground, it's lifeless eyes looking up at me.

Peadar experiments with a different kind of narrative, and in his story about a panda cub, Poy, raised in captivity, he also seeks to balance retrospection and anticipation. In comparison with the other two, his is perhaps a less assured shaping of the narrative, as it is not entirely clear whether the first two sentences are supposed to be part of the dream from which Poy is awakened at the end of the extract. However, in some respects there is greater complexity in what he is trying to achieve:

> I stood there in a summer medow the grass licked with rain. My paws wobbled slitly on the uneven ground. I faintly rememberd the separation from me and my mum as I was put in captivity from a extremly yonge age.! The space was rather good and plenty of bamboo shuts and water to disscover. Suddenly! there was a deffning crash. The noise vibrated racing and bouncing on the wall.
>
> It was ko-toy my keeper 'poy poy poy'. I responded with a growl as he had woken me from my nap.

Following a further description of Ko-toy the keeper, Peader arrives at an anticipatory ending, a cliff-hanger of sorts, which is reflected in the dramatic, almost theatrical cadences of Ko-toy's speech:

> you know young Poy young o young Poy i wish you good luck good luck as you will find your destainy tomorro?

Peader's writing also successfully draws on the separation narrative of *War Horse*, as is apparent from Poy's fleeting memory of his mother and the impending changes that Ko-toy's words signal.

In these first-person narratives the writers communicate a sense of being inside the story and a genuine feeling of empathy for the uncertain plight of their animals. The extracts, which are taken from longer accounts, also demonstrate how they have found and sustained a voice for their animals, as Morpurgo does. This has been supported by the teacher enfolding the anthropomorphic experience of *War Horse*, explored through play and dramatic activity, into written composition, allowing the experimental physical 'language' of the drama to inform the necessarily more crafted language of the students' narratives.

Developing a writerly disposition

It is undoubtedly a complex pedagogical challenge to provide students with opportunities that motivate them to write. First and foremost, learners must believe in themselves as creators/writers and in their ability to generate ideas for writing. The stimulus must be capable of firing their imagination and desire to write. The forms of writing that they undertake should sustain their interest and the contexts for writing (whether real or imagined) offer a degree of authenticity. Having some sense that an audience or reader would want to engage with their writing is also important. We are, therefore, interested in the ways in which drama motivates writing and builds on learners' potential as writers.

As is clear from the *War Horse* example, a drama-in-English approach offers the students an impetus to write and a register and style with which to experiment. Similarly, the Brisbane-based *Υ Connect Project* (Dunn and Jones 2022), mentioned in Chapter 1, suggests how dramatic approaches in English lessons 'create opportunities for enhanced self-expression' and 'nourish creative ideas, enabling students to imagine new possibilities' (p. 316) in both their speaking and writing. Whilst benefitting all the students involved, the project also seeks to address concerns about the disengagement of some. This is an issue, identified in a number of reports quoted by Dunn and Jones, which affects 'up to 20% of all secondary students' (p. 314) in the Australian context. In their US-based Literacy to Life programme, Lee et al. (2017, p. 5) point to a problem of 'low efficacy for writing'. This term encompasses both the types of anxieties experienced by the learners when they are about to embark upon a writing task and their ongoing fears about meeting writing expectations, a particular problem in a test-driven curriculum. The authors argue that the value of drama-based teaching lies in the opportunities it provides 'to collaboratively invent, improvise, and play with words and meanings that expand students' writing, along with an increased sense of their potential to author and enjoy creative storytelling' (p. 3).

Describing Heathcote's practices, Wagner (1999) demonstrates how Heathcote used the drama to 'press for language' (p. 197); to 'lure' (p. 197) learners into reaching for the 'more precise or apt' (p. 199) vocabulary and the 'greater eloquence' (p. 197) that the situation demanded. This was achieved by her conscious modelling of language use, when, in role herself, Heathcote would introduce new vocabulary and support the learners to expand their own repertoire and rise to the demands of the specific characterisation and/or dramatic context. Her press for language was carried over into the different types of writing that the learners produced. For example, sometimes Heathcote would pause the drama to allow learners to reflect in writing, or she would deliberately call a halt at a point of high tension to prompt an urgent recording of their thoughts and feelings in the immediacy of the moment. If artefacts such as a scroll or a letter were important to the fiction, the learners would produce these, often collaboratively, and share them for use in the drama as it progressed Or sometimes the writing was a way of summing up the story. Heathcote's learners also wrote in role when in the thick of the drama, an approach to writing that is analysed in detail as part of the much later *We're Writers* project (Grainger et al. 2005). These researchers understand role in a similar way to Heathcote, and they make a strong case for an integrated approach to drama and writing in which the teacher looks for opportunities to 'seize moments in the drama when writing seems both appropriate and necessary' (Grainger et al. 2005, p. 109). This is writing that happens 'from inside the imagined experience' (p. 103). Julie Dunn, Annette Harden and Sarah Marino (2013) report on three research projects undertaken with learners of varying ages, including those in the early stages of literacy development, in primary schools in Australia and New Zealand. In one of their studies they describe how the nature of the role itself can create the impetus to write and encourage a positive disposition. The learners are positioned as expert writers pursuing a range of interesting writing activities, and as a result 'Writing was something they wanted to do all the time' (p. 250).

When it comes to writing about texts, we acknowledge that learning to write within a 'lit crit' formula to address examination requirements is also a necessary part of English, but it is detrimental if this is the overwhelming focus of writing activity (and, indeed, of literary analysis). As Teresa Grainger, Kathy Goouch and Andrew Lambirth (2005, p. 6) remind us, 'children construct their understandings from the opportunities, experiences and priorities created in their schools', warning that 'the perceived nature and purpose of writing can become skewed' if the prevailing and oft-reinforced message that learners receive is all about writing as test preparation. We want to suggest that drama-in-English can be used effectively to motivate and prepare learners for examination writing, because it supports them in developing opinions and a critical perspective on the text they are studying. As part of our case study research, we sought views on this matter from a small group of Year 11 students who had all experienced some drama activity as part of their English lessons throughout their secondary schooling. They were fast approaching the end of their compulsory education and were now in the revision period for their GCSE examinations. The focus group participants were drawn from the same Year 7 class we had observed engaging in drama-in-English activities four years earlier. They were asked to reflect on a number of statements that describe different aspects of and attitudes towards drama-based learning in English. Amongst these statements were:

- Drama-in-English is about playing with ideas and texts.
- Drama-in-English gets in the way of what you should be studying in English.
- Drama-in-English helps you to come up with ideas for your writing.

Given the timing of the focus group it was unsurprising that the students' discussions periodically turned to the topic of the impending examinations. In their comments the students Zemar and Ricky suggested that there might be such a thing as a writerly disposition for examination purposes and considered how drama-in-English had helped them to develop it. Zemar explained how drama-in-English had supported him in developing his ideas about the texts he was studying, and chose the statement about playing with ideas and texts as of most importance to him:

> . . . once we've finished getting ready, like getting your act ready, every-one performs their acts then you get to learn about other people's ideas and how like they think of the text, and how they've interpretated [sic] the text as well, and also you find out different views and that. And also when like you're talking to people in your group, you also find different views then as well so that's why I put that [the statement] up at the top because then you get attitudes to the text.

Here Zemar highlighted the collaborative nature of the learning at all stages in the drama-in-English process, noting how he and his peers developed their improvisations, shared textual interpretations during presentation of their work, and interrogated each other's ideas. His reference to developing 'atti-tudes' towards the texts read in class suggested that a productive interplay between personal perspective and collaborative interpretation had supported his growing independence as a learner, particularly important for the individ-ual facing an examination situation.

Ricky, whose creative writing as a Year 7 student we have quoted previously in this chapter, explicitly referred to the issue of learner independence when he considered the way in which drama-in-English had helped him prepare to write about GCSE texts. Whilst acknowledging that the exam is 'all about the individual, and it's all about what you think and your ideas and your reasons for justifying that', he expressed some confidence that the shared experience of drama-in English would support him in the pressurised context of the high stakes exam:

> And in a Literature exam they'll talk about explaining . . . it won't be explain but it'll be like . . . it would look at how the writer has depicted

a character, and it'll want you to talk about how they've done that. And I think it helps, when you've maybe acted as the character or seen them almost live action, to, like, understand them better.

Whilst Ricky believed that there was room within the examination system for his interpretations to be validated, his fellow student, Joel, was more sceptical about the capacity of drama to ameliorate exam constraints. Unimpressed by the statement 'drama-in-English gets in the way of what you should be studying in English', he nevertheless accepted that 'leading up to that Year 11 stage where you have to know what an examiner wants you to do, I can see, like, what it means'. Similarly, he rejected the idea of the one 'right' interpretation of a text, but suggested that, for the purposes of the exam, there might well be such a thing. Joel favoured instead the statement 'drama-in-English helps you to come up with ideas for your writing'. When interviewed at age 12 he had not hesitated in talking about himself as an avid creative writer, and at age 16 this was still a very important part of his writerly identity: 'I like to write novels in my spare time, I write a lot and I write about kind of personal experience'. He attempted to unpick how drama-in-English had supported his approach to creative writing:

> I know from personal experience, like, with drama you can pick up on certain mannerisms, certain ways that people try to kind of adapt the text into like a physical kind of thing and with that physical interpretation of the writing there's kind of more combinations of words you could use to explain it.

Here Joel pointed to the 'physical tuning up' (Barrs 1987, p. 10) of the drama work as 'a way of getting into the right linguistic gear'. His words also echoed Kempe's (2001) analysis of how drama activity supports writing development. Although Kempe's research is with upper primary learners, it is useful in demonstrating how they imbue their writing with the visual and auditory sign-making of their drama activity, a process that requires conscious manipulation of language. It is clear from their comments that Zemar, Ricky and Joel had all found their experiences of drama-in-English to be both motivating and purposeful in terms of honing their writing skills, whether for examination purposes or as an expressive act in itself.

Role and writing

The research of Neelands et al. (1993) into the effects of drama on the writing development of adolescents in four schools in Toronto, Canada, over a six-month period, provides a way to begin thinking about the types of writing that drama activity inspires. They identify *writing for the drama* such as planning and research, 'or to find new directions as the drama develops' (p. 11); *writing about the drama*, which would include reflection and evaluation; and w*riting within drama*, that is, writing-in-role. Focusing on the last of these, it is worth noting that Hoard was one of the earliest practitioners to recognise the power of adopting roles in writing. In her reflections on 'Dramatization' (1940), a collaborative approach to reading stories and literary texts which combines drama activity, discussion and writing-in-role, she notes how 11-year-old Margaret is even motivated to write in role during an exam, composing an imagined conversation between Don Quixote and Christian, the protagonist of *Pilgrim's Progress*, notable for the way she 'unconsciously borrowed in style from both books' (p. 152). Whether consciously or unconsciously achieved, certainly Margaret's response is indicative of the intellectual endeavour that goes into both the production of this type of writing and the dramatic exploration of the texts that leads to it.

Heathcote (1980), like Hourd, demonstrates how writing arises from dramatic engagement with texts, and in her pamphlet for NATE she writes about a lesson sequence based on Shelley's poem *Ozymandias*. Heathcote's sequence of activities provides opportunities for different types of language use (poetic, exploratory and so on), as appropriate for 'the particular qualities of each situation' (p. 22), and this informs the learners' writing in different genres. For example, a formal report to a historical society, written in role as archaeologists on a dig to reveal the fallen effigy of Ozymandias, provides a way of reflecting on the 'evidence' the learners find during the drama.

Like the *Ozymandias* drama, much of the research into enactment as a stimulus and a model for writing has been conducted in primary/elementary school classrooms, which is unsurprising given the widely accepted links between play, drama and literacy development (see, for example, Booth and Neelands 1998; Lee et al. 2017; McNaughton 1997). Crumpler and Schneider's (2002) cross-study analysis of the writing of children in Grades 1–3 (6–8 years) in American schools, for example, focuses on the ways in which role-play and 'composing in role' help the children to negotiate the complexities of taking a stance in their writing, stance being defined as 'how writers place themselves in relation to their texts as well as their emotional and intellectual attitudes towards text' (p. 75). This idea of exploring stance is just as relevant to older learners and is reflected in our work with a PGCE English cohort to plan and undertake a range of integrated drama activities for teaching the KS3 novel *Stone Cold* by Robert Swindells.

The student-teachers experimented with a writing-in-role task that was preceded by both in-role and out-of-role work and which was based on the story thread dealing with the reporter Louise, who goes undercover as a homeless young person. She presents the reader with one of the narrative's 'indeterminacies' (Iser 1980, p. 112) – until the very end readers know her as 'Gail', someone living on the streets and befriended by the main protagonist, Link, although the author does offer some hints that she may not be all that she seems. Louise's other life as a reporter was exploited by the student-teachers for particular English-related ends. Half the group took on the role of Louise as her reporter self. These student-teachers conducted a series of in-role interviews; her interviewees were carefully selected characters from the book, either someone who had come into contact with the homeless youngsters on which the novel focuses or a relative of one of them. The reporters were set the task of finding out as much information as possible about these characters, their opinions on the plight of the homeless young people and if they had heard any rumours about strange disappearances amongst the homeless community in London. Whilst the Louises planned their questions, the interviewees looked through the novel to remind themselves of the part played by their assigned characters.

The paired interviews followed, and each reporter periodically moved around the room to interview a new character, jotting down a few key notes from what was said. The tutor listened in unobtrusively and selected one or two conversations to spotlight briefly as a way of sharing ideas and approaches. At the end of this round of interviews, the reporters went back to update their editors, having synthesised all the information gleaned so far. The student-teachers who had previously played the other characters took on the editor role, and the tutor briefed them that the editor was looking for a sensational story, whereas the Louises, in keeping with her characterisation in the novel, were told that she was hoping to write a probing feature article about homelessness and its dangers. These contrasting positions framed the paired discussion between Louise and her editor, and when the tutor again briefly paused the action to spotlight some of the conversations, the idea of newspaper stance, and indeed bias, was thrown into stark relief.

Although the student-teachers had experienced interviewing processes and editorial pressures as real reporters might, they felt that their KS3 learners might need more support to grasp the ways in which bias operates in a newspaper article. They devised an out-of-role, small group activity during which learners would closely compare a news story that had recently been reported in both a tabloid and a broadsheet, and respond to some focused discussion points about each report's structure and what the use of language conveyed about the newspaper's stance on the topic. Following this the student-teachers tried out the task of writing the article based on *Stone Cold*, taking either Louise's or the editor's perspective.

Whilst providing the opportunity for this particular type of writing-in-role, the *Stone Cold* lesson sequence also ensured that the novel's literary content and the issues it raised for the student-teachers (and that they thought it would raise for their learners) remained central. Other drama activities, for example, focused on the dual narrative and unreliable narrator aspects. Thus, the integration of literary and literacy learning served both elements of the curriculum well, and as an approach it chimed with that favoured by Barnes and Moffett discussed in Chapter 2.

The student-teachers also tried out some writing-in-role that happened whilst in the thick of the action. Following a rushed farewell between Link and his sister at the railway station, a short scene improvised spontaneously by the student-teachers in pairs, Link wrote a letter to her whilst on the train, expressing all the thoughts and feelings left unsaid. This gave an immediacy and urgency to their writing and ensured that the drama carried on inside their heads as they wrote, an approach that Teresa Cremin and her colleagues (2006, p. 277) aptly refer to as '"seize the moment" writing'. Cremin et al.'s (2006) year-long research into writing integrated with process drama suggests that the tense scenarios engendered during role-play provide the impetus for the type of writing which has 'A clear sense of focus and empathy, powerful language choices, the inclusion of details and an often emotively engaging voice' (p. 279). This is because drama activity involves 'thinking, feeling, visualising and creating multiple possibilities' (p. 289), and the physical and vocal enactment of these processes is subsequently reflected in the learners' writing. During the act of writing learners are able to 'shape their understanding further' (p. 289), which as Neelands et al. (1993, p. 12) put it, ensures that the writing 'is no longer an isolated task, but an extension of the whole experience'.

Paving the way for writing

i. Setting up the role(s)

Barrs (1987) suggests that the passage between role-play and writing can be a smooth one. As long as the writer has a clear '"sense of a reader"' (or audience), and if their role has been well-defined, they can 'sustain [it] just as well on paper' (p. 9). The importance of how the role is set up is also noted by Lee et al. (2017) in their description of the Literacy to Life programme. They recount how the teaching artists in the project present themselves as 'Story Wranglers' (p. 9) who have lost all their stories. They enlist the help of the students, in role as their assistants, in order to create (or wrangle) more stories through drama and writing. This immediately establishes the students' sense of expertise and purpose, as well as communicating the need for sustained collaboration. By highlighting the practices that are an expected part of the assistant story wrangler role, the teaching artists provide a context and reason for the ongoing exploratory improvisations and presentations of work-in-progress that are integral to the writing and redrafting process.

ii The text as the teacher

In 'The Reader in the Writer' (Barrs and Cork 2001), a research project concerned with the writing development of upper primary school students, the authors highlight how learners benefit from in-role activities in response to literary texts. They note the importance of working in ways that we have explored previously in Chapter 4, such as using drama to pre-figure the text's fictional world and its themes. The project's drama work based on *The Green Children* by Kevin Crossley-Holland has a discernably positive effect on the learners' written responses: 'in most classrooms it led to writing which was thoroughly imagined and qualitatively different from what had gone before' (2001, p. 209). Barrs and Cork conclude that in-role activity provides an imaginative space for learners to meet and engage with the work of skilful authors whose texts open up exciting possibilities for those experimenting with their own language use.

The choice of text and investment in the roles adopted are, therefore, key factors in learners' engagement with writing tasks. This is evident from Grainger et al.'s (2005) study with a class of 10–11-year olds. These researchers describe the hook that the text provides, in this case Louis Sachar's novel *Holes*, and they report on the tension created during in-role activity based on one particular scene. As journalists interrogating the teacher, in role as the Warden of Camp Green Lake, their questioning picks apart the pointless and cruel forced labour that the juvenile inmates of the camp have to endure. Both the heated dramatic interaction and the ensuing out-of-role discussion lend an urgency to the learners' production of 'leader columns, diaries, letters and Camp records'. This attests 'to the generative power of the drama' (p. 114) and to its significance as a stimulus for writing, which is enriched by learners assuming the stances, registers and words of the characters in the novel. The researchers conclude that this alliance of drama and writing enables learners to communicate creatively and effectively with 'voice and verve' (p. 119).

The writing that the student-teachers produced at the end of the *Frankenstein* drama, the project we describe in Chapter 4, displays these qualities. They were asked to write very briefly in role as Frankenstein addressing his maker about what he remembers of the traumatic circumstances of his birth. Having created the dramatic moment of the creature coming to life and then switching perspective to emphasise the horror of those who witness it, many of those writing started with the creature's first physical actions and/or the first thing that he sees. The writing of the student-teachers Rachel and Bethan takes the reader to the visceral moment of coming into being that they had physicalised in their scenes; the tone is Gothic in its emphasis on the grotesque and there is a sense of nihilism and despair. Bethan writes, 'I sucked life into my aching lungs and made my eyes wide, to see your world. I saw emptiness and I saw the bile rise in your throat'. Rachel's writing similarly captures what the creature is confronted with on opening his eyes for the first time, 'All I see is unknown. Nothing. Nothing. Nothing . . . Send me back to the darkness'. These student-teachers have captured his isolation from the human world, which is a theme that has such significant consequences in the novel.

iii The teacher's interventions

The question of teacher intervention to support learners in discovering 'what they want to say and advise on the forms available for saying it' (Neelands et al. 1993, p. 15) is highly pertinent to planning the shift from drama to writing. When drafting their writing it is likely that learners receive teacher guidance on their work-in-progress, and similarly, as a role-play develops, the teacher intervenes in particular ways. In Chapter 4 we developed our argument around teacher-in-role as a particularly effective way of questioning and provoking ideas and, when necessary, moving the drama on or developing it in a new direction. However, we were also clear that the teacher's intervention may be quite brief and low key, and does not require any particular or specialist acting skill. Rather, what is important is the teacher's pedagogic or 'educator artistry' (Dunn and Jones 2022, p. 318), a concept very familiar to English teachers. They have the specialist knowledge of 'how the various forms of tension work' in literary and dramatic texts, how such texts 'create and communicate a sense of place and time' and how students can be supported 'to engage with, understand and manipulate these elements for themselves' (p. 318) in their writing. After all, as Scholes (1985, pp. 24–25) puts it in his seminal work on literary theory and the teaching of English, the skill of the teacher is not simply to transmit or 'intimidate' learners with their 'superior' knowledge (p. 24). Instead it is to offer them appropriate ways to identify and explore 'the codes upon which all textual production depends' and encourage 'their own textual practice' (p. 25). Thus we advocate teacher-in-role and teacher-as-narrator, both discussed in Chapter 4, as ways to employ what Scholes refers to as 'the pedagogy of textual power' (p. 39).

English teachers are accustomed to using their pedagogic artistry when reading aloud to the class. They are very familiar with and understand the value of employing 'their voices in artful ways to heighten student engagement with the language included in poems, prose and plays' (Dunn and Jones 2022, p. 318). Teacher-in-role and teacher-as-narrator employ these exact same skills and can be used to help learners achieve an understanding of the important features of their drama activity.[2] Kempe (2001) provides practical examples[3] of his use of both teacher-in-role and teacher-as-narrator as a means to develop learners' textual practices. He describes employing 'a soft narrative voice' (p. 3) to create atmosphere and 'Speaking in a slow, sombre voice' (p. 3) to narrate a moment of increasing tension. On one occasion when he moves into role, he adopts 'a portentous voice' and makes the symbolic yet simple action of 'drawing invisible patterns on the floor with a staff' (p. 4) as an immediate way of delineating Prospero's persona. Each activity leads swiftly to writing-in-role, and Kempe recounts how his in-role and narrator interventions have inflected the learners' written responses. Learners are shown experimenting with and building upon the different perspectives, vocabulary use and speech rhythms introduced by Kempe from within the drama, as well as the 'visual patterns' (p. 4) of the actions that he has modelled. Furthermore, their writing draws creatively on the tension and atmosphere that they have experienced once his narration has 'enticed' (p. 3) them into role.

To demonstrate the effectiveness of teacher-as-narrator and teacher-in-role as interventions to support learners' writing, we return now to the *Beowulf* project. A significant finding from this research (Bryer 2020) was that the drama's visual evocation had a powerful effect on the writing-in-role that the student-teachers produced. The tutor made a key, albeit brief intervention at a particular point in the narrative, to focus attention on the dramatic moment that would provide the inspiration for writing-in-role. The warriors were waiting for Beowulf to return from his quest to kill the monster, Grendel's Mother, which involved a day-long plunge into a sinister 'mere' or haunted lake. As we have explained elsewhere (Burn et al. 2016; Coles and Bryer 2018), for those listening and watching, the tutor's careful choice of words and syntax, and the way that she moved and used her gaze, prompted a shift in narrative perspective (from the hero's followers to that of Grendel's Mother):

> Deep in the waters is Grendel's Mother. She has lost her son, he is mutilated – here she is in the cold, cold water . . . She knows that someone is come, someone is coming to revenge, she is waiting in the water, with the arm of her son.

A noteworthy aspect of this improvised text is the way in which the tutor described the monster's body within an imagined landscape. The monster's positioning was reinforced by the sense of depth evoked as the tutor crouched in front of the assembled group of student-teachers and then fleetingly appeared to look up, as if awaiting the inevitable attack. Situating the characters within a landscape that is highly pertinent to the action was a feature of most of the student-teachers' writing. It is clear that at the point at which they had to commit their ideas to paper, the visualisation of the location and the characters within it acted as a conduit to the character's thoughts or the insights that the learners chose to express.

As noted in Chapter 4, Grendel's Mother is granted neither voice nor name in the poem, and she is famously ignored by Tolkien (2002) in his seminal critical essay on *Beowulf* from 1936. The tutor's brief narrative disruption opened up a more inclusive reading of the poem, reflective of recent feminist critical interpretations (e.g. Chance 2002). It prompted a moving response from some student-teachers who, like Sophie (quoted below), chose to write from the more intriguing and unconventional perspective of the female monster, rather than that of the male warrior who wants the monster dead:

> Icy cavernous depths, thick with fear. I clutch him to me, all there is left, all I have left. And he is coming to seek me out, even here – I sense him and I am afraid. Dark memories blacken the waters around me,

stories that will never be sung in great halls and echo through time. When he takes my life, I will fade into obscurity, a flicker in his memory, a footnote in *his* story. All these years I've had no one upon which to unburden my thoughts and so they linger here, polluting the mere that he now wades through. He is coming.

Sophie's affective engagement with the predicament of Grendel's Mother, prompted by the tutor's brief but significant moment of enactment, is evident in her writing. The start of Sophie's piece is highly dramatic, taking the readers/listeners straight to the heart of the monster's isolation and terror through reference to where she is located, in the 'icy cavernous depths'. Sophie emphasises the word *his* (in '*his* story') which suggests that she is consciously exploiting the gaps in the *Beowulf* poem to give sympathetic voice to this otherwise voiceless character. The tutor's intervention has applied a different lens to this key event from the poem, enabling the student-teachers to witness it from a fresh angle.

And finally

In this chapter we have proposed that, from a range of perspectives and across all levels (university to primary), in-role drama activity powerfully realises both creative and critical processes in the development of learners' writing. We can think of no better way to end than by quoting Barrs' (2000, p. 57) succinct explanation of why this is the case. Writing-in-role:

> . . . moves them out of their personal language register and into other areas of language. It involves them in writing in first person – in a way that they are accustomed to and that is an extension of their speech. But it also involves them in taking on a different persona – in a way that enables them to get inside other experiences and other ways of talking, thinking and feeling . . . to access language that is beyond their normal range.

Notes

1 In the USA, Title 1 schools – those with a higher-than-average percentage of students from low-income families – qualify for additional funding from government agencies. This is often directed towards additional test preparation rather than more creative learning resources.
2 At the Interactive Research Conference held at the, then, University of Central England in 1996, Heathcote and Bolton identify this use of teacher-as-narrator. See www.mantlenetwork.com/basic-principles
3 Kempe's examples come from workshops on Shakespeare's *Hamlet*, *The Tempest* and the story of *Theseus and the Minotaur*.

6

'ACTIVE SHAKESPEARE'

A special case?

If there is one area of the secondary English curriculum that has been routinely linked with drama and performance-related pedagogies it is Shakespeare, a connection that even pre-dates the 1921 Newbolt Report. Obviously, Shakespeare wrote plays to be performed, but for over a century there has also been a growing sense that Shakespeare presents a special curricular case, almost an exclusive category of literature in its own right. It is, moreover, a highly protected category: the assumption that Shakespeare should form a core component in any secondary English course is rarely questioned officially (in England, at least), a manifestation of both Shakespeare's iconic cultural status and political opportunism.[1] Policy discourse has instead tended to steer attention towards the practicalities of teaching and assessment, rather than fundamental questions about disciplinary scope and purpose. As a consequence, the development of 'active', drama-based approaches has been largely driven by concerns about access to 'difficult' texts.

By devoting a separate chapter to the teaching of Shakespeare, we acknowledge that we, too, are affording Shakespeare particular privileges not granted to other writers. However, it is our intention to unpick rather than reproduce some of the assumptions about Shakespeare's cultural authority, particularly in the way they relate to the use of drama in English.

Political Shakespeare

The association between drama and Shakespeare was formally cemented by policy-makers in Britain at the inception of the National Curriculum in 1989, when Shakespeare became a statutory component of the state education system in England and Wales. Analysing the ideological imperative underpinning

DOI: 10.4324/9781003290827-6

this historic moment reveals some of the complexities inherent in the relationship between English, Shakespeare and drama. A good illustration of this occurred in 1993 when Prime Minister John Major outlined his Conservative government's new 'back to basics' campaign for schools: 'People say there is too much jargon in education, so let me give you my own: Discipline, Tables, Sums, Dates, Shakespeare' (cited in Wilson 1997, p. 64). That politicians were weaponising Shakespeare to perform the same authoritarian function as rote learning and 'discipline' would have come as no surprise to any English teacher who had been following debates about the implementation of the first National Curriculum for English from the late 1980s onwards. Nor would it be the first time that crisis-stricken British politicians had reached for Shakespeare, more often than not as part of a nationalistic exercise in manufacturing nostalgia for a mythical Golden Age. How Shakespeare came to be invested with this level of cultural and political authority has already been explored by a number of commentators from a range of perspectives (see, for instance, Sinfield 1985; Taylor 1990; Trivedi 2011) and does not need rehearsing here. Instead, what we are paying specific attention to in this chapter are the contradictory ways in which drama has functioned in this contested area of curricular English.

Statutory Shakespeare

> Almost everyone agrees that [Shakespeare's] work should be represented in a National Curriculum. (DES/Welsh Office 1989, para 7.16)

This deceptively simple statement, taken from the Cox Report, forms the clinching argument for making the study of Shakespeare a statutory part of every 11–16-year-old's schooling in England and Wales. Shakespeare's special status (as the sole-named compulsory author) is thus rooted in the rhetoric of common sense, obviating the need to produce evidence or engage in debate. Over the intervening years Shakespeare's uniquely privileged position as the nation's cultural and educational touchstone has been carefully preserved, surviving eight Prime Ministers to date and four major government-authorised revisions of the English curriculum.

Professor Brian Cox, chair of the inaugural National Curriculum working party, claimed his report represented 'the new consensus between the traditional and the progressive which had become dominant in Britain during the 1980s' (Cox 1991a, p. 5). At the same time, Cox was claiming elsewhere that his English curriculum was 'revolutionary' (Cox 1991b, p. 2) in its break with conservative tradition. It is somewhat ironic, then, that the nomination of Shakespeare as the only compulsory author in the new National Curriculum was at the time attacked by critics from both the right and the left, perhaps reflective of the internally contradictory nature of the overall document (see Jones 1992). To his credit, Cox had indeed resisted right-wing political pressure to produce a literature curriculum anchored to a prescriptive list of canonical 'set texts'. Cox was keen to defend his committee's decision to broaden the range of reading material, declaring trust in teachers' professionalism to make judgements about content and appropriacy (see Cox 1991a), yet when it came to teaching Shakespeare apparently the same degree of professional trust did not apply. Justifying the special, statutory status afforded to Shakespeare, the Cox Committee sounds distinctly less 'revolutionary', particularly in its appeal to 'universal values' (DES/Welsh Office 1989, para 7.15), a rationale that is reminiscent of Newbolt in 1921. Despite Cox's determination to avoid a canonically centred curriculum, as Thomson and Hall (2022, p. 2) argue, in singling out Shakespeare in this way 'the Bard is positioned as synecdoche for British culture and the "quality" literary texts that the nation's school children must read and appreciate'. Indeed, in the pages of the Cox Report the authors show some awareness that their political compromise is not entirely satisfactory. Somewhat undercutting their own assertion of universalism, they acknowledge that some teachers may take a more culturally analytical view of Shakespeare and want to encourage their students 'to think critically about his status in the canon' (para 7.16). Rather than confront these contradictions, Cox and his committee merely point teachers towards the 'active' drama-based approaches of Rex Gibson's national Shakespeare and Schools Project. In doing so, they effectively sidestep unresolved questions about cultural theory and disciplinary knowledge by recommending a progressive-sounding teaching method. A somewhat similar oversimplification is performed when they equate 'traditional' pedagogy with 'desk-bound pupils read[ing] the text', whilst claiming that it has been 'advantageously replaced' by the project's 'exciting' approaches (para 7.16).

The report's authors applaud active methods for successfully enabling secondary pupils 'of a wide range of abilities' to 'find Shakespeare accessible, meaningful and enjoyable' (para 7.16). It needs to be remembered that until the introduction of GSCE in 1988 Shakespeare had traditionally been the preserve of high-achieving 14–16-year-olds taking 'O' Level examination courses in academically selective grammar schools and 'top' streams of some comprehensives.[2] Moreover, in the first few years following the introduction of GCSEs, Shakespeare did not yet form a mandatory component in examination board specifications, allowing individual English departments some flexibility and choice. In that context, Cox and his committee were clearly aware that the summary imposition of compulsory Shakespeare for all state-school secondary students would be regarded by many teachers as a controversial step. The strong inference of the Cox Report, however, is that a focus on method – drama-inflected 'active Shakespeare' to be specific – should allay any English teachers' concerns. It is a pedagogical move that dissociates drama from its socio-cultural associations with learning, and instead enlists it simply as a pragmatic mechanism by which students will be afforded 'access' to Shakespeare as part of their government-endorsed entitlement.

The roots of the 'active Shakespeare' movement

In the UK the 'active Shakespeare' movement is perhaps most commonly associated with the late Rex Gibson's Shakespeare and Schools Project (1986–94), endorsed as an exciting innovation by the Cox Committee and subsequently praised by James Stredder (2009, p. 5) as 'the most influential specific initiative in Britain in the last twenty years'. While Gibson's teacher-centred, participatory model of professional development and funded secondments was indeed distinctive, the idea of approaching Shakespeare plays through drama-based approaches was by no means unique. Other 'active Shakespeare' projects were being developed contemporaneously in both the USA and in Australia, one of the most significant and enduring of which is based at the Folger Shakespeare Library in Washington and owes its creative vision to Peggy O'Brien, appointed as Director of the new education department in 1981. The Folger initiative began with schools Shakespeare festivals, subsequently expanding into provision of professional development for educators and the publication of a wide range of teaching materials and other texts. Meanwhile, the education department at the Royal Shakespeare Company (RSC) was also beginning to offer workshops for schools and professional development programmes for teachers in the UK. Joe Winston (2015) offers a historical account of the RSC's involvement in school Shakespeare and identifies Cicely Berry, the RSC's venerable, long-standing voice coach, as highly influential in the developmental trajectory of its work, particularly in physicalising Shakespeare's language and recognising the potential for transferring rehearsal room techniques to classroom contexts. There is some evidence of cross-fertilisation between Gibson's project and Cicely Berry's work,[3] although Winston (2015) is somewhat sceptical about Gibson's legacy in relation to the development of the RSC's distinctive 'rehearsal room' pedagogy (an issue we discuss in Coles and Pitfield 2022b).

Although the 1980s witnessed a transatlantic burgeoning of creative Shakespeare pedagogies, as we indicated in Chapter 2 the idea of approaching the plays as drama scripts was far from new. In the first two decades of the 20th century, several performance-related references to teaching Shakespeare are documented. In Britain, The English Association, founded in 1906 to support the development of English as a fledgling school subject, designated the teaching of Shakespeare as the appropriate topic for its first ever pamphlet (1908). Its advice incorporates three core tenets of the 'active Shakespeare' movement which have endured for over a century: voicing scripts aloud, taking parts and seeing a live performance. Early classroom drama pioneer Caldwell Cook (1919) draws heavily on Shakespeare in his 'playmaking' approach to literature, based on his conviction that Shakespeare was the master of 'dramatic conventions' (p. 185) and theatrical 'craftsmanship' (p. 189). The Newbolt Report (1921) recommends treating the plays as drama scripts, one benefit of which, the authors suggest, is to help children overcome problems associated with Shakespeare's 'remote' and 'unfamiliar' language (p. 312).

Exactly ten years later, the Chair of Trustees at Shakespeare's Birthplace Trust in Stratford-upon-Avon published a plea for 'Making Shakespeare Live' in *The New Era* journal (Flower 1931) in terms that could almost have been written by Gibson half a century on. In the article, Archibald Flower warns against the danger of Shakespeare being 'rammed down our throats' (p. 82) at school, proposing instead that pupils should all have the chance to see a live theatre performance and take pleasure in speaking Shakespeare's words out loud for themselves. Meanwhile, over in the US, early 20th-century contributors to the *English Journal* bear witness to a thriving community of educators employing a surprisingly wide range of drama-related Shakespeare pedagogies, as evidenced by Joseph Haughey's (2012) overview of archived issues of the journal between 1912 and 1917.

A more recent tendency by successive British politicians, whether from Conservative, Coalition or New Labour governments, has been to promote cultural 'entitlement' as a key aim of schooling, emphasising the benefits of fostering an apparently common culture through compulsory Shakespeare, all in the name of social inclusion (Coles 2013a; Olive 2015). It is argued that pupils from the least advantaged backgrounds will benefit academically and socially from the opportunity to encounter Shakespeare and other canonical writers at school, based on the assumption that this would not happen unless Shakespeare is made compulsory. This policy position is, of course, shot through with contradictions: Shakespeare is meant to be self-evidently beneficial for learners, yet teachers need to be coerced by means of legislation lest they omit it; Shakespeare is regarded as part of 'our' common heritage, yet at the same time we are told that it is absent from most students' lives outside of school; Shakespeare conveys 'universal' meanings and yet when studied by the masses it needs to be mediated via explanatory texts and special theatre-inflected pedagogical approaches (see Coles 2013b).

What is 'active Shakespeare'?

'Active Shakespeare' has become the term most commonly used in the UK to denote these special approaches (sometimes known as 'performance pedagogy' in the US). Broadly speaking, it signifies methods which are drama-related or have some basis in performance (often involving, for instance, role-play, still-image, mime, improvisation, choral reading). Framed by the Cox Report's rejection of 'desk-bound' Shakespeare (see above), it became associated with physicalised, performance-related activity, rather unfortunately encouraged by the RSC's 'Stand up for Shakespeare' slogan adopted in 2008 calling for pupils to learn Shakespeare 'on their feet' (see O'Hanlon 2008). Yet it is clear from what Gibson says in his seminal text, *Teaching Shakespeare* (1998), that for him 'active' signifies more than this: 'Active methods comprise a wide range of expressive, creative and physical activities' (p. xii). Gibson encourages 'personal engagement' which is both 'critical' and 'appreciative', through which students 'become the agents of their own learning' (pp. xii–xiii); and, indeed, two of the foremost principles underpinning his whole project are to make Shakespeare 'learner-centred' (p. 9) and 'social' (p. 12). While the majority of the activities Gibson offers in *Teaching Shakespeare* clearly have their roots in educational drama, they also invite learners to respond in a range of other imaginative and artistic modes, including creative writing, drawing, collage or film (a range that is reflected in the Gibson-inspired Cambridge School Shakespeare editions of individual plays).

Peggy O'Brien's long-running project in the USA shares some similarities with Gibson's, particularly in the desire to 'Give up Shakespeare worship', one of the 'foundational principles' listed on the Folger education webpage;[4] and the basic conception of the plays as scripts (famously, Gibson introduced his teacher workshops with a collective 'oath' chorused by participants holding copies of plays aloft: 'This is not a text; this is a script').[5] There are, however, some differences in emphasis. O'Brien's initial pedagogic rationale – which over time has developed into a distinctive 'Folger Method' – is set out in her *Shakespeare Set Free* series of texts (O'Brien 1993):

> The man wrote *plays*. So is this about *acting*? No, it's about *doing*. Students get his language in their mouths, take on the work of actors and directors, get to know a play from the inside out. Don't worry . . . that students moving about a classroom can't possibly be *really* learning anything. Make no mistake: learning Shakespeare through *doing* Shakespeare involves the very best kind of close reading. (p. xii) [italics in the original]

Whereas, like Gibson, she rejects any suggestion that 'the body and thinking can't be engaged simultaneously' (p. xii), her definition places greater emphasis on physical activity than his, possibly a consequence of the original Folger project's performance roots.

The RSC's brand of active Shakespeare, rooted in theatre practice, has in recent years been marketed as specifically benefitting from 'rehearsal room techniques',[6] an approach which, according to Jonothan Neelands and Jacqui O'Hanlon, 'takes the artistry and critical engagement of its pedagogy beyond the conventional uses of "active methods"' (2011, p. 240). Winston (2015, p. 44) praises the 'playful edginess and deep theatricality' underpinning the RSC's pedagogy, which he contrasts with the more classroom-focused roots of Gibson's. Yet, despite their different origins, the fundamental principle for both initiatives is that Shakespeare wrote plays to be performed. Moreover, both are framed by the language of social constructivist understandings of learning. For the RSC this theoretical position developed out of a ten-year (2005–15) partnership with academics from Warwick University (the Learning and Performance Network, or LPN). In describing key elements of the RSC's method, Neelands and O'Hanlon, both former LPN practitioners from Warwick University and the RSC Education Department respectively, draw attention to learners working as an 'ensemble', involving 'participation, collaboration, trust and mutual respect' (2011, p. 246). In their independent evaluation of the RSC's outreach work with schools, Thomson et al. (2010, p. 16) highlight how 'Learners act as co-constructors of the meanings created through work on a Shakespeare text. Ensembles are built in and through the time/space of the rehearsal room'.

The Globe Theatre in London offers its own distinctive version of active Shakespeare by capitalising on the opportunities afforded by its unique playing space. Encouraging school students to see a live performance in its replica Elizabethan theatre lies at the heart of its education programme: 'the perfect way to introduce young people to Shakespeare . . . to break down walls to cultural access . . .'.[7] Adapting a different play each Spring specifically for school audiences, the Globe allocates thousands of free theatre tickets for state-funded schools, supported by drama-based workshops for students and teachers in preparation for their Globe visit.[8] Online teaching and learning materials on the Globe website centre around the specific productions. Fiona Banks, a former Globe Education practitioner, describes the Globe 'as a space of experiment and discovery' (Banks 2014, p. xi) and adds, in a clear echo of the RSC, that 'creative exploration is to be found in the rehearsal room' (p. xi). Although 'creative Shakespeare' is the term she applies to the Globe's approach (also the title of her book), she acknowledges the debt Globe Education owes to Gibson's work, not least the principle that creative approaches 'are active, physically and/or intellectually' and can even be experienced 'at a desk' (p. 5).

As we indicate in Chapter 8, there appears to be some consensus amongst the writers of handbooks for English teachers that drama-based activities offer a model of best practice in relation to Shakespeare. Yet active Shakespeare is not without its critics. One of the most high profile, for example, is Shakespeare scholar Kate McLuskie (2009), who has characterised the Shakespeare and Schools approach as replacing 'thinking' with 'dancing' (p. 130), serving to shift attention away from language and meaning: 'The plays in this form of pedagogy', she warns, 'are released from their texts' (p. 131). Similarly, teacher and writer John Haddon (2009) cautions that 'acting out' (p. 91) and improvisation often lead to 'inert remakings' (p. 81) and focus almost exclusively on 'story' at the expense of serious engagement with Shakespeare's language. He is even critical of tableau work, a popular 'active' strategy often used to explore metaphorical language, on the grounds that it tends to produce 'word pictures' (p. 30) that are so visually obvious as to close down the full range of interpretive possibilities. Richard Wilson (1997, p. 63), another Shakespeare academic, is sweepingly dismissive of Gibson's playful approach, calling it 'charismatically anti-intellectual in its exhortation to joy'. In *Reading Shakespeare through Drama* (Coles and Pitfield 2022b) we argue that these negative judgements are based on misrepresentations of 'active approaches' and we provide examples of practice observed in secondary English class-rooms that counter these criticisms. This does not mean, however, that we are wholly uncritical of Gibson's project as well as those marketed by the RSC and the Globe, none of which, we believe, are sufficiently focused on the process of reading in classrooms, nor pay adequate attention to learner identity and representation in the context of Shakespeare's iconic cultural status.

Some of the problems inherent to Gibson's project arise out of the loosely progressive framework it rests on. His own passionate enthusiasm for all things Shakespeare led him to embrace an eclectic range of participants' accounts of their own practice which sometimes reflect contradictory attitudes to learn-ing and to the process of reading. A good illustration of this can be found in teachers' contributions to the project's final publication, *Secondary School Shakespeare* edited by Gibson (1990), a number of which describe activities that are heavily teacher-led, offering limited scope for students to produce their own meanings. That being said, Gibson's trust in teachers' agency, given time, space and encouragement to develop their practices in positive ways both individually and collaboratively, remains a core strength of his philosophy.

Our concerns with the theatre-inflected approaches promoted by arts-based institutions such as the RSC and the Globe fall into two categories. The first of these focuses on matters of sustainability, for example in terms of resources (both are heavily reliant on external funding to support educa-tional projects), space and models of training. Issues with the cascade model of professional development are highlighted by Thomson et al. (2010) in their review of the RSC's LPN project, observing a '"dilution" effect . . . as the work ripples out from the central RSC experience' (p. 26). Debra Kidd's account (2011) of creative practitioners leading a school-based *Macbeth* pro-ject leaves her wondering 'Whether this was more than a quick fix' (p. 83). In our own research we also point to concerns with 'special event' versions of active Shakespeare, with their own potentially disruptive demands on time and space (Coles and Pitfield 2022b).

Our second area of concern involves the different ways arts organisations position themselves in relation to teachers as professionals (see Coles and Pitfield 2022b). This is where the RSC's approach is most clearly at divergence with that of Gibson's. Shakespeare and Schools was a genuinely 'bottom-up' developmental model, reliant on the enthusiasm and expertise of a national network of participating teachers, many of whom were offered full-time secondments to the project with the objective of developing and shar-ing new ideas with other colleagues in their locality. In his writings Gibson (e.g., 1998) leaves the reader in no doubt as to his respect for teachers' professional skills.

Although the RSC's outreach project developed with Warwick University has engaged schools in what have undoubtedly been productive, long-term professional relationships (see, for instance, evaluations by Galloway and Strand 2010; RSC 2016), and has encouraged participating teachers to 'see themselves as belonging to a "community of practice"' (Neelands and O'Hanlon 2011, p. 246), it is disappointing that on occasion the rhetoric is of professional deficit on the part of regular English teachers. For example, Neelands and O'Hanlon (2011, p. 246) promote the benefits of RSC 'interventions' in the following terms:

> . . . teachers often lacked confidence in key areas of competence, for instance, in basic knowledge of the plays, using drama and theatre techniques in their English classrooms . . . they also tended to lack confidence in key pedagogical skills associated with the RSC approach such as the use of sophisticated questioning skills, group work and setting tasks that encourage higher order thinking.

In the same article, Neelands and O'Hanlon produce a daunting list of pedagogic skills which they claim are necessary for successful Shakespeare teaching, but they devote rather less detail to the ways these relate to the day-to-day business of being an English teacher. The overriding impression from Neelands and O'Hanlon's repeated emphasis on the 'authentic' (e.g., p. 242) skills of theatre practitioners is that, when it comes to teaching Shakespeare, the RSC are the real experts and at times it is unclear what pedagogic or subject expertise English teachers are able to contribute. Similarly, according to the Globe website, its theatre practitioners represent 'the lifeblood' of bringing Shakespeare to life in creative ways for young people, implying that is where the necessary expertise is located. But as Sarah Olive (2015) points out, institutions such as the RSC and the Globe are ultimately governed by a 'commercial imperative' (p. 98) that has a tendency to conflate Shakespeare as a cultural figure with the signature characteristics of the individual organisation. So, as far as both the Globe and the RSC are concerned, Shakespeare simply *is* theatre, albeit stamped with their own unique selling point – whether that be 'rehearsal room approaches' (RSC) or the cultural experience of seeing a live stage performance (the Globe). We share Thomson et al.'s (2012, p. 47) concern about 'top-down' attitudes to professional development which do not fully acknowledge the different professional skill-sets contributed both by creative practitioners and teachers, and which are not attentive to the 'complex frame of national policy, public expectations and local institutional interpretations of policy and educational purposes' within which teachers work.[9]

Cultural baggage and moral panics: Shakespeare, not Ronald McDonald!

The specific challenges of 'doing' Shakespeare at school are manifold and complex, not least of which is how to deal with Shakespeare's cultural baggage. Malcolm Evans (1989, p. 34) borrows the term 'incrustation' from Pierre Macherey to capture the sense in which Shakespeare becomes weighed down by socio-historical layers of signification, like shells sticking to a rock. Having been invested with immense cultural and political authority, Shakespeare's more recent fate has been to trigger periodic moral panics about its cancellation by so-called left-wing culture-warriors. Peaking in the mid-1980s, these 'crises' were bound up with alarmist rows in the UK about English as a school subject, where lurid headlines and reactionary think-tank pamphlets (see, for example, Marenbon 1987) declared that multiculturalism was threatening to replace Culture, and notions of correctness were being lost in a quagmire of progressive relativism. Determined to privilege a particular form of cultural heritage, ring-fencing the Western canon became a core aim of those fighting the so-called 'culture wars' on both sides of the Atlantic, at the centre of which Shakespeare was 'celebrated as a pillar of a superior Western civilisation' (Shapiro 2020, p. 227).[10] Just to debate publicly the place of Shakespeare in the curriculum was to result in a national frenzy of manufactured outrage, as teachers and academics speaking at 'The Future of English' conference at Ruskin College in Oxford (1991) found to their cost (see, for instance, Coles 2013a; West 1996).

Rejecting the Cox Committee's attempt to find some ideological consensus, the Conservative government's response in England and Wales was to police what was actually being taught in classrooms by imposing a national Shakespeare test for all state-educated 14-year-olds in 1993. The justification was as absurd as it was pernicious, here articulated in a speech by John Patten, then Secretary of State for Education:

> I am afraid that the interests of children are not being served either by some of the examination boards. One recently defended the use of a hamburger advertisement in a public exam by claiming that it provided just as much 'food for thought' for children as our great literary heritage . . . They'd give us Chaucer with chips. Milton with mayonnaise. Mr Chairman, I want Shakespeare in our classrooms, not Ronald McDonald. (Cited in Coles 2013a, p. 100)

The mass circulation British newspaper the *Daily Mail* (1 July 1992) considered the background story worthy of front page exposure, running the headline: 'SHAKESPEARE BACK IN CLASS', adding underneath, 'Patten drops *Neighbours* to make way for the Bard', a misleading reference to a culturally eclectic list of background texts which had been suggested by one exam board to enrich the rather more conventional literary diet of GCSE English Literature set texts. But the moral panic, that children would be denied 'some understanding of the national culture' as the *Daily Mail* story put it (cited in Coles 1996, p. 61) was triggered, with Shakespeare once again representing elite culture and all things British.

Fast forward almost exactly 30 years and the latest manifestation of this phenomenon raises the spectre of Shakespeare being replaced 'by any number of black and female authors', as Katharine Birbalsingh (by popular reputation, 'The UK's strictest headmistress') warns in an article in the *Guardian* (Wheale 2022), a liberal British newspaper. In this instance, the moral panic pivots around the imminent 'loss' of Shakespeare as a result of 'woke culture', including pressure to decolonise the curriculum following resurgent Black Lives Matter activism during 2020–21. Birbalsingh counters: 'Dead white men have something to offer us . . . The ideas in Shakespeare are universal'. A controversial review of English published by Ofsted (2022) similarly warns that the selection of a broader range of literary texts which 'address contemporary issues' can lead to 'significant, influential texts being removed from the curriculum'.

Students are not immune to these various 'culture-war' narratives; they pick up a confusing mix of assumptions and expectations about Shakespeare, shaped by a range of external influences. It is not uncommon for secondary English teachers to be met by resistance from their classes upon embarking on a Shakespeare scheme of work. It is a widely recognised phenomenon (see Coles 2013a; Kidd 2011; Neelands 2008; Yandell 1997) where students' initial assumptions are that Shakespeare is for 'posh' people, will be boring or too hard. Attitudinal surveys of students engaged in the first three years of the RSC's LPN outreach project point to the initial difficulty in shifting young people's deep-seated antipathy to Shakespeare (Galloway and Strand 2010) even in the context of a generously resourced intervention programme.[11] Indeed, such attitudes may persist into undergraduate study: the survey undertaken by the Higher Education Academy English Subject Centre (Thew 2006, p. 7) notes university teachers' concern about students' 'dangerously self-fulfilling' expectations that Shakespeare will be too hard for them. Outside of the UK context, Ansurie Pillay's (2021) South African student-teachers' post-colonial response to Shakespeare is, unsurprisingly, initially one of outright rejection.

One of our ongoing concerns as researchers is the capacity of 'active Shakespeare' pedagogies to chip away at these cultural accretions in a way that privileges young people's voices and is responsive to their diverse experiences and cultural practices. Such matters are rarely addressed in 'active Shakespeare' handbooks, and tend to be only obliquely referenced in accounts of classroom-based research.[12] It is, therefore, refreshing to read Pillay's (2021) analysis of 'active' practice which has enabled her student-teachers to 'talk back to Shakespeare' by means of hot-seating and other in-role work: 'students were able to set the agenda for interrogating and resisting forms of knowledge usually deemed worthy' (p. 286). One strategy we developed many years ago (Coles 1991), and have incorporated into our work with student-teachers (Franks et al. 2006), is to frame a Shakespeare unit of work by asking students explicitly what they know (or think they know) about Shakespeare, and then to probe where those ideas and assumptions have come from. Nevertheless, our own classroom observational data gathered over many years have revealed few moments in which precious classroom space has been allocated by teachers for exploration of these issues, even as part of 'active' pedagogy (Coles and Pitfield 2022b). Yet time and time again, our lesson transcripts indicate individual students' readiness to challenge Shakespeare's authority in potentially interesting ways, invariably as part of the 'unofficial script' of a lesson and therefore more likely to be closed down or ignored by teachers working in the context of high-stakes tests and exams (Coles 2013a). Since Shakespeare's central position in the KS3 and KS4 Literature curricula in England is rooted in politicians' nationalistic-tinged notions of heritage, we believe that it is vitally important to unpick how students see themselves in relation to Shakespeare as a cultural icon, and this should be included as an explicit facet of drama-in-English pedagogy.

High stakes Shakespeare

Not only is Shakespeare embedded in the Common Core State Standards in the US, but also enshrined as a compulsorily assessed component of the National Curriculum in England. Written response to a Shakespeare play forms a key element of English Literature examinations at both GCSE and 'A' Level, circumstances under which teachers are likely to play safe and rein in experimentation (Dymoke 2002; Hutchings 2015; Irish 2011). In fact, occasional surveys (e.g., Batho 1998; Wade and Sheppard 1994) indicate that the use of 'active methods' to teach Shakespeare is not as widespread as teacher handbooks and some commentators have suggested. Elliott (2021, p. 51) even suggests that there is 'a large proportion of teachers (40%) who do not know what active methods are'. Data from surveys we have undertaken with student English teachers asking them to identify practices observed in their placement schools imply that 'active Shakespeare' is by no means the dominant classroom approach (Pitfield and Coles 2013). Fewer than half of the student-teachers surveyed across two years' cohorts in two university departments reported witnessing any active methods, although they indicated that most teachers they had worked with or observed appear to have been using film to support the study of a Shakespeare play.[13] A snapshot survey we undertook with PGCE English/Drama students at the time of writing in 2022 echoed the 2012–13 data in respect of film, but suggested even fewer English teachers were employing active methods (although this may represent a legacy of the Covid-19 pandemic). Available case study research, while not extensive,[14] presents a mixed picture, suggesting that the integration of active Shakespeare methodology into everyday classroom routines is by no means straightforward. Jennifer Kitchen's (2018) research suggests that implementation of 'ensemble' pedagogy into a school context may be subject to a process of 'domestication' (p. 10), whereby the more radical aspects of the approach are constrained by institutional factors. In Kitchen's study, it is a looming performance festival deadline that dilutes the potentially democratic, collaborative and culturally aware practice of the teacher (in this case, a Drama teacher). One of our own case studies indicates ways in which tensions may arise in the context of high-stakes assessment (Coles 2009), and elsewhere we cite concerns voiced by English teachers about classroom control and time constraints (Coles and Pitfield 2022b). However, Tracy Irish's positive account of a particular LPN teacher's successful adoption of an 'ensemble' approach to Shakespeare indicates the potential benefits in taking what might appear to be a pedagogic 'risk'.

Inclusive, culturally responsive 'active Shakespeare'

Despite the complex cultural, ideological and practical challenges we allude to above, our classroom-based research indicates that 'another Shakespeare is possible' (Coles and Pitfield 2022b, p. 85) by means of an inclusive, sustainable form of reading through drama pedagogy. This form of active Shakespeare is at once playful *and* critically rigorous. Importantly, by privileging students' voices, it has the capacity to connect with learners' lived experiences and be receptive to their diverse cultural lives as part of the collaborative process of meaning-making and knowledge production. In one urban school we video-recorded a mixed attainment Year 10 class engaging with *Henry V*. Across the series of lessons, the object of students' textual study was transformed multimodally through a combination of film adaptations, movie stills and printed playtext, all supported by frequent moments of in-role spoken and written work woven into the fabric of their day-to-day English lessons. Improvisatory predictions at key moments in Shakespeare's playscript ensured that understandings of Henry as a dramatic figure were playfully rooted in the (multi)cultural life of the classroom, dialogically produced over the series of lessons and never allowed to become an academic abstraction (Coles and Pitfield 2022b). In another school, we observed a teacher reading *A Midsummer Night's Dream* with her Year 7 class. Throughout the scheme of work, she skilfully and confidently incorporated a wide range of drama-based approaches into her English lessons alongside, and as part of, discussion, writing and textual analysis. In one lesson she very effectively drew on dramatic play to focus on the moment that Titania, under the influence of a love-potion, awakens to fall in love with the first creature she sets eyes on. This learning sequence was notable for the way in which the teacher moved the all-male class of students on from playful portrayals of forest creatures into more challenging – and uncomfortable – dramatic territory, freezing the love-struck moment. Potentially subversive 'dark play' (Schechner 1988) prompted by the boys' real-world self-consciousness about sexual identity, was constructively harnessed by the teacher, to be unpicked in a later whole-class discussion that allowed meaningful connections to be made with those thematic aspects of the play so often avoided when studied with this age-group (see Coles and Pitfield 2022b). The play is no longer an inert package of elite knowledge because these approaches reconstruct Shakespeare as a living, socially situated practice (Coles 2013a).

It is important to stress that these reading through drama approaches are equally applicable to more advanced level literary study. Working with undergraduate students at the University of Warwick, Paul Prescott (2013) provides an account of teaching *Measure for Measure* which embraces a 'hybrid' methodology integrating drama-based activity, seminar discussion and textual analysis of historical documents and images. His work is based on the premise that learning should 'encourage collaboration', be 'grounded in discovery, enquiry and action', and 'recognise both cognitive and embodied knowledges' (p. 64).

In our roles as teacher-educators, we have been involved for a number of years in running 'A' Level Shakespeare workshops in a local sixth form college. Far from regarding the deployment of drama as merely an initial 'way in' to complex 'A' Level texts, part of our aim has been to demonstrate to our student-teachers that reading through drama approaches offer a particularly productive and meaningful way of working with texts throughout the period of study, even including preparation for terminal exams. For example, our 2018 *Hamlet* workshop was specifically framed by an authentic exam question: *'Claudius' court is a stage: a place of performance and pretence'. Show how far you agree with this statement.* Working in a similar manner to Prescott, our workshop explored the question in a number of ways and from a range of intertextual perspectives – importantly, this included treating the embodied texts produced by students themselves (as part of various drama activities) as worthy of critical scrutiny. After every activity or stage of the workshop, we revisited the exam question with fresh insight. We set up our opening drama activity, for example, by considering a contemporary portrait of the then aging Elizabeth I (the 'Rainbow Portrait', c1600),[15] a visual piece of political propaganda depicting a youthful-looking, bejewelled queen holding a rainbow, wearing a golden cloak symbolically studded with the eyes and ears of the state. We then turned students' attention to the grand entrance of Claudius and Gertrude into the Great Hall of Elsinore Castle at the opening of Act 1, scene 2. In groups of ten the students were asked to create a wedding portrait (in the form of a freeze-frame) as if commissioned by Claudius. Selection and positioning of participating characters along with consideration of the overall performative function of this moment all came into play as the groups set up their versions of the picture. After an initial showing, each group of students was invited to design a visual symbol (drawn on paper) that might have been added later to the portrait by the court artist (for example, one group created a regal crest for Claudius consisting of a capital C within the rays of the sun, topped by a crown). Following a re-presentation and collective analysis of their portraits with these symbolic additions, subsequent discussion focused around the themes of performance and pretence, drawing on textual references (the stark contrast of the idealised portraits with what we later learn about the politics of Claudius' court, for instance), contextual knowledge and a developing understanding of *Hamlet* as a piece of theatre. Later collaborative, drama-in-English activities included close linguistic analysis of a piece of dialogue, consideration of 'The Mousetrap' (the play within the play, Act 3, scene 2) as metatheatre, and to what extent Hamlet consciously assumes the role of revenge tragedy protagonist (e.g., Act 3, scene 3). Comparison of stills taken from film adaptations introduced a discussion about the ways in which different directors have interpreted Denmark as 'a prison', a place of surveillance and pretence (for example, Grigori Kozintzev's 1964 film setting it in Stalin's Russia; Gregory Doran's 2008 *Hamlet* as if viewed through CCTV cameras; Vishal Bhardwaj's controversial 2014 Hindi version set under military occupation in the disputed territory of Kashmir), not only adding an international dimension to the workshop but also providing opportunities for students to reimagine *Hamlet* for themselves. As Prescott (2013, p. 67) says, it is all about 'making the texts we teach leap off the page and into the brains, bodies and hearts of our students', whether they be learners in a comprehensive school or undergraduates at university.

In each of these examples, what students bring to the literature classroom (for example, in terms of experience, beliefs and identity) forms a core aspect of learning. Importantly, it involves an understanding of literary knowledge production that is undaunted by the prospect of studying the arch-canonical Shakespeare. Finding points of contact enables students to 'live through' the text as part of the collaborative, in-class experience of reading; it also encourages students to reposition themselves in relation to a writer who may otherwise present as alienating. It is worth listening to the poet Benjamin Zephaniah reflect on discovering Shelley's works for himself once he had left school: 'As a young, angry black man in the 1980s, it was a revelation to find a dead white poet that made sense to me. Good poetry has no age, and no colour'. [16] This is not about 'access', nor is it a claim to Shakespeare's or other canonical writers' so-called 'universality' (as promoted by Birbalsingh, cited earlier). What we are instead suggesting is that by giving voice to students in the drama-in-English classroom, they are more able to locate ways in which Shakespeare means something specific and personal to them. It is an agentive process of active dialogic engagement conducted on multiple levels at once, combining the affective, physical and intellectual.

Throughout the period of its inclusion in the National Curriculum, Shakespeare has remained a site of contestation and debate. Rather than deploy drama techniques in a way that may serve to mask awkward questions about literary knowledge and cultural authority, it is our contention that a truly drama-in-English classroom has the capacity to meet – and illuminate – these challenges.

Notes

1 Significantly, in the new Education Wales/Addysg Cymru curriculum (2020) Shakespeare has been rendered non-compulsory. See https://hwb.gov.wales/curriculum-for-wales/languages-literacy-and-communication/statements-of-what-matters/

2 'O' (Ordinary) Levels, introduced in 1951, were designed for a minority of the school population in England and Wales. The majority followed lower status Certificate of Secondary Education courses. Both were replaced in 1988 by the more inclusive GCSEs.

3 The inaugural issue of Gibson's *Shakespeare and Schools* 'Newsletter' (Autumn 1986, p. 6) announces a forthcoming Cicely Berry workshop for the team of teachers seconded to the project in the following Spring.

4 https://teachingshakespeareblog.folger.edu/

5 Like Gibson, we prefer the term 'script' to convey the provisional, unfinished nature of Shakespeare's dramatic works prior to enactment.

6 See www.rsc.org.uk/learn/schools-and-teachers/teacher-resources/rehearsal-room-approaches-to-shakespeare

7 See the Globe's website at www.shakespearesglobe.com/learn/

8 For an evaluation of the Globe's Playing Shakespeare initiative, see Yandell et al. (2020).

9 It is worth adding that the Shakespeare Schools Foundation initiative, the UK's largest youth drama festival, appears to offer teachers and students creative licence, supporting them to interpret half-hour versions of the plays for performance in local theatres, see: www.shakespeareschools.org/

10 Originating in US academia, these 'culture wars' arose in humanities faculties and involved the polarisation of competing beliefs, typically between 'progressive' and 'reactionary' views of society and culture (see Graff 1992).

11 Although researchers reported statistically significant improvements in student attitudes to Shakespeare a year later – for details, see the chapter co-written with Strand in Winston 2015, pp. 133–158.

12 Stredder (2009) and Neelands and O'Hanlon (2011) raise it as an issue, both claiming that versions of active approaches help students take ownership of the plays. Neither, however, provides evidence of students contesting Shakespeare's high cultural status, nor, indeed, pays particular attention to what learners bring to the texts themselves in terms of their own experiences and beliefs.

13 Most commonly this entailed the showing of a single film, rather than comparison of different film versions. For a discussion of teaching Shakespeare with film, see Coles (2015).

14 As Olive (2015) points out, compared to the large quantities of Shakespeare textbooks and teaching manuals published each year, empirical research which analyses what is actually happening in classrooms is surprisingly sparse.

15 See www.hatfield-house.co.uk/explore/the-house/the-rainbow-portrait/. For an account of Elizabeth's regime of espionage and surveillance, see Stephen Alford (2013). We are grateful to our former colleague Anne Turvey for designing this part of the activity.

16 *Percy Shelley: Reformer and Radical* (2022) BBC Sounds: www.bbc.co.uk/sounds/play/m00193rw

7
MULTIMODAL MEANING-MAKING THROUGH DIGITAL MEDIA

Our vision for drama-in-English is one that takes account of rapidly expanding systems of communication in the digital era, including changes in the ways texts are produced, read and interpreted. In Chapter 4 we explore how assuming a role encourages learners to draw on the resources of their bodies and cultural repertoires. Here we consider forms of pedagogy that enable learners to bring further cultural and technical resources to bear on the collaborative processes of media production. Our approach is underpinned by a social semiotic theory of multimodality (Hodge and Kress 1988; Kress 2010; Kress and van Leeuwen 2001), a 'theory of communicative practices' that takes account of all the modes or ways in which meaning may be expressed (Cannon, Potter and Burn 2018, p. 181). Kress' (2010) account of social semiotic theory underlines the significance of the socio-cultural and linguistic resources that learners bring to the processes of meaning-making and interpretation. A distinguishing feature of Kress' (2010, p. 54) theory is his focus on what he terms the '*motivated*' sign, highlighting how individuals who are 'agentive and generative' engage in 'sign-*making* rather than sign *use*' [italics in the original]. This means that we attribute a degree of authorial intent to the ways that learners negotiate their ideas and make informed choices in the creation of the drama and media texts that are the focus of this chapter.

A rationale for media production in the English classroom

Burnett et al.'s (2014, p. 161) 'Charter for Literacy Education' identifies nine '*Dimensions of literacy in experience and action*' [italics in the original] that align with our vision of a creative English classroom. In this chapter we focus on the second of these dimensions, 'Multiple modes and media', which

DOI: 10.4324/9781003290827-7

involves 'understanding how socially recognisable meanings are produced through the orchestration of semiotic resources' in the creative and collaborative practices of textual making. In reflecting on possibilities for media production in English classrooms, we offer a rationale for *why* teachers might consider incorporating these pedagogical approaches. We consider how creating media texts expands learners' understanding of genres, themes and the socio-cultural location of the novels, plays, poems and non-fiction texts that they study in English.

An obvious justification for bringing digital media into the English classroom is that works from the English literary canon, including those authored by Dickens, Shakespeare, Shelley and Stevenson (referenced later in this chapter), have been interpreted in the medium of film or TV for well over a century. Maurice's (1900) less than two-minute film of Sarah Bernhardt playing *Hamlet* involved a pre-record of the actors' voices, played over the silent footage, and by 1907 Méliès had developed a multi-scene, silent version. There are more than 120 stage and film versions of Stevenson's *The Strange Case of Dr Jekyll and Mr Hyde*. Convergence across different media means that we experience literature in a variety of forms. Pullman's *Northern Lights* (1995), for instance, exists as a novel, a film (*The Golden Compass*; Weitz 2007), a TV series (*His Dark Materials*; Bad Wolf and New Line Productions 2019), a play (*His Dark Materials;* Wright and Pullman 2004) and a computer game (*The Golden Compass*; Shiny Entertainment 2007).

In proposing an integration of English, drama and media, both conceptually and pedagogically, we draw on an expanded definition of what is generally understood as English (Coles and Bryer 2018; Franks, Durran and Burn 2006). The approach outlined here is aligned with a longer tradition of filmmaking and media production in educational contexts and particularly in English classrooms (Buckingham, Grahame and Sefton-Green 1995; Burn and Durran 2007; Sefton-Green 1995). Our argument is premised on the understanding that 'Literacy is transformative and *creative*. It does not simply involve understanding a text – it involves, to different degrees – remaking that text' (Burn and Durran 2007, p. 2) [italics in the original]. This form of reading through media production is one that we have been experimenting with for over a decade, facilitated by the increasing availability of digital devices. Franks et al.'s (2006) argument for a shift in critical attention to the full range of expressive tools, particularly the body and forms of technology in English, has provided the inspiration for a series of research projects (e.g., Bryer 2020; Bryer, Lindsay and Wilson 2014; Coles and Bryer 2018). We have explored how the processes of adapting literary texts in different media support learning about distinctive aspects of the printed versions, including genre, narrative tropes and different perspectives. In particular, we have identified how taking on a role informs learners' engagement with a variety of media in productive ways (Bryer 2020; Coles and Bryer 2018).

Burn (2022, p. 16) suggests that English teachers might shift their focus from the ways in which *Pride and Prejudice* becomes a different text (often regarded as inferior) when adapted in the medium of film, to 'How is *Pride and Prejudice already* like a film?' He argues that:

> In this case, the metaphors of frame, lens, editing, soundscapes and the general management of time and space in the moving-image may prompt complex considerations of how stories are told both in literature *and* film. (2022, p. 16) [italics in the original]

Working with a group of student-teachers (see Chapter 4) we became aware of the filmic qualities of the Old English poem *Beowulf*, particularly its shifts in narrative perspective (Bryer 2020; Coles and Bryer 2018). Indeed, medievalists Nickolas Haydock and Edward Risden (2013) use technical film terminology associated with camera shots and angles to explain how the *Beowulf* poet depicts Beowulf's fight with Grendel's Mother at the bottom of a deep lake. Haydock and Risden analyse the significant shift from Beowulf's perspective as he swims down, searching for her at the bottom of the 'mere', to Grendel's Mother, on the lookout, far below. As part of our *Beowulf* project, we asked student-teachers to make this switch explicit through the ways that they filmed and edited their own versions of this dramatic interaction, leading to productive discussions about the construction of narrative tension and the identification or evocation of empathy with both hero and monster.

Burn (2022, p. 2) further suggests that exploring how *The Tempest* is like a videogame is a productive question for 21st-century learners to address. Our own research involving computer game-making (Coles and Bryer 2018; Coles, Bryer and Ferreira 2021) and animation convinces us that taking account of the rendering of narrative in different media makes an important contribution to textual study in contemporary English classrooms. From a dramatic perspective, computer games involve role-play and improvisation, generating dynamic and interactive texts that emerge through the processes of playing (Burn 2022; Carroll 2002). We have also been involved in projects related to filming the news, like the BBC News School Report project[1] and making journalistic films in the style of Al Jazeera's AJ+[2] social media items (Bryer 2019). In this chapter we have chosen to focus on activities related to drama as an aspect of filmmaking that are particularly accessible for English classrooms and relevant to our interest in reading through drama.

We regard filmmaking on a shared trajectory with improvisational drama because it involves forms of role-play and dramatic action, albeit recorded and mediated through lenses, screens and editing software or apps. We are interested in the ways that this situates learners' production work in a cultural context that will be familiar to them, as audiences of multiple narratives that play out, on small and large screens – or are played in the form of digital games. It is important to highlight that the forms of media production we are referring to here are those specially adapted for classroom contexts, with outputs that inform learning rather than mimicking those produced in film or TV industries; creating what might be termed film sentences rather than feature films, for example.

A range of roles

In our experience, a distinctive aspect of the ways that media production activates learning in the English classroom is that it ushers in a range of different roles for learners to assume as they make and create, providing focus and a sense of purpose. Anderson and Miranda Jefferson (2009, p. 123) make a case that those engaged in classroom camera, sound and editing work be considered as 'technical actors' – an interesting recognition of the students' overriding engagement in film narrative. David Cameron, Michael Anderson and Rebecca Wotzko (2017), our Sydney-based *Beowulf* project-partners, note the ways that the participants alternated the roles of 'directors, actors, puppeteers, game designers and film-makers' (2017, p. 133) through the processes of devising and performing. It is from this integration of elements that they identify the emergence of an 'experimental intermedial drama-making model' (p. 137). The authors underline that the function of the narrative was not only to provide a platform for this convergence of tasks or roles, it also determined the students' responsibilities as they engaged in re-telling the story in different media, developing their understanding of the text through the process. Burn and Durran's (2006, p. 292) focus on the social dynamic of the classroom as a site of production draws attention to the way that the roles of 'critic, media analyst, or even the academic' become available to learners invited to engage in the processes of making. We recognise the criticality inherent in these processes and see the benefits in their accessibility: for many learners, making drama and media texts is the most meaningful way to engage in forms of critical analysis and dialogue. We share further examples below.

Working with literary texts

In our experience particular texts lend themselves as a stimulus or pre-text for short filmmaking in ways that offer the potential to explore aspects of genre, language, mood and atmosphere. Our approach involves developing short sequences using moving-image (digital video or shots) and still-images (photographs), edited together using user-friendly software such as iMovie. Gothic literary texts like Coleridge's *The Rime of the Ancient Mariner*, Poe's *The Raven* and Stevenson's *The Strange Case of Dr Jekyll and Mr Hyde* offer possibilities for forms of adaptation that activate learners' knowledge of horror, providing opportunities to reflect on the links between that and the

Gothic tradition. For instance, we (Bryer et al. 2014) have asked school students to make two-minute sequences prompted by the intriguing end of the fourth stanza of *The Raven*:

> "And so faintly you came tapping, tapping at my chamber door,
> That I scarce was sure I heard you" – here I opened wide the door; –

We have also asked learners to respond to similar instances of terror and suspense in relation to the moment when the sailors come back to life in zombie form in *The Rime of the Ancient Mariner*, or when Mr Utterson and Mr Enfield spy Dr Jekyll at the window about to transform into Mr Hyde. These carefully chosen stimuli provide a prompt to capture dramatic Gothic imagery, drawing on the modes of gesture, facial and bodily expression, costume, location, lighting, colour, sound and the possibilities of shifting camera angles indicating different perspectives in expressive ways.

The introduction of cameras and editing software offers learners the opportunity to manipulate time and space, to make actors disappear, to transform their garments and the environment they inhabit and to speed up or slow down their movements. The magical realism of Rushdie's *Haroun and the Sea of Stories* has proven an excellent stimulus for filmmaking with a focus on the transformation from the routine and everyday to the fantastical that happens when Haroun and his father set off from the 'sad city' in the country of Alifbay. We worked with an English teacher and her class of 11- and 12-year-olds in an inner-London school, to make short films that captured this tonal switch in a variety of imaginative and surprising ways, including characters disappearing and reappearing and shifts from black and white to colour, that students were able to enact when editing. Those playing characters clearly enjoyed reacting to these changes with a comic, exaggerated style of acting that was entirely appropriate to the tone of the novel. Most striking was the opportunity that students found to comment on the dramatic action through witty voiceovers, echoing Rushdie's wry humour. When we interviewed the class at the completion of their *Haroun* unit of work, several students reflected on how memorable the process of filmmaking had been and how it had changed their relationship with the novel, giving them a sense of ownership. They also said how much they had enjoyed making work that they could share with their peers, generating laughter and appreciation for the significant ways that they had deployed their technical expertise.

Some of the short films were clearly enriched by the students' cultural knowledge of films and stories that Rushdie alludes to, including *The Arabian Nights* and *The Wizard of Oz*, capturing significant aspects of the genre and the specific literary qualities of the novel. Distinctive cultural insights informed similar creative decisions in other filmmaking projects. A teenager engaged in directing a short film explained that she chose to reveal the identity of the protagonist through a slow-moving camera shot from low to high angle (from his feet to his face) because of her appreciation of the way that villains are introduced in some Hindi-language films (Potter and Bryer 2017).

One of the ways that emerging technology has shaped the evolution of a particular genre of classroom filmmaking relates to sound. Poor sound quality, associated with cheap digital cameras, has led to a focus on music and sound effects rather than dialogue in-situ. As mentioned above, students added voiceovers to their films inspired by *Haroun and the Sea of Stories* to explain aspects of the narrative action. In another project, having shown the class films without dialogue, like *Le Ballon Rouge* (Lamorisse 1956), we noted the ways that 'the student actors clearly recognized that an expressive or heightened form of acting was being required of them to communicate the story' (Potter and Bryer 2017, p. 122). There have been developments in the use of sound more recently that may reflect the popularity of podcasts and possibilities for sound editing. Heidi Höglund's (2022) research in Finland provides an analysis of the way that learners voice the poem that they are working on and juxtapose this with other sound effects and recorded dramatic action, in order to interpret the text in significant ways.

It works well to identify a moment of tension, when drawing on the stimulus of a text that is more naturalistic. The incident in Malorie Blackman's *Noughts and Crosses* when in Chapter 11 Sephy saves a seat for her friend Callum in the classroom and he enters, provides an engaging starting point (see Bryer 2019). Novice filmmakers need a clear focus, in this case to make choices about Callum's reactions and those of the other students captured in the form of close-ups on faces and hands. This provides a hook, enticing learners to further immersion in the world of the novel as well as drawing their attention to the ways that the characters' reactions are communicated to the reader in the written text. The moment when Sephy stops the fighting at the school gates on Callum's first day, that subsequently appears on the TV news in the novel, might provide a stimulus for students to create recorded interviews with witnesses. This dramatic action references the iconic media images of the 'Little Rock Nine' making their way to school in Arkansas in 1957, following the desegregation of schools in the USA. Comparing the novel and pupils' own work with the footage from 1957 offers a contextual reference point to expand learners' understanding of the text and its themes. It is also worth comparing the version of these moments from the BBC TV adaptation of the novel (2020) and the play version (Cooke 2007).

Reading through media production

Here we develop our argument about the ways in which generating multimodal readings supports learning about texts in English, providing more detailed examples and analysis from our research. The *Beowulf* project was undertaken to explore the pedagogical possibilities in teaching a classic text through forms of media production. When we undertook our research, the links between the Old English text and popular cultural heroic fantasy narratives were particularly vivid for the student-teacher participants, exemplified by the *Lord of the Rings* trilogy of films, (Jackson 2000, 2002, 2003); *Game of Thrones* (Benioff and Weiss 2011–19); and *Beowulf* itself as a TV series (*Return to the Shieldlands*, ITV 2016). We started by situating the learners' media production in this popular cultural context by sharing images from these and other adaptations. Alongside the illustrated literary adaptations for young people (e.g., Crossley-Holland and Keeping 1982), images of 3D models and a graphic novel (Hinds 2007), we showed excerpts from film versions (e.g., Baker 1999; Zemeckis 2007). The learners were invited to consider the extraordinary variety of ways that the monster Grendel's Mother has been represented, from the graphic novel's (Hinds 2007) depiction of a screaming, harpy-like older woman, with messy hair, wrinkles, a pot-belly and fangs, to Angelina Jolie's air-brushed appearance (Zemeckis 2007). Our questions about gender and the forms of representation at work in these images were suggestive of the degree of criticality that we expected learners to exercise in their own creative choices. The learners' discussions about the cultural references associated with the images were enriched by forms of embodiment, such as clawing and other monstrous gestures. We have argued elsewhere (Bryer and Coles 2022) that these animated, multimodal responses represent a 'flickering' (Fleer 2014, pp. 126–128) in and out of role, triggered by working with visual images within a narrative or storytelling frame. Through the process, a range of insights about filmic associations were brought into play, realised not only through the learners' verbal interactions, but also as they appeared to try on roles of the protagonists in the images that they were editing.

As tutors, we communicated our excitement about both the narrative and the extraordinary ways in which it has been adapted through our storytelling tone (see Chapter 4). We invited the student-teachers to address the textual gaps generated by the sparse descriptions of the female monster in the Heaney version (2000), including 'hell-dam . . . troll-dam . . . brutal grip . . . savage talons . . . wolfish swimmer . . . swamp-thing from hell . . . grim embrace', through the creation of short recorded sequences. With this prompt to the imagination, we encouraged a creative interpretation of the text within tight parameters and with close reference to the perspective of either the hero or monster, indicated by excerpts from the script that we gave to different groups. Looking at the images, learners had been reminded of *Avatar* (Cameron 2009) and *Pan's Labyrinth* (del Toro 2006) – fantasy films that involve complex make-up and computer-generated images. They did not have motion-capture technology, costumes, stage make-up or props at their disposal, other than a few lengths of coloured cloth that we provided. But of course, as with the other activities that they engaged in, the constraints they had to navigate were key to the creative process. We were prescriptive in our instructions to take about five still-images and two or three moving-images with a view to editing them together. We gave the groups 20 minutes to shoot, yet they did not appear daunted by the demands of the task or frustrated that what they made could only approximate how they might envisage a final product. A significant aspect of this approach lay in the learners' playful orientation towards each other – the ways that they appraised, responded and built on each other's contributions, in and out of role – and that they inserted themselves, their bodies and their ideas into the narrative, through the process.

The introduction of technology in the form of an iPad came with a particular set of teacherly instructions and emphases; some encouragement to hold the tablet still and in landscape rather than portrait mode, to avoid backlighting and to consider the power of close-ups. We have often been struck by the ways that learners respond to everyday technology such as tablets and mobile phones, although they do not look like traditional cameras, with respect for 'the signifying systems, cultural frameworks and social production processes' associated with the histories of film and TV production (Burn 2007, p. 520). This knowledge informs learners' attempts to refine their material and to create media texts that have some legitimacy in and beyond the classroom. Thus, we assume that learners' prior experience is likely to guide their fingers, as it does their aesthetic responses in shaping their work, something that may be reassuring for English teachers who do not feel they have particular technical expertise. However, in the *Beowulf* project working with cameras and editing software did not signal an obvious disruption to the playful, collaborative approach initiated by the preceding live drama or engagement with the fiction. This is one of the reasons that we regard this form of filmmaking as on a shared pedagogical trajectory with drama-in-English.

Representation

Through Franks' (1996) analysis of children filming their performances in a devised soap opera, he recognises how learning through the body brings questions of representation into play. The spontaneity and invention of much improvisational classroom drama has the potential to open up debate about casting and other issues, but the practical processes of shooting and editing, and the discourses associated with media education, tend to acknowledge questions of identity and representation in more salient ways, through the transformation of students' bodies into images on-screen. Film and its association with popular culture also seem to deliver it into the hands of young people, so that they are less obviously positioned by particular ways of working in the classroom. Of course, for learners seeing themselves in-role, on-screen provides a marker of referents of a wider cultural realm (of TV or YouTube, for example). Media production creates a bridge between the canonical texts encountered in English classrooms and those that learners are familiar with outside school, rendering the curriculum 'permeable' (Dyson 1993). The student-teachers' representations of the powerful female antagonist, Grendel's Mother, are suggestive of the way the poem has reverberated through time, including the obviously gendered and sexualised Jolie incarnation (Zemeckis 2007). They also touch on wider cultural associations, as exemplified by the terrifying female monster in Cameron's (1986) *Aliens*. In our view, an awareness of these intertextual connotations is integral to reading and understanding a text like *Beowulf*.

Creating images, inviting reflection

English and Drama teachers appreciate the convention of the still-image, tableau or freeze-frame because it offers opportunities to draw learners' attention to the semiotic potential of bodies, faces, hands, emphatic gestures and use of space (often referred to as 'levels'). This intensity and specificity are prompts to students to recognise the impact of their physical selves, facilitating close analysis. Similarly, the use of still-images in the form of photographs has been a feature of classroom media production, as free software has facilitated the sequencing of photographs into forms of narrative, *Photo Story* (Microsoft 2006), for example. Like animation, we find these approaches interesting because they encourage learners to consider the meaning and impact of particular moments or details, presented for contemplation in an accessible way, exerting a discipline in the creative choices that they make.

There are analogies between the ways that the spaces for dramatic action in film and on stage have been conceptualised. Augusto Boal (1995, p. 28) claims that the stage space becomes 'telemicroscopic', enabling those involved to see things that might otherwise 'escape our gaze'. Jill Nelmes (2003, p. 242) suggests that images in film are 'concentrated, symbolic and highly charged; they have a super-charged meaning'. The specificity of this medium offers the makers of this form of dramatic narrative a particularly powerful tool to direct the gaze of their audience so that both audience and characters' perspective on the action – their sympathies, interests and engagements – are influenced by 'the angle of the camera, the depth of field, the distance from the object and so on' (Jackson 2007, p. 162). This is partly why we encourage learners to take close-ups that capture nuances of gesture and gaze in considered ways.

The large tablet screen supports a reflective pause; a point at which a small group might view a still (photograph) or moving-image (shot), critique their embodiments of particular roles and make choices about their next shot or photograph in response (Bryer et al. 2014). The process of making and reflection opens up possibilities for review and criticality, allowing for a degree of control or agency in relation to the dramatic action, as Sumaya, one of the student-teachers involved in the *Beowulf* project, explained:

You were able to kind of look and go, oh that's really good, do that again or pose like that (gesturing with her arm in the air) and we'll take a picture. You know we had that control . . . You've got to use your body to kind of create the story.

The link that Sumaya makes between the body and the narrative also explains how the role of filmmaker enables learners to draw on the resources of their bodies for expressive purposes, in conscious and selective ways.

Some of these choices were more or less considered in the fast-paced process that the student-teachers engaged in. Several groups of learners framed and sequenced their shots carefully, starting with visually arresting establishing shots. Others tended to play out the action in front of the hand-held iPad camera, a more haphazard and spontaneous process that captured something of the energy and enthusiasm with which younger pupils engage in role-play. Either approach offers opportunities for interpretation and learning, particularly when learners become editors of the material that they have generated.

The significance of space and location

Multimodal social semiotics point to the significance of the orchestration of meaning through the specifics of particular contexts or environments for learning (Franks 2015; Kress et al. 2005). Franks (2015, p. 229) draws on Vygotsky's account of the psychology of actor training to consider how 'the materiality of particular socio-spatial environments frames, mediates and affects learning'. The impact of the environment on drama activities is often significant; the quality of the acoustics and lighting can generate a sense of intimacy, for example, even if students have to contend with desks and chairs in a classroom space. The transformation into the medium of film means that all that is captured through the camera lens, including the background, becomes salient to the meaning-making processes. When we set up the *Beowulf* filmmaking task, we pointed out the constraints and possibilities of the environment that the learners were working in. We explained that although there were no obvious natural sources of water, the building's stairwells and lifts offered opportunities for a suggestion of the depths of the haunted lake or mere that is Grendel's Mother's home. From our experience we know that re-appropriating familiar, institutional spaces can surprise and delight an audience that is likely to recognise the transformations being wrought, as space and the material world are co-opted into the narrative frame (Bryer et al. 2014).

One group used translucent blue cloth to transform a long stairwell so that it became suggestive of the watery depths. An image of a face glimpsed through the cloth appears fleetingly in a long transition, a cross-fade that captures a sensation of Beowulf's movement as he travels down, through the water. There is an ambiguity in the actor's dazed expression, looming towards the viewer. Transforming the location in this way enabled the learners to create a sequence that captures glimpses of Beowulf from Grendel's Mother's point of view as she, 'sensed a human/observing her outlandish lair from above' (Heaney 2000). In another group's film, called *Descent of Beowulf*, the learners developed a symbolic reinterpretation of the watery depths starting with a shot of water disappearing down a plug-hole juxtaposed with a high angle shot of heavy green and yellow cloth, slowly falling down the gap between some bannisters. It takes 15 long seconds for the cloth to hit the bottom. Another group chose a stark concrete stairwell, outside, for the establishing shot of their film, *Diving into the Deep* (see Figure 7.1). Their choice of location emphasised the distance that Beowulf has to travel (a day's journey) to contact the monster lurking in the shadows at the bottom of the mere. There is a hint of the hero's potential reversal of fortune in the way that his passage downwards is delineated by the line of the concrete stairwell and the blue cloth hanging over it.

The ways that the learner playing Beowulf found to move down the stairs, circling his arms as if swimming, were integral to this plan (see Figure 7.2).

FIGURE 7.1 *Diving into the Deep*. Beowulf is seen appearing above a concrete stairwell with the female monster below. Photograph

FIGURE 7.2   *Diving into the Deep*. Beowulf's arm makes a circular motion above a blue cloth-covered wall. Still from video

That he checked the impact of his movement as soon as the shot had been taken was suggestive of a degree of intentionality. But the group could not have planned the bright autumn light, and the looming shadow at the bottom of the stairwell, with all its symbolic associations – maybe a chance occurrence. Manipulating time and space through digital means often provides such opportunities to incorporate aspects of the random elements that constitute our everyday environment into a critical re-imagining that includes a role for objects, spaces and even people (Burn and Parker 2003). We have learnt to expect that everything that appears in the frame of a photograph or shot to have been placed there with intent, to be mediated and therefore meaningful. The role of the imagination to transform what is captured by the camera into a narrative sequence that we recognise as a film is a fascinating affordance of working in this medium – offering possibilities for close viewing and interpretation and bringing the makers into a more intense relationship with the text that they are adapting.

For a group of women in a familiar location, indulging in some 'serious play' created a platform for them to take up more space than they might normally, as they assumed those most potent of roles, hero and monster in mortal combat. There are analogies here with research by Kathy Mills and colleagues (2013) and John Potter (2010), and the ways in which they identify that the children involved use the cameras to frame themselves in a specific and significant relationship with their environments and to develop narratives for their films around this placing, referencing shared histories and identities. The effect of learners producing images of themselves, in a familiar context – being playful, inventive and assertive and acting in ways that are not necessarily sanctioned – is not insignificant. Several of the student-teachers commented that this was what they most enjoyed about the film-making; 'the freedom we had to discover our own space around the building', as one expressed it in her written evaluation. In our own experiences of teaching in school we were able to negotiate some flexibility in allowing groups of students to film outside the classroom for short periods of time. We are aware that these freedoms may be harder to arrange in contemporary school contexts but opportunities like this can prove surprisingly memorable and worthwhile. We have found that the echoes of such activities remain so that the spaces themselves remind us on a daily basis that things can happen differently, that roles can be recast and culture be remade through the process.

The editing process

Drama draws on a selection of the signs that we use to make meaning in our everyday interactions with other humans or social actors, through gesture, gaze, dialogue, movement and positioning, for example, and its meaning emerges with reference to the socio-cultural, political and intellectual aspects of our lives. Yet these selections may be arrived at in ways that often appear quite spontaneous, haphazard even. Editing has the potential to offer more control over learners' transformations than live enactment, since once still- and moving-images are fixed on a timeline, nuanced and minute choices of dramatic action are made more visible, available for critical debate, further revisions and enhancements. It is satisfying to observe the excitement of children and adults alike as they engage in shaping their representations of characters, dramatic action, space and atmosphere and their stories emerge through the processes of editing. The experiences are akin to writing a critical English essay, involving introducing a particular point of view about a source text and then making careful selections through refining, redrafting or editing emerging arguments. As they edit, learners are able to dissect the action through sequencing and cutting, underlining aspects of the actors' physicality and meaning-making, on-screen. This can have the effect of amplifying the powerful affordances of assuming a role in live drama. The choices learners make about how to represent characters go hand-in-hand with choices about how they want to appear; a highly motivating endeavour that involves a form of graphic immersion in a narrative.

Interestingly, Heathcote (2015b, p. 77) favours approaches to role that, 'Unlike television with its fast-moving action/images . . . function more like still photographs or photographic slides, causing infinitesimal decisions to be made by the children'. In making the *Beowulf* films, taking still- as well as moving-images and editing them together to create an impression of animation facilitated the slowing down of time and the potential for a closer interrogation of the stages in the violent encounter between Beowulf and Grendel's Mother. The process enabled the editors to render the battle in a way that felt convincing for their peers – stylised, aestheticised and emotionally powerful. In some of the films this was enhanced by deliberately slowing shots down: as Beowulf appears to leap over the wall to surprise Grendel's Mother or the hero swishes his sword. Some of these shots were enhanced by a careful edit to a musical soundtrack. The starkness of a live drum beat provides emphasis for every emphatic move in the film *Diving into the Deep*.

Our observations of learners, clustered around iPads as they edited, threw up insights about how the process of 'self-spectatorship' (Bolton 1998, p. 278, see Chapter 3) appeared to become a collective endeavour, as the screens reflected back what the learners had created and as they re-worked their material. We have written elsewhere (Bryer and Coles 2022) about how three female student-teachers, seeing themselves enacting a fight on-screen during the processes of editing, share their pleasure in and appreciation of each other's movement by mirroring the sword-brandishing, clawing and wrapping gestures (see Figure 7.3).

The ways that the three editors tried on roles as they viewed themselves acting on-screen might be recognised as a form of story-dwelling, involving the drama extending beyond the shoot to the edit.

FIGURE 7.3 Sophie mirrors Hope's on-screen claw action, as the *Beowulf vs. Grendela* filmmakers edit. Still from video[3]

Sharing work

The *Beowulf* films were shot and edited in a little over an hour. In our experience a double-period of lessons is plenty of time for this kind of filmmaking. Yet the intensity of the experience involved learners in careful choices about degrees of sympathy in their representation of figures engaged in bloody combat, taking inspiration from the ambiguities of characterisation, action and motivation that emerged from their readings of the text. One of the affordances of media production is, like drama, the motivation provided by the expectation of sharing their work with their peers. For nine- and ten-year-old children who made films in their primary classroom, it was anticipating how their work would be received by a very particular audience that appeared to provide a coherent frame, integrating the children's actions and shaping their work in a providential way (Bryer 2013). There was a 'flow' (Csikszentmihalyi 1997) in the children's approach that manifested in the ways that different elements seemed to combine in the creation of a particular aesthetic. Many of the student-teachers seemed similarly driven, keen to generate the laughter that confirmed that they had found the right tone and were communicating with their audience – accommodating teacherly demands and yet finding space for their own shared interests and humour in subtle ways.

Reflexivity and criticality

The move from live to recorded drama in the *Beowulf* project played its part in sustaining the flow of work by presenting the learners' improvisatory drama back to them, offering them further possibilities for revision and transformation in the way that Mills (2016, p. 68) describes – prompting 'evaluative and generative thinking' through the process. This reflexivity and criticality seemed key to the ways that learners assumed different roles: of the actor, hero and female monster, and of directors, camera-operators and editors. The touchscreen technology and its affordances played their part in encouraging a degree of provisionality and flexibility. Of course, although digital technologies provide opportunities to enable people to engage in collaborative and 'distributed' learning (Lankshear and Knobel 2011), the impact of the introduction of digital devices into an educational context is complex and contingent on many factors. This conjunction of English, drama and film was productive because of the ways that the playful and spontaneous dramatic response became potent images, available to support communication and understanding and open to further manipulation.

As one of the learners involved in the *Beowulf* project put it, reflecting on both the shoot and the edit, 'By the mere fact of working creatively with the text, taking on roles, moving parts of the text around, or chopping them . . . you are immediately deciding how you view the story'. We attribute this to an invitation to engage in an embodied analysis of the text – highlighting questions of power and social relations, with a view to re-writing the script. Transforming bodies and the environment and making the familiar strange represents a significant cultural intervention in educational contexts. Here we interpret the intensities of learners' interactions as evidence of their responses to a heightened awareness of each other's bodily presences off- and on-screen, as they transitioned between processes of enactment, direction and editing. We want to put emphasis on the trajectory of the sign through these sequences of dramatic engagement with digital media. Yandell (2014, pp. 73–74) explains the work of a class reading and remaking *Julius Caesar* in similar terms, underlining how the text becomes 'productively multimodal' as it is 'instantiated in talk, in movement, in gesture'. The forms of role-play that patterned our *Beowulf* project had a generative quality, providing a facilitating link between the learners' work in different media that enabled them to make imaginative leaps and to articulate and to realise their creative purposes.

Our suggestion is that spending a lesson or two on a focused filmmaking task, or even setting these kinds of activities for homework, can open up a text, sensitising learners to its genre, tone and construction. Such playful, technical approaches offer significant opportunities to harness the 'meticulously selective and complete signing system' (Heathcote 2015b, p. 71) that drama has to offer the English classroom. The processes can encourage learners to scrutinise excerpts of text and to recognise and forge intertextual links. Editing and viewing texts provide further opportunities for critical analysis, opening up meaningful questions of perspective and representation in accessible ways and transforming learners' relationships with curriculum material.

Notes

1 BBC News School Report project (www.bbc.co.uk/programmes/b01rs4sk).
2 Al Jazeera's AJ+ (https://global.ajplus.net/english/home).
3 This video still was also reproduced in Bryer and Coles (2022).

8

THE FORMATION OF ENGLISH TEACHERS

How might beginning English teachers' dispositions towards educational drama be fostered during initial training and beyond? And what models of teacher education might aid this development? Our own research over the last two decades (see Pitfield 2006, 2011, 2020; Pitfield et al. 2021) suggests that feelings of hesitancy and confusion are commonly experienced by student English teachers in respect of their role in incorporating drama. Added to that are concerns voiced by Drama student-teachers about the danger of their subject being reduced to 'a collection of exercises' (Pitfield 2011, p. 66) in curricular versions of English.

Combined English with Drama initial teacher education (ITE) courses remain comparatively rare in England,[1] sometimes regarded with a degree of suspicion as being 'neither fish nor fowl' (Franks 1999, p. 40). However, most secondary English training courses do contain some elements of drama in recognition of its statutory place within the National Curriculum, although our own experiences working as external PGCE examiners over the past 20 years suggest that precise interpretations and degrees of emphasis differ across institutions – borne out by our analysis of English teaching handbooks (which we explore below). Historically, there is some evidence that drama has been an established part of English PGCE courses for over half a century, although a 1965 NATE special 'Oracy' Bulletin indicates that 'activities which involve speech, such as drama, scripted or unscripted' were as yet unlikely to be part of primary teachers' courses in Colleges of Education (Stone 1965, p. 35). In contrast, a reference to the 1951 PGCE course at King's College, London in Medway et al.'s (2014, p. 74) account of post-war English teaching makes it clear that drama approaches were already being included in that institution. We can personally attest to the embedding of significant elements of

DOI: 10.4324/9781003290827-8

drama from our own student-teacher experiences in the late 1970s/early 80s (for example, at the University of Nottingham where the English and Drama PGCE courses were closely integrated). Meanwhile, in the USA the NCTE produced a *Statement on the Preparation of Teachers of English* (Larson et al. 1976) which suggests a growing transatlantic consensus that initial training of English teachers should include drama, particularly in relation to the teaching of literature:

> Today many teachers invite students to say how they as individuals re-spond to a work of literature – what it says to them and about their lives, about other human beings, and about human life in general. The idea that 'English' includes whatever one does with language (maybe even: whatever one does with symbols) has broadened the activities of the English classroom beyond what most of us would have envisaged ten years ago. 'Dramatic' activities, such as improvisation and the enact-ment of literary texts, are now encouraged. (p. 197)

The NCTE Standing Committee authors recommend that student-teachers should be required to engage in the kinds of activities they expect their pupils to perform, including 'keeping a journal, writing poetry, writing to different audiences in different voices, taking part in dramatic improvisations, making films – and analyzing at some point the processes they pass through in doing these' (p. 207). This way of working accords very strongly with current prac-tices that are familiar to us from our own more recent work as PGCE tutors in England.

Until very recently in the UK, the conventional model for postgraduate ITE has been the one-year PGCE led by university Education departments working in collaboration with a pool of partnership schools providing sub-stantial 'teaching practice' placements for student-teachers in specific subject departments. However, over the last 20 years official policy in England has encouraged the establishment of school-based training routes as part of an ideological shift towards a skills-based apprenticeship model of training.[2] At the time of writing, UK government proposals[3] aim to diminish the influence of university education departments and to hand over a considerable degree of control to the new Institute of Teaching,[4] led by a national consortium of semi-autonomous Academy chains. We address the implications of this reor-ganisation for English and drama at the end of the chapter.

Before considering broader issues around teacher education and subject knowledge development, first we turn our attention to publications marketed as handbooks for beginning English teachers, focusing particularly on the ways in which these texts attempt to induct new entrants into disciplinary and pedagogical understandings of the English–drama relationship. Since the majority of the authors or editors of these volumes have had experience of working as PGCE English tutors in UK university Education departments, the variable treatments of drama may well be indicative of the range of current practice in the training of English teachers.

English teaching handbooks

The following sample of UK-published texts are, in our experience, broadly representative of those frequently recommended by ITE tutors, nominated on core reading lists and to be found easily in university libraries: *The Complete Guide to Becoming an English Teacher*, edited by Stephen Clarke, Paul Dickenson and Jo Westbrooke (2010); *Learning to Teach English in the Secondary School: A Companion to School Experience*, edited by Jon Davison and Caroline Daly (2019); *English Teaching in the Secondary School: Linking Theory and Practice*, by Mike Fleming and David Stevens (2015); *Teaching English in Secondary Schools*, by John Gordon (2015); *Becoming a Reflective English Teacher*, edited by Andrew Green (2011); *Teaching Secondary English*, by Mark Pike (2004); *How to Be a Brilliant English Teacher*, by Trevor Wright (2012). The dates of these publications span three versions of the National Curriculum (DfE 2014; DfEE/QCA 1999; QCA 2007). As we outline in Chapter 1, the latest (2014) curricular revision signals the narrowest conception of drama's role within English, yet interestingly this reduced role for drama-in-English is not necessarily reflected as such in the most recently published textbooks.

While all of these handbooks attest to drama's place within the English curriculum – and, with the exception of Pike (2004) where Drama is addressed in a chapter entitled 'Reading for Meaning: Media, ICT and Drama', all routinely include a chapter dedicated to the topic of drama – they reflect contradictory understandings as to the nature and scope of the English–drama relationship. At one end of the spectrum, drama extends little further than its constrained National Curriculum boundary and is largely associated with the reading of plays (e.g., Gordon 2015); at the other end, drama is, to a greater or lesser extent, embedded in the editors' and/or contributing authors' overall conception of English as a subject. Within the volumes taking the latter approach, consideration of drama within English extends beyond the discrete chapter, emerging organically within other chapters dealing with, for example, Speaking and Listening (Davison and Daly 2019), the reading process (Davison and Daly 2019; Fleming and Stevens 2015) or responding to texts at 'A' Level (Green 2011). Contributing the drama chapter in Davison and Daly's edited volume, Franks and Bryer (2019, p. 153) summarise their broad concept of drama in English as 'a whole spectrum of activity that stretches from asking pupils to take on the role of characters in a novel and perhaps writing a diary entry or a letter, to moving into a performance space to enact whole scenes, whether scripted or devised. . .'.

In other handbooks the vision for drama appears to be rather less integral to the day-to-day work of an English teacher, perhaps best exemplified by Wright's (2012) publication in which the drama chapter is the only one not written by the main author, implying that even 'brilliant' English teachers require specialist help. What emerges from both Wright's book and that edited by Clarke et al. (2010) is the tendency to regard drama as a specialised, potentially risky pedagogy which, since 'space is a prerequisite' (2010, p. 234), best takes place outside of the normal English classroom. Caveats that 'workshop leading' can feel 'exposing' (Wright 2012, p. 155) logically progress on to discussions of complicated ground rules which have to be negotiated by the inexperienced practitioner. Indeed, the title of the chapter in Clarke et al.'s volume, contributed by Mick Connell, 'Doing Drama: Standing Up for English' (p. 231), serves to reinforce this notion of drama as physicalised workshop, despite the opening positional statement in which the author claims that drama is 'a key contributor to pupils' development in all aspects of the English curriculum' (p. 231). The chapter concludes with a toolkit of 20 drama conventions such as 'captioning', 'essence machine', 'forum theatre' and 'hot-seating' (p. 236), a list which may strike the reader as either deceptively straightforward or daunting, depending on their experience and perspective.

Fleming and Stevens (2015) and Pitfield (in Green 2011) are alone in attempting to locate drama historically and to provide a brief account of its complex relationship with English. Where the various handbook writers appear to converge, however, is around acknowledgement of drama's 'engaging, playful' qualities (Clarke et al. 2010, p. 232), 'motivational value' (Fleming and Stevens 2015, p. 159) and its capacity to encourage 'children to go further' (Pike 2004, p. 119). However, Fleming and Stevens add the codicil that drama's association with playful engagement is not always straightforward. In their drama chapter they make a clear conceptual distinction between 'dramatic play', 'drama as art' and 'role-play or simulation' (2015, p. 160) and go on to cast some doubt as to the value of dramatic play, warning of its tendency to be 'superficially fun but in the end unrewarding' (p. 161). This is no doubt true if 'dramatic play' is regarded as an end in itself, but as we note in earlier chapters, dramatic play can undoubtedly provide a valuable springboard into productive English activity; it therefore feels somewhat counterproductive to accentuate the negative in a textbook aimed at the novice practitioner.

Coming from a different perspective, Gordon's drama chapter mostly focuses on drama as the performance of dramatic literature. More particularly, he promotes drama's unique capacity to help learners recognise (and enjoy) humour in literary texts, particularly Shakespeare. For example, Gordon suggests using clips from radio comedy in order to draw attention to the way verbal humour works, and clips from silent films to explore visual gags. Whilst Gordon's conception of drama may be limited in its scope, the practical examples he gives do at least appear to be designed to encourage the unconfident English teacher to integrate simple moments of what might be called desk-drama into literature lessons. In direct contrast, Connell in Clarke et al. (2010) categorically states that 'unless the work is at some point made to "stand on its feet", to be "performed", it can hardly claim to be drama', p. 234.

On a pragmatic, organisational level, varying degrees of classroom-focused advice are offered to the readers of these handbooks, broadly falling into two categories; these are neatly, if inadvertently, epitomised in one sentence in Wright's volume: 'The freedom of drama can be alarming but it's also stimulating and exciting' (2012, p. 155). The implication is that drama's potential to enrich practice comes at a cost, raising understandable concerns around level of risk. The particular emphasis placed by the different writers on one side or other of this apparent dichotomy largely depends upon their overall concept of drama-in-English. For instance, Pike highlights its social and affective aspects and the way drama, along with media and ICT, 'address important issues regarding meaning and are concerned with the way we make, interpret and communicate meanings' (2004, p. 117). Interestingly, although he discusses 'challenges' associated with the introduction of media and other technology in English, the same concern is not applied to drama (overall, drama is afforded a shorter section within the chapter than for either media or ICT). Fleming and Stevens warn against adopting 'a sense of drama as something rarefied . . . hard to recreate in the classroom' (p. 161) and, instead, suggest ways in which it can be integrated into the study of texts, whether involving reading, writing or spoken work. In terms of classroom organisation, they advise that the 'newcomer to drama' (p. 168) start with pairs work, moving incrementally into structured small-group activity. While Pitfield (in Green 2011) likewise promotes the use of drama approaches particularly in support of literary study, she is realistic in her acknowledgement of the pressurised, test-oriented context within which teachers are operating; she therefore prompts her readers to articulate their own justification for the use of precious curriculum time on such activities, a strategy designed to pre-empt potential institutional objections. Connell (in Clarke et al. 2010) draws a different kind of attention to concerns expressed by 'teachers new to drama . . . about discipline and control in lessons' (p. 234) and goes on to devote a significant section of the drama chapter to establishing 'ground rules and protocols' (p. 234). This is not surprising, given the earlier prescription for an 'adequate, self-contained space' (p. 234), apparently necessary for the 'devising, performing, evaluating' (p. 234) phases of learning to progress.[5]

As explored in Chapter 6, the use of drama in English has been long associated specifically with the teaching of Shakespeare, and it is interesting to investigate to what extent drama methods are promoted. Shakespeare is often afforded its own dedicated chapter within these teacher handbooks, although Wright is unique in choosing to open his volume in this way. In fact, he uses the teaching of Shakespeare to make a more general pedagogic point: the crucial principle of planning learning from a learner's point of view. He illustrates what he means by way of an example of students' initial contact with *A Midsummer Night's Dream* and points to a number of 'unpromising' barriers encountered right from the opening of the play: a group of nobles with unpronounceable names, fairies listed in the cast list, and 'of course', the language which 'presents serious difficulties' (p. 5). Such obstacles, he argues, are only to be avoided if the teacher has first been able to locate a meaningful point of connection between the learners and the text. Whereas for some other practitioners this might be a cue for the introduction of drama-based approaches, this is not the case for Wright, although discussion and other oral work are very much at the heart of the lesson fragments he goes on to describe within the chapter. By way of contrast, Yandell and Franks' Shakespeare chapter in Davison and Daly (2019), owes a recognisable debt to Gibson's 'active Shakespeare' initiative, employing strategies such as choral speaking, tableaux, role-play and performance – albeit framing their approach with popular cultural references, film adaptations and production histories. Taking yet a different approach, Gordon (2015) commences his Shakespeare chapter with an analysis of a student-teacher's lesson, the focus of which is dramatic tension in a scene from *Henry V*. Gordon suggests ways in which the lesson might have been improved. With the explicit intention of helping students understand emotional undercurrents in the scene, he offers several alternative ways of extending students' learning, including the use of a film clip and a much-simplified form of Boal's forum theatre.[6] The latter drama-based strategy is, perhaps, an unexpected suggestion in a handbook which is otherwise limited in its vision of drama's role in English. That being said, the whole-class or small-group adaptations of forum theatre Gordon outlines here are offered in relation to a specific teaching-point in a classroom context. The advantage over toolkit-style lists of drama conventions as proffered by other authors is that this example of quasi-forum theatre is completely embedded as a collaborative teaching and learning episode in a classroom-based English lesson.

Predictably enough, taken together these teacher handbooks reflect the nature of ongoing debates about the connection between English and drama, representing a range of views. Where an individual writer or editor's position on the English–drama relationship is not stated explicitly, it is left up to the reader to construe from the overall structure, overarching philosophy and specific content of each book. This lack of clarity surely presents a bewildering conundrum for novice English teachers and an uncertain pedagogic terrain to navigate. What, in our view, would help is a move towards a much clearer consensus amongst English educators as to what contribution drama can make to English – along with suggestions for sustainable ways in which it might be integrated into day-to-day classroom practice.

The collaborative and social nature of teacher education and development

We now turn our attention to models of ITE and early professional development, exploring ideas about the relationship between knowledge and practice, and the formation of teacher identities.

In direct contradiction to the charismatic 'hero-teacher' narrative promoted in popular culture and government teacher recruitment campaigns, a recurring theme that runs through research around the formation of teachers, whether during their initial training, early career or later, is the importance of being part of a learning community (Brady 2009; Ellis 2007; Findlay 2006; Heilbronn 2010b). This understanding of the collaborative and social nature of teacher development runs counter to the individualistic model of skills acquisition as promoted through official policy and measured routinely until recently in England by means of standardised lists of competencies against which beginning-teachers are judged, a prerequisite for accreditation (DfE 2011/2021). The discourse around teaching 'standards' reflects a regulatory, commodifying tendency that is not restricted to policy in England (Doecke 2015; Stewart 2012). In the one-dimensional skills-based approach to teacher education enshrined in government thinking, the 'skills that define great teaching' are reductively summarised by a previous Secretary of State for Education in the UK as 'managing behaviour, constructing compelling narratives, asking the right questions, setting appropriate tasks' (Gove 2013a). What is essentially an apprenticeship model of learning to teach lies behind the Westminster Government's long-held aim to remove teacher education from institutions of higher education ('the classroom is the best place for teachers to learn as well as to teach', Gove 2013a). However, as Ruth Heilbronn (2010a) points out, the attempt to define 'good teaching' in terms of a universally applied set of descriptors serves to minimise the significance of contextual variations, whether social, geographical or institutional; consequently, it over-simplifies a developmental process frequently described by researchers as 'complex' (Ellis 2007; Heilbronn 2010a), or as Sarah Steadman (2020, p. 60) puts it, 'messy, recursive and intense'.

In the contested landscape of teacher accreditation and development, terminology matters. For a number of years those learning to teach in England have been routinely described in official documentation as 'trainees', and teacher qualification programmes as 'initial teacher training'. The term 'training' suggests to us that learning to teach largely involves the acquisition of skills, what Alex Moore (2004, p. 141) terms 'the pragmatic turn' in how teacher education is positioned (as opposed to 'the reflexive turn'); instead, our thinking about the development of English and drama teachers is underpinned by a Vygotskyan understanding of learning as a socio-cultural process, shaped by the material contexts within which the teaching experiences take place. In recognition of this complexity, we prefer the term 'initial teacher education', indicative not only of the broader intellectual and emotional aspects of the enterprise, but also of the open-ended nature of learning to teach, which in many respects continues throughout the professional life of a teacher. For similar reasons, we adhere to the term 'student-teacher' rather than 'trainee' in recognition of the theoretical understandings that need to combine with practical experience to aid successful development as a teacher.

For Heilbronn (2010a) questions about the nature of practice-based knowledge and understanding are essentially epistemological. At the heart of the matter lie arguments about knowledge as a concept, specifically the kinds of knowledge a teacher needs to develop as part of their professional growth – including how those sets of knowledge are acquired. At play is a complex and dynamic interaction between theory and practice, and knowledge and experience, a combination of processes that most new entrants to the profession find at once intellectually and emotionally challenging (Daly 2004; Steadman 2020). According to Anderson (2003, p. 46) professional development involves a forceful combination of 'identity and context': in the early stages of their career, he argues, beginning-teachers 'reflect on emerging aspects of their own teacher identity in a developing understanding of themselves as teachers within a subject and schooling context'.

It is often assumed that the 'subject context' Anderson refers to here should be a straightforward aspect of development for entrants to secondary teaching, given that the vast majority of students enrolled on traditional secondary PGCE courses are in possession of a degree in their chosen subject specialism. Indeed, surveys undertaken by Blake and Shortis (2010) suggested that more than 90% of those enrolled on PGCE Secondary English programmes in England during 2008–09 held degrees in English, or subjects very closely related to English. Nevertheless, at the instigation of Ofsted, most initial teaching programmes in England have routinely begun with a 'subject knowledge' auditing exercise. Typically, individual students have been required to measure their existing academic knowledge against the content of the relevant National Curriculum subject document, undertaking to address any identifiable gaps over the period of the course. The expectation is that a period of 'teaching practice' in school classrooms will gradually transform each student's academic knowledge into a more accessible, classroom-ready form, what is often termed 'pedagogic content knowledge' (Shulman 1987) or 'subject knowledge for teaching' (NASBTT 2020). With our current project in mind, these kinds of subject audits might seem to offer a productive point of intervention in raising English student-teachers' awareness of drama. However, the way in which this dominant policy discourse constructs subject knowledge as a commodity that can easily be audited and codified is problematic, 'an apparently simple public token to exchange for professional status' (Ellis 2007, p. 448). As Yandell (2017, p. 588) argues:

> To treat knowledge as an entity that can become the possession of an individual is to reify it, to remove it from the social semiotic processes that are implicated in the production of knowledge.

By way of illustration, Yandell considers the real-world case of a student English teacher struggling to engage his classes, whose hesitancy in dealing with subject-related questions by students is diagnosed by both his tutor and mentor as subject knowledge deficiency. The same student-teacher's remarkable turnaround in his second school placement, a particular context within which he felt more confident, leads Yandell to argue that it was not 'knowledge in the abstract' that was the problem, 'but knowledge in the context of the pedagogic relations of schooling' (p. 588). It therefore seems to us that ticking off a list of topics on a subject knowledge audit is a wholly inadequate method of gauging a beginning teacher's subject expertise or of attempting to broaden the scope of disciplinary understanding. Significantly, such auditing takes no account of the diverse ways in which these fragments of disciplinary knowledge might be understood to fit together or be variously interpreted in a range of cultural, social and institutional contexts.

The making of English (drama-in-English) teachers

Turning to English specifically as a subject, 'pedagogic content knowledge' becomes all the more problematic as a notion, not least because, as noted by Ben Knights (2015, p. 14), English is a much-disputed, even 'embattled', disciplinary field. Indeed, Simon Gibbons (2016, p. 35) argues that it is 'ludicrous' to suggest English could be considered to be anything but a political subject:

> The insights of Vygotsky tell us that our ability to command language is critical in the formation of our intellect, and in developing consciousness through language we are internalising the culture in which we grow. Our ability to use, interpret and analyse language – the essential work of the English curriculum – is critical in defining our relationship to the world and in forming and refining our concept of self and others . . . In literature, politics is similarly inescapable; I can't think of many texts that pupils in the secondary school will encounter that don't raise questions about society, ethics and beliefs.

Perhaps for that very reason, English has been prioritised for ideological interference by UK politicians at key moments of curricular reform (for example, see Cox 1991a; Elliott 2014). In these terms, interrogating how beginning-teachers of English arrive at an understanding of what it means 'to be an English teacher' becomes as much a question of identity and ideology as of academic subject expertise. The implications of such a contested disciplinary terrain mean that student-teachers bring to their secondary English ITE programmes very different ideas about their chosen subject specialism not only in terms of content, but also in terms of theoretical frameworks and scope – even allowing for the apparent bias in favour of Literature-based degrees reflected in PGCE admissions procedures noted by Blake and Shortis (2010). Caroline Daly's case study research (2004) helps to illuminate how novice English teachers' subject knowledge evolves during the period of their ITE programme. She describes it as a process of 'struggle' (p. 189) that may require the 'unlearning' (p. 196) of assumptions gained from previous educational experiences, as student-teachers attempt to adapt their stores of knowledge to the socio-cultural spaces of unfamiliar classroom contexts. According to Daly, this requires 'intellectual creativity' and a degree of 're-invention' (p. 196), further identified by Green (2006) as a process of realignment between old and new forms of knowledge, 'a painful and difficult process to manage, personally and academically' (2006, p. 112). At the interface between 'the teacher, the students and the curriculum' (p. 121), Green argues that each student-teacher develops their own 'personal deliverable model' (p. 115) of subject English, a reconciliation between what must be taught, what they are able to teach, and what they are happy to teach. This clearly has significant implications when considering the embedding of drama in English teachers' pedagogical repertoires.

Research suggests that a crucial element in an ITE student's emerging identification as an English teacher is that of collegiality and the recognition that their personal and professional development is situated in the social worlds of the various training contexts (see, for instance, Coles and Pitfield 2006; Daly 2004; Pitfield et al. 2021; Stevens et al. 2006). Part of this process involves being inducted into what Étienne Wenger (1999) calls 'communities of practice', defined as 'an ongoing, social, interactional process' (p. 102) with groups who share the same passion or interest and who collectively learn from each other. The roles of school-based mentors and departmental colleagues are undoubtedly an important part of this (for example through ongoing professional dialogue, team teaching and so on), but Stevens et al. (2006, p. 104) point to student-teachers valuing 'new ways of working . . . most of all with pupils'. In an echo of Eaglestone's comments about the nature of literary knowledge (see Chapter 1), they further add that student-teachers' sense of English 'becomes transformed by and enmeshed in pedagogical awareness of the subjectivities of their pupils and this means that the "meaning of a text" is constructed jointly with pupils in ways that can be both exciting and unsettling'. However, this is rarely a straightforward process, complicated not only by the contested nature of English but also by the overt – and sometimes awkward – duality of a student-teacher's role, at once a learner and a teacher. For those beginning-teachers in Steadman's (2020) detailed study who are enrolled on PGCE programmes, the university-based part of the course provides a welcome bridge between being a student and a teacher. Nevertheless, Steadman notes that navigating the professional relationships between university tutors on the one hand and school mentors on the other may still be fraught with contradictions. This is neatly illustrated by Steadman in reference to the widespread practice of 'PEE',[7] the essay writing orthodoxy exercised by each of the student-teachers' placement English departments yet sharply criticised by tutors at university. In these circumstances, the student-teachers were most likely to conform to school expectations. As Steadman puts it, 'Acquiescence might be bruising, but it is also safer' (p. 198). Based on anecdotal evidence gathered in our PGCE tutor roles, we would add that similar tensions arise with regard to the deployment of drama-based approaches, with concerns voiced by mentors around issues of curriculum time and classroom control.

Anne Turvey and Jeremy Lloyd (2014) provide us with an interesting, partly autobiographical account of a student English teacher (Lloyd) working through, and reflecting upon, his own 'personal deliverable model' of English. We witness Lloyd's attempt to reconcile the tensions between the teacher he wants to be (drawing on his own personal history and values, further influenced by his readings at university) and the institutional expectations (framed by dominant discourses of regulation and accountability) he encounters during school placements. Unlike the tendency amongst Steadman's research subjects, Lloyd persists in his pursuit of a socio-cultural classroom practice that bears out Bruner's (1986, p. 123) insight (cited by Lloyd): 'culture is constantly recreated as it is interpreted and renegotiated by its members'. It is a position arrived at through Lloyd's ongoing dialogic 'renegotiations' with his university tutors and fellow student-teachers, colleagues in school, the students in his class and, presumably, the process of writing his own reflexive narrative account. According to Turvey's optimistic summing up, Lloyd's experiences demonstrate 'what can happen when a teacher takes seriously in the context of a contemporary classroom the cultural productivity of "ordinary" school students' (p. 76).

One example taken from our own research suggests that other English teachers may find it takes rather longer for a satisfactory 'personal deliverable model' to evolve. Shona, an experienced teacher of English, is observed routinely embedding drama within her day-to-day classroom practice in an inner London boys' comprehensive school (Coles and Pitfield 2022b; Pitfield 2020). In interview, Shona expresses her sincere commitment to a vision of English within which drama is an essential pedagogic component. Yet, as a student-teacher she recalls being immensely sceptical of drama-in-English sessions on her PGCE programme (Pitfield 2020, p. 151):

> **Shona**: . . . it was almost as though we were affronted that we were being asked to do something active, that we wanted the passive delivery,

we were in a university. We wanted the passive delivery of having to sit there and make notes or stare into space and leave, you know, and we were really resistant to being asked to do this what we thought was a little bit beneath us, we were going to have to get up and show things. But it was, as it turns out, you don't know, do you, at that moment, it was some of the most useful stuff, some of the most relevant. All the other, where we sat there passively making notes, I can't remember any of it, or very little of it.

A key aspect of Shona's subsequent 're-invention', to use Daly's (2004) term, has arisen out of her deep engagement with specific communities of practice. She appreciates the value of working in a particularly collaborative environment at her current school, where professional learning is regarded as a shared endeavour, involving staff colleagues as well as students as co-experimenters. Above all, Shona's practice has been supported by a very stable, experienced English department, confident in articulating – and defending – their agreed philosophy and preferred ways of working. It has also been invigorated by a whole-school 'Learning Community' initiative which emerged out of participation in a Creative Partnerships[8] programme for which Shona had been a school co-ordinator.

Shona now rejects any notion of a view of teachers as 'technicians who implement the educational ideas and procedures of others' (Alexander 2004, p. 11), although she recognises that this was her expectation of learning when she started out. But it is interesting that the drama-in-English content of her PGCE, which she initially rejected, is the aspect which she now cites as having the longer-lasting impact on her current practice. Shona's understandings of the contribution drama makes to her English teaching repertoire have developed gradually over time and through the vehicle of classroom experience (Pitfield 2020, p. 153):

> **Shona**: I've never taught drama as a discrete subject but I have used it sort of over the last 14 years in English, very frequently I think, obviously not to teach dramatic techniques but as a way of exploring ideas in literature or ideas in how to use language, ideas about communication, across all year groups.

From this description it is clear that, for Shona, drama-in-English is rooted in the social, communicative and literary practices that are the bedrock of the discipline. Much of Shona's 'transformation' as an English teacher has occurred in spite of increasingly restrictive curricular and assessment policy constraints (although, it must be said, most of her development took place prior to the even tighter post-2014 revisions). Nevertheless, her pedagogic journey stands as a sharp reminder that teachers are not without agency even under such regimes. Indeed, Shona herself is well aware of the constant challenges creative English teachers face in retaining their hard-won sense of professional identity (Coles and Pitfield 2022b, p. 48):

> **Shona**: We lose confidence then in the value of this work [drama-in-English], even though instinctively we know it has great value for our students, we lose confidence in our ability to explain its value in a culture which is. . . which can often feel, you know, this sort of notion that you've got to be able to show progress for everybody by the end of the lesson. We lose confidence in our ability to explain how that is visible in this kind of lesson [a drama-based English lesson].

Similarly self-aware sentiments are expressed by Jamie, a newly qualified English teacher at another London school. He acknowledges that what is holding his practice back is his uncertainty about 'where it [drama] fits in' and 'finding ways you can integrate it as a bit of a lesson' (Pitfield 2020, p. 125). Yet, he perseveres despite concerns articulated by some of his departmental colleagues about behaviour issues:

> **Jamie**: It's having the time to think about it sometimes, and also worrying about, I mean it is a double-edged sword because I worry, I worry about behaviour but actually I find behaviour often improves because of drama but it's taking that first risk. (p. 125)

Final thoughts

A key conclusion reached by Daly (2004) and Stevens et al. (2006) is that the role of teacher-educators is crucial in encouraging beginning-teachers to adopt reflexive attitudes, 'a view of teaching and learning that is research-based, sympathetic to critical enquiry and able to sustain change' (Daly 2004, p. 105). Reflecting upon the dialogic nature of learning to teach, Turvey (2005, p. 6) emphasises the multi-layered discourses of education that play a significant part in the formation of English teachers:

> Above all, it is the sense of the collective nature of learning which emerges. . ., collective in the sense that it is the product of many 'voices' whose power to shape practice is constantly called upon, questioned and challenged by the learners.

Shona's case also highlights the importance of the school environment within which teachers work: 'The emotional climate of the school and classroom will affect attitudes to and practices of teaching and learning' (Day et al. 2006, p. 612), and thus influence the teacher's ability to adopt a transformative approach towards their pedagogy. Shona is acutely aware that her sense of what constitutes English has been re-worked in the context of a collaborative school culture, an environment within which she is able to reflect upon, and experiment with, the drama-based approaches first introduced during her PGCE. There are, we think, instructive parallels to be drawn with the agentive 'self-educative' groups of teachers formed in the early days of LATE, as described by Gibbons (2013). The history of LATE, he notes, 'is a case study of a network of professionals that effectively fostered change and progress, informing policy and practice in the professional development of teachers. . . emphasiz[ing] the key importance of engaging members through working in small groups' (p. 85); and, significantly, the LATE archive shows that a 'drama in the classroom' study group existed as early as 1948 (Gibbons 2008, p. 126). Tony Burgess, one of Gibbons' interviewees, recalls: 'You would draw stuff from your own classrooms. That was the point of those groups, they were groups of working teachers but fed by intellectual and theoretical interests as well' (2013, p. 86). The assumption underlying these LATE collaborations was that 'practice always informed the theory and vice versa' (p. 86). There is here a recognition that ideas about teaching and the concept of subject knowledge continue to evolve in the light of experience, reading and dialogue with other teachers and learners, both during initial 'training' and continuing throughout teachers' careers. This has serious implications for the way in which teacher education is conceived. As Gibbons argues, if teacher development continues to move towards delivery of 'apparently proven methods for the classroom' it will serve to '[inhibit] teachers from identifying and researching areas of their concern, and undermines their professional and personal identities' (p. 86). For this reason, we have concerns about the imminent break-up of current university-led ITE structures, a move that appears designed to reduce the opportunities for encountering a range of ideas, pedagogies and understandings about what it means to be an English teacher. Our own interviews with student English teachers across different training routes, including school-based employment programmes, indicate how much they have valued regular contact with fellow English students, a social space within which they could be both teachers and learners together (Coles and Pitfield 2006). Camilla Stanger (Pitfield et al. 2021, pp. 14–15), now involved in teacher education herself, articulates very clearly how that mixture of mutuality and experimentation has been important to her subsequent identity as an English teacher:

> And then we were out on our placements, hit by the realities of 21st century London schools with their (sometimes) competing goals of academic success and care for their students, and hit equally by the sheer energy and fire of the young minds we were challenged to nurture within the English classroom, with all of its possibilities. All this was a baptism of fire – for me at least – and all of it we had been prepared for by the PGCE which was at once a cocoon and a laboratory – a place to learn, build strength, find ourselves as teachers, wake up and experiment. But

this growing and experimenting never took place alone – it was always as a community if not a family of sorts, one we returned to on Fridays to regroup and remember why we were doing all this. And it is in this that I can't help but think of the PGCE as home.

The proposed fragmentation of substantial university PGCE subject cohorts, with trainees spread across numerous individual training schools, promises to be less conducive to the formation of these dialogic communities. This, we believe, to be of crucial importance when considering drama-in-English, the development of which is so intimately bound up with issues around teacher agency, professional confidence, creativity and generative attitudes about subject knowledge.

Notes

1 In Spring 2022, nine English with drama 'postgraduate teacher training' courses were listed across England on the Government website out of a total of 690 English courses (conventional university-led PGCE courses as well as small school-centred training programmes). See www.find-postgraduate-teacher-training.service.gov.uk/results?age_group=secondary&l=2&subject_codes%5B%5D=Q3
2 A process which began in the 1990s with the long-stated intention of breaking up 'the monopoly of the teacher training colleges', to use the words of a Conservative Schools Minister (quoted in Protherough and Atkinson 1991, p. 45). Conservative-leaning think-tanks accused higher education institutions of promoting left-wing educational theory at the expense of practical classroom skills (see Lawlor 2004).
3 See the 2021 *Initial Teacher Training (ITT) Market Review* at www.gov.uk/government/publications/initial-teacher-training-itt-market-review
4 See www.gov.uk/government/news/new-institute-of-teaching-set-to-be-established
5 These three phases of learning echo the 'making, performing, responding' formula proposed by Arts Council England (2003, first published in 1992) in respect of Drama as a school subject. They are, in turn, replicated in the *Drama Objectives Bank* (DfES 2003), published as part of the UK Government's KS3 Strategy.
6 Forum theatre emerged out of Boal's work with poor communities in Latin America in the 1960s and 70s. During live performances he invited his audiences to actively engage as 'spectactors' in tackling the issues of social injustice and political oppression portrayed, and by dramatically exploring the different ways in which scenes might be played out. See *Theatre of the Oppressed* (Boal 2008).
7 Point Evidence Explanation: a formulaic approach to the structuring of paragraphs commonly taught in UK secondary schools in respect of writing literary critical essays.
8 A well-funded flagship project of the New Labour Government, designed to bring creative professionals into schools to work with teachers (2002–11).

9
CONCLUSIONS

The value of drama-in-English

We began this book by asking what kinds of English lessons stand out as being particularly memorable, and indicated the positive ways in which young people in our research have responded when prompted to reflect on drama-based English lessons they have experienced. In this final chapter it seems fitting to return to a related question about the purpose and value of this way of working, especially in the inhospitable face of the knowledge-rich turn (Elliott 2021) so beloved by current policy-makers. We start by approaching this issue from the perspective of the learners themselves, in this case Ricky, a Year 11 boy, interviewed as part of a whole-class discussion in the run-up to final GCSE examinations (see Pitfield 2020). His recollection of a memorable English lesson touches on the complex interplay between students' own experiences, the social life of the classroom and the world of the text, while indicating the longer-term benefit of re-creative classroom activity.

Back in KS3, Ricky's class had been exploring Steinbeck's *The Pearl*. In a mock-trial episode prompted by the novella's denouement, Ricky had taken the role of the main character, Kino, a poor pearl fisherman being tried for murder as part of a whole-class role-play. Whilst Ricky emphasised that, in his view, this had been a 'good lesson', and clearly the in-the-moment, tense courtroom scenario had stayed with him for some time after the event ('it got quite heated, that day'), a real-life sense of grievance about the ways others had played their parts ('there were some biased people on the jury so they weren't, like, impartial') resurfaced when he was recounting it to us in the social forum of the classroom. The connections between Ricky's direct in-role experience and the themes of injustice and corruption in Steinbeck's novel hardly need pointing out, but what is interesting is that on the day of

DOI: 10.4324/9781003290827-9

the role-play any spontaneous reaction that Ricky might have made, such as challenging his 'biased' classmates, had clearly been subordinated to the rules of the drama, in this instance, the formal nature of the trial and the relative powerlessness of Ricky-as-Kino as set against the power invested in the jury. We are reminded of Vygotsky's (2016) insights into the dual nature of play activity, which suggest to us that participants are capable of being immersed in the drama whilst remaining critically distanced, a doubleness of perspective that can lead to productive forms of tension as Ricky discovered. It is in such friction, between the personal and the social in the dramatised context, that the seeds for an active discourse around social change can be sown. This, according to Brian Edmiston (2003, p. 223), is why the 'doubled reality of drama is so significant' because 'the social and cultural meanings that we make in one space-time affect the meanings in the other'.

Ricky is not alone amongst students we have interviewed in suggesting that drama-inflected lessons represent 'good' and memorable practice in English from a learner's perspective; the sample of student comments we include in the opening section of Chapter 1 suggest some of the reasons why that might be the case. Throughout this volume we have sought to support our observations about practice with reference to a range of international research that goes some way towards building a credible qualitative evidence-base. What is deemed 'good' learning by current policy-makers and their outriders, however, depends upon factors that are more ideological than epistemological. England's powerful schools inspection agency, Ofsted, provides a perfect illustration of what we mean, despite its claims to an 'arm's length' relationship to Government. At the time of writing, Ofsted's latest English-related publication, a 'curriculum research review' (Ofsted 2022), is uncompromising in its promotion of a reductive knowledge-transfer model of curriculum and learning in English.[1] This not only conveys a joyless and arid version of the subject we have loved to teach, it represents a considerable philosophical and pedagogical shift from Ofsted's own position a decade previously, when it characterised English as 'a creative, interactive subject' (Ofsted 2012, p. 34). In a series of reports between 2005 and 2012 based on observational evidence collated from routine school inspections, Ofsted inspectors provide examples of classroom practice that they are happy to mark out as outstanding, such as English teaching which is designed to engage and motivate students, encourage a love of reading, make links with students' lives beyond the classroom and respond flexibly to learners' needs in unexpected ways during the course of a lesson (see Ofsted 2012). Presumably this is why, in a set of case studies entitled *Excellence in English* (Ofsted 2011), inspectors highlight an 'emphasis on drama in English' as a marker of an 'effective English department' (p. 36), and stress 'the need to make English an active and discursive experience for students, one which engages their interest and gives them a voice' (p. 19). The references to hot-seating, role-playing and writing-in-role in these Ofsted documents are all the more remarkable given that, throughout this period, teachers continued to be subject to the relatively constricting curricular and assessment system we refer to in Chapter 1, a system that did little to encourage the integration of drama within English. In fact, Ofsted's own overarching inspection protocol with its insistent focus on individual schools' formal assessment data was clearly identified by researchers at the time as a contributing factor in the narrowing of pedagogical range (Perryman et al. 2011). Nevertheless, the English inspectors' surprisingly positive observations of what might have been regarded as examples of unconventional practice are testament to English teachers' creative resilience. Likewise the teachers whose principled practice we describe in this book have all, to some extent, pushed back against institutional or national discourses of constraint. It is worth reminding ourselves that top-down policies never wholly reflect what happens in classrooms, and that it is not only in Britain that official attitudes to drama within English are subject to ideological fluctuations. Manuel et al. (2008) note that in Australia, too, policy interventions have at times been less restrictive than in recent years.

The relationship between policy and practice raises an interesting question: should a government's English curriculum carry statutory force (beyond a broadly agreed framework), or should it be merely advisory? If the latter (our preference), the structures, resources and continuing professional development have to be in place to support English teachers in experimenting with and embedding their drama practices, as we imply in Chapter 8. A similar point is made by Dunn and Jones (2022) with regard to the Y Connect Project, and by Saunders and Ewing (2022) in their account of the wide-reaching School Drama programme, both in Australia. As revealed by our brief historical overview in Chapter 2, significant developments in drama-English pedagogy, however much welcomed when instigated, have rarely left a lasting, broad-based legacy. If policy documents offer an incoherent rationale, or merely equivocate about the need for drama-in-English, then teachers receive a clear message that they should regard any drama activity beyond the reading of plays as, at best, optional. And if, as is presently the case in England, there is an almost total neglect of drama in the statutory curriculum for English, it implies that drama represents an unjustifiable distraction from the 'real' work of the English classroom.

Reclaiming English as a creative, humane subject

We also want to return to the thorny question about the 'fractured' and 'contested' (Elliott 2021, p. 26) nature of English as a subject, central to which is the way knowledge in English is understood and acquired in the social space of a secondary classroom. It will be evident from the preceding chapters that we regard English in its fullest sense to have the potential to be 'central to young people's emotional, social and intellectual development and a foundation for developing an understanding of self, others, cultures and modes of communication' (Thomas 2022, p. 64). The personal, interpretive and exploratory aspects of English are probably what drew many of us to it in the first place, as we imply in our Introduction. A good example from beyond the world of English teaching is the immense popularity of adult book-groups, which rests on the collective enjoyment that is to be derived from interactions with fellow readers. Whether for adults or for young people in a classroom, an essentially Vygotskyan view of learning applies, whereby meanings are constructed socially and dialogically, rooted in the experiences and cultures of the participants. This understanding underpins our core proposition: that drama is an embedded form of learning in English. Embodiment enriches the processes of meaning-making in an English classroom, especially in relation to texts, bringing 'the writer and the reader together in an experience that is apprehended sensorially and emotionally as it is comprehended cognitively' (O'Toole and Dunn 2020, p. 3).

Nowhere is the interplay between the creative, the affective and the critical more apparent than in the concept of 'living through'. From their different perspectives Heathcote, Rosenblatt and Barrs provide accounts of living through, and a synthesis of their ideas is an integral part of our drama-in-English framework. For Heathcote, it is vital that learners work from inside a situation, with all the in-the-moment thinking that such an approach implies. However, in her own practice she would regularly halt the action for learners to reflect on its implications, thus oscillating between the dramatic and evaluative modes, each informing the other. In this model the creative and the critical are co-dependent, the evaluative function putting the creative responses under scrutiny so that they serve as fresh stimuli and prompt further learning. Similarly, Rosenblatt's aesthetic and efferent reading exist on a continuum in terms of reading activity. The aesthetic implies that readers are immersed in the world of the text whilst always reading from the perspective of their own worlds, both of which inflect what they then take away for further thought and action (the efferent). When brought to life through drama-in-English activity, this can have a profound effect, as Ricky's account from earlier in this chapter suggests. In supporting both literary reading and creative writing, living through for Barrs means enactment that is often playful and always imaginative, exploiting the full range of learners' linguistic and physical resources.

It must be emphasised that this expansive, creative model of English should not be regarded as the preserve of younger learners or students in non-examination classes. In Chapters 5 and 6 we give examples of integrating a drama-in-English approach into advanced level literary study. The large North London sixth form centre that hosted our PGCE Shakespeare workshops for a number of years has, in the words of the then head of English Literature, 'a deep commitment to the view that the language of literature – and I mean just about any literary text – is inextricably linked to actions, and if our students can insert themselves into the unfolding *activity* of the text we know that they'll bring their own insights and feelings into their study'. For the team of 'A' Level English specialist teachers, drama-based approaches form a day-to-day part of their classroom practice, including the use of re-creative writing, 'as a further way of grappling with the dynamics of literary texts'.

The flexibility of role

The important thing for English teachers to remember is that drama-in-English work is about *learning*, not acting. Enactment as a concept provides a key to understanding ways in which reading and writing may be brought alive in an English classroom, and in-role work is a central component of this process. Not only does role facilitate entry into a fictional world with remarkable speed and efficiency, it can also serve to heighten learners' critical awareness, particularly when the dramatic action is carefully framed. As we suggest in Chapter 4, the immense flexibility of role represents its unique pedagogic strength, whether as part of responding to a pre-text, generating moments of insight during reading, or looking back once the reading is completed. In its most obvious form, role-play might entail the inhabiting of a well-drawn character from a fiction; on the other hand, it might involve a more symbolic way of working, perhaps through the embodiment of *ideas* rather than identifiable people, as we demonstrate with the *Frankenstein* activities around Gothic motifs described in Chapter 4. The *Beowulf* sequence of learning illustrates the ease with which the teacher might themselves adopt a role. After all, telling and reading stories expressively are a staple feature of English teaching, and in Chapters 4 and 5 we argue that this is only a short step away from teacher-as-narrator and teacher-in-role, neither of which require specialist acting skills, but are simply part of the artistry of being an English teacher – as our student-teachers discovered when exploring how to make hot-seating a meaningful activity with secondary school students. In Naidoo's research (1992), mentioned in Chapter 2, she and the class teacher make effective use of other appropriate adults who are willing to be hot-seated as characters from novels that deal with controversial or sensitive topics. Importantly, in all of these examples students are encouraged to question, interpret and reflect both during and following the in-role activity.

Adopting others' gestures, mannerisms and voices forms a natural part of humans' communicative repertoire, and above all, we have emphasised the everyday quality of being in role. As we indicate in Chapter 7, on one occasion we were fascinated to observe a small group of student-teachers responding to viewing themselves on-screen by spontaneously embodying each other's roles. This example suggests that adopting a role carries differing degrees of intentionality. Elsewhere in our research, whether working with adults or in schools, we have routinely noted the ease with which learners take up roles when invited to do so, sometimes prompted by a simple but carefully selected prop or even a length of coloured fabric. Furthermore, as the student-teachers in Chapter 4 discovered, engaging adolescent learners in creating their own role-related artefacts represents a logical extension of the kinds of re-creative activities that constitute everyday English classrooms, helping to bridge the experiential spaces between the students' own lives and those of characters in a text. More broadly, the range of personal and cultural resources learners draw on when being in role help to enrich their encounter with literary texts that might otherwise remain impersonal and inert. O'Toole and Dunn (2020, p. 3) express it in this way:

> Embodying and animating the text in order to bring it off the page works for all literature, since it is always about human beings and their relationships – in a truism, it illuminates the human condition and its world of ideas. And the human condition includes bodies and senses and emotions and instincts, not just words about them.

One of the Year 11 students we invited to reflect upon their experiences of drama-based English lessons told us that it had helped him take up an 'attitude' to each of his GCSE Literature texts, an independence of thought which he believed would stand him in good stead when taking his final examinations. We suggest that the *Stone Cold* activity we describe in Chapter 5 provides a good illustration of how this might work in practice: adopting the role of the undercover journalist in the novel requires students to ask probing questions, gain a range of opinions regarding characters and events, and, ultimately, consider how they position themselves in relation to their written investigative report. At the same time as immersing learners in the imaginative world of the text, this activity demands a high level of critical inquiry.

Inclusive practice

Drama-in-English offers an inherently inclusive way of working. The degree to which in-role work can motivate and critically engage a wide and diverse range of secondary-aged students is a discovery that pleasantly surprised our group of student-teachers (see Chapter 4), an insight, we should emphasise, that is amply supported by our own observation and interview data collected over many years. Not only does in-role activity offer rich opportunity to open up spaces within which learners can bring their own experiences and understandings to bear on the matter in hand, it encourages them to read and understand the signs of each other's bodies and facial interactions more readily. As Year 11 student Joel suggests in Chapter 5, this can provide a conduit to expressive writing. Importantly, process drama also makes demands on learners to 'imagine themselves differently, to re-frame or to re-create themselves as "others"' (Neelands 2011, p. 170), and thus expands their horizons of experience beyond what they already know and recognise.

As we argued in Chapter 1, we are committed to a vision of English that takes account of a broad range of cultural traditions. However, working in the context of policy-driven emphases on canonised forms of knowledge, national identity and the assimilation of difference, it becomes all the more important for English teachers to work in ways that start with their students, enabling learners to discover for themselves personal points of contact with all aspects of the English curriculum. As we indicated in relation to teaching Shakespeare, this is not the same as seeking out an illusory universal relevance; instead, by using drama to 'read from the inside out', it is possible to open up dialogic spaces within which a plurality of meanings can be made and contested.

Enabling students to draw on their knowledge of popular culture facilitates a productive, critical interplay between the formal disciplinary knowledge of school and the informal experiential knowledge learners acquire in their lives outside of school. For example, for the students exploring *Haroun and the Sea of Stories* (in Chapter 7) their existing knowledge of folk tales and films helped them to develop an understanding of magical realism, shaping the inventive ways they crafted their films. In other research projects we have observed students of South Asian heritage drawing on their familiarity with popular Hindi-language films, for instance in carefully selecting a specific shot-type (Potter and Bryer 2017), or in considering how *Macbeth* is structured (Coles 2020).

Drama-based re-creations of key moments in literary texts offer a valuable strategy for raising questions about representation and exposing assumptions that might otherwise remain hidden. The account we give of the *Beowulf* project in Chapters 5 and 7 indicates the ways in which meanings change when point of view is flipped, in this instance from the conventional perspective of the male warrior-hero to that of the grieving mother, and how that plays out either in written first-person accounts or the subsequent combat episode when re-creating it in the format of an edited film. Providing 'A' Level students the opportunity to 'write back' in role as Goneril helps them construct the beginnings of a feminist reading of *King Lear*.

As alluded to in Chapter 7, the use of voice-overs to accompany a short film or series of stills offers opportunities for students to combine linguistic features of the source text with their own language(s), what might be called 'the reader in the voice-over', to misquote Barrs and Cork (2001). Thus, the students creating *Haroun* films reaped obvious enjoyment from blending Rushdie's dry, witty style with their own voices; student-teachers threaded Old English words and kenning-like phrases into their various *Beowulf* commentaries; and one of the Year 9 students taking part in the wider *Beowulf* project created a bilingual voice-over (in Kurdish and English) as part of his videogame adaptation (see Burn et al. 2016).

A key advantage of the drama-in-English classroom experience is its capacity to appeal to a wide spectrum of learner dispositions, encouraging students individually to take ownership of their work through collaborative engagement.

Working multimodally in English

English, drama and media represent three interrelated domains, yet there remain what Franks, Durran and Burn (2006, p. 65) identify as 'legacy traces' stubbornly ascribing a hierarchy of curricular and cultural worth. Nowhere is this more apparent than in the 2014 revision of the National Curriculum in England which fetishises traditional forms of printed text almost to the total exclusion of other modes of communication. Indeed, Burnett and colleagues (2014) suggest that this is an international phenomenon associated with systems of accountability in relation to literacy education. Assessment frameworks have tended to ignore learners' complex engagements with digital media, so that 'there is a real danger of reducing meaning-making to a set of relatively simple skills that are easy to assess' (p. 158).

The *Beowulf* project exemplifies the benefits of integrating English, drama and media in such a way as to enable the three domains to 'cast new light on each other's special ability to tell the tale, involve the audience, represent the world, spin fantasies, dramatise ethical conflict' (Burn 2022, p. 56). In our two-day workshop with student-teachers we explored ways in which a piece of canonical literature could be adapted successfully through the media of drama, film, game and creative writing in the form of *skaldic* poetry. In discovering the narrative possibilities each mode afforded, the project revealed unexpected connections, most noticeably highlighting the pliable properties of role and its capacity to illuminate the significance of narrative perspective in different versions. Across the various stages of the project, the participants' own roles shifted between audience, producer, storyteller and player, expanding what it means to be an active reader of texts. As McCallum (2012, p. 63) argues, the value of this kind of re-creative activity lies in helping students 'take control of learning, refashioning texts in keeping with their own worlds and world views', opening up a dialogic relationship between the source text, the reader and the newly created, co-authored piece.

Playfulness and enjoyment

Back in 1981, lamenting the direction of educational policy under Thatcher's Conservative government, Harold Rosen observed in his inaugural professorial lecture that '"The pleasure of the text"' was being 'appropriated and turned to ashes. Like so many other things, children are not to be trusted with it' (2017b, p. 77). His words resonate afresh all these decades later. Across the preceding chapters we have drawn attention to play and pleasure as important elements in the learning process. Common to both play and in-role activity is an imaginative and motivating form of pedagogy that can be used to draw participants deftly and quickly into a fictional world. In Chapter 6 we give the example of a teacher who used play as a disarmingly free prelude to risky and demanding explorations of sexuality in *A Midsummer Night's*

Dream. Far from creating a distraction from the serious business of rigorous study, it became clear that, in fact, the teacher had very high expectations of her 12-year-old students personally, emotionally and intellectually. Of course, in most circumstances, playfulness and enjoyment go hand in hand. Whilst Vygotsky does not regard pleasure as 'the defining characteristic of play' (1978, p. 92), he nevertheless recognises its effectiveness in motivating and incentivising the type of '"good learning"' that is always 'in advance of development' (p. 89). Given the body of evidence that suggests young people in England are not as enthusiastic about reading as they might be (McGrane et al. 2017; OECD 2018), we propose reading through drama as an approach which supports criticality *and* enjoyment. On one level, we are invoking reception theory notions of textual playfulness; on the other, we are seeking opportunities to exploit learners' inclination to share a joke with an audience of their peers, such as when one group of student-teachers wittily located Grendel's Mother's underwater lair in the university's rather dank basement toilets (see Coles et al. 2021).

The heart of English

What kind of English teachers we want to be is bound up with how we see our subject. A passion for literature is often cited as justification for becoming an English teacher by new entrants to the profession. To that we would add the love of talking about texts, enjoyment in making our own texts and pleasure in using language creatively, to name but a few. Words like 'passion', 'love' and 'enjoyment' suggest that the affective and personal aspects of English are as important as the intellectual; indeed, as Vygotsky argues, art, literature and the fostering of imagination should be regarded as absolutely fundamental to the well-being of society as a whole.

Transmission models of teaching are antithetical to this vision of English. We need a classroom pedagogy that recognises – and does justice to – reading and writing as complex, socio-cultural processes, and which releases English from its utilitarian constraints. Conversations about texts, the language of texts and how we make and re-make meanings are at the core of our subject. Caroline Daly (2004, p. 196) suggests that effective English teachers 're-invent every time they teach the same poem'. This is what Daly calls 'the intellectual creativity of teaching', a notion that underpins our drama-in-English approach. The examples of practice we describe in the pages of this book make clear that English teachers already have the professional resources to work in this way, but frustrated by policy and institutional pressures may feel unable to engage fully with the English that they came into the profession to teach.

Our English is about so much more than 'knowledge'. Our English is a creative, imaginative, interactive and deeply humane subject that, with drama at its heart, affords students the communicative resources to make sense of their lives and their worlds, and gives them the agency to shape their futures.

Note

1 Little of the peer-reviewed research cited by the authors in support of Ofsted's position is specific to secondary English: see www.englishandmedia.co.uk/blog/review-of-ofsted-curriculum-research-review-english

REFERENCES

Adichie, C. N. (2009). *The Danger of a Single Story*, TED Talk. Retrieved from www. ted.com/talks/chimamanda_ngozi_adichie_the_danger_of_a_single_story

Alexander, R. (2004). Still no pedagogy? Principle, pragmatism and compliance in primary education. *Cambridge Journal of Education*, **34**(1), 8–33.

Alford, S. (2013). *The Watchers: A Secret History of the Reign of Elizabeth I*, London: Penguin Books.

Anderson, G. (2013). Exploring 'The Island': Mapping the shifting sands in the landscape of English classroom culture and pedagogy. *Changing English*, **20**(2), 113–123.

Anderson, M. (2003). Beginning secondary Drama and English teaching. *English Teaching: Practice and Critique*, **2**(1), 43–53.

Anderson, M. (2012). *MasterClass in Drama Education: Transforming Teaching and Learning*, London and New York: Continuum.

Anderson, M., Hughes, J., & Manuel, J. (eds.). (2008). *Drama and English Teaching: Imagination, Action and Engagement*, Sydney, Aus: Oxford University Press.

Anderson, M., & Jefferson, M. (2009). *Teaching the Screen: Film Education for Generation Next*, Crows Nest, NSW: Allen & Unwin.

Andrews, R. (2001). *Teaching and Learning English: A Guide to Recent Research and its Applications*, London and New York: Continuum.

Arts Council England. (2003). *Drama in Schools*, 2nd edn, London: Arts Council England.

Banks, F. (2014). *Creative Shakespeare: The Globe Education Guide to Practical Shakespeare*, London: Bloomsbury.

Barnes, D. R. (1968). *Drama in the English Classroom*, Champaign, Illinois: NCTE.

Barnes, D. R. (1976). *From Communication to Curriculum*, Harmondsworth: Penguin.

Barrs, M. (1980). Introduction. In *Drama as Context*, Aberdeen: National Association for the Teaching of English, pp. 1–3.

Barrs, M. (1987). Voice and role in reading and writing. *Language Arts*, **64**(2), 8–11.

Barrs, M. (2000). The reader in the writer. *Reading* (July), 54–60.

Barrs, M. (2022). *Vygotsky the Teacher: A Companion to his Psychology for Teachers and Other Practitioners*, London and New York: Routledge.

Barrs, M., & Cork, V. (2001). *The Reader in the Writer: The Links Between the Study of Literature and Writing Development at Key Stage 2*, London: Centre for Language in Primary Education.

Batho, R. (1998). Shakespeare in secondary schools. *Educational Review*, **50**(2), 163–172.

Bishop, R. S. (2012). Reflections on the development of African American children's literature. *Journal of Children's Literature*, **38**(2), 5–13.

Blake, J., & Shortis, T. (2010). *Who's Prepared to Teach School English?* London: Committee for Linguistics in Education.

Boal, A. (1995). *The Rainbow of Desire: The Boal Method of Theatre and Therapy*, London and New York: Routledge.

Boal, A. (2008). *Theatre of the Oppressed*, translated from Spanish by C. A. McBride, M.-O. L. McBride & E. Fryer, New edn, London: Pluto Press.

Bolton, G. (1998). *Acting in Classroom Drama*, Stoke on Trent: Trentham Books.

Bolton, G. (2007). A history of Drama education: A search for substance. In L. Bresler, ed., *International Handbook of Research in Arts Education*, Dordrecht: Springer, pp. 45–61.

Bolton, G., & Heathcote, D. (1997). Dorothy Heathcote reflects with Gavin Bolton. In D. Davis, ed., *Interactive Research in Drama in Education*, Stoke on Trent: Trentham Books, pp. 7–40.

Bomford, K. (2022). Critical or creative? The creature writes to Victor Frankenstein. *Changing English*, **29**(4), 421–439.

Booth, D., & Neelands, J. (eds.). (1998). *Reading, Writing and Role-Playing across the Curriculum*, Hamilton, Ontario: Caliburn Enterprises.

Bourdieu, P., & Passeron, J.-C. (1990). *Reproduction in Education, Society and Culture*, London: SAGE.

Bousted, M., & Ozturk, A. (2004). 'It came alive outside my head'. Developing literacies through comparison: The reading of classic text and moving image. *Literacy*, **38**(1), 52–57.

Bowell, P. (2006). The Drama teacher in time plays many parts. *Drama: One Forum – Many Voices*, **13**(2), 24–29.

Brady, L. (2009). 'Shakespeare reloaded': Teacher professional development within a collaborative learning community. *Teacher Development*, **13**(4), 335–348.

Brady, M. (2014). On being (and not being) Mrs Curley's wife. *Changing English*, **21**(4), 334–347.

Bruner, J. (1986). *Actual Minds, Possible Worlds*, Cambridge, Massachusetts: Harvard University Press.

Bryer, T. (2013). An audience for the aliens. *Changing English*, **20**(3), 253–265.

Bryer, T. (2019). Working with digital technologies. In J. Davison & C. Daly, eds., *Learning to Teach English in the Secondary School: A Companion to School Experience*, 5th edn, Abingdon: Routledge, pp. 135–151.

Bryer, T. (2020). *What Are the Affordances of Role in Learning through Transmedia Forms of Pedagogy?* (PhD), University College London.

Bryer, T., & Coles, J. (2022). Re-animation: Multimodal discourse around text. *Literacy*, **56**(2), 150–159.

Bryer, T., Lindsay, M., & Wilson, R. (2014). A take on a gothic poem: Tablet film-making and literary texts. *Changing English*, **21**(3), 235–251.

Buckingham, D., Grahame, J., & Sefton-Green, J. (1995). *Making Media: Practical Production in Media Education*, London: English and Media Centre.

Bundy, P., Piazzoli, E., & Dunn, J. (2016). Sociocultural theory, process drama and second language learning. In S. Davis, B. Ferholt, H. Grainger-Clemson, S.-M. Jansson, & A. Marjanovic-Shane, eds., *Dramatic Interactions in Education: Vygotskian and Sociocultural Approaches to Drama, Education and Research*, London and New York: Bloomsbury, pp. 153–170.

Bunyan, P., Catron, J., Harrison, L., McEvoy, S., Moore, R., Welburn, B., & Williams, J. (1998). *Position Paper: Drama*, Sheffield: NATE.

Burgess, S., Rawal, S., & Taylor, E. (2022). *Characterising Effective Teaching*, London: The Nuffield Foundation. Retrieved from www.nuffieldfoundation.org/project/characterising-effective-teaching-2

Burn, A. (2007). The place of digital video in the curriculum. In R. Andrews & C. Haythornthwaite, eds., *The Sage Handbook of E-Learning Research*, London: SAGE, pp. 504–524.

Burn, A. (2022). *Literature, Videogames and Learning*, Abingdon: Routledge.

Burn, A., Bryer, T., & Coles, J. (2016). Playing Beowulf: Bringing literature, drama, media and computing together in English for the new curriculum. *Teaching English*, **12**, 63–69.

Burn, A., & Durran, J. (2006). Digital anatomies: Analysis as production in media education. In D. Buckingham & R. Willett, eds., *Digital Generations: Children, Young People and New Media*, Mahwah, New Jersey: Lawrence Erlbaum Associates, pp. 273–293.

Burn, A., & Durran, J. (2007). *Media Literacy in Schools: Practice, Production and Progression*, London: Paul Chapman.

Burn, A., & Parker, D. (2003). *Analysing Media Texts*, London and New York: Continuum.

Burnett, C. (2015). Investigating children's interactions around digital texts in classrooms: How are these framed and what counts? *Education 3–13*, **43**(2), 197–208.

Burnett, C., Davies, J., Merchant, G., & Rowsell, J. (eds.). (2014). *New Literacies around the Globe: Policy and Pedagogy*, Abingdon and New York: Routledge.

Burnett, C., & Merchant, G. (2016). Boxes of poison: Baroque technique as antidote to simple views of literacy. *Journal of Literacy Research*, **48**(3), 258–279.

Byron, K. (1986). *Drama in the English Classroom*, London and New York: Methuen.

Caldwell Cook, H. (1919). *The Play Way: An Essay in Educational Method*, 2nd edn, New York: Frederick A Stokes Company.

Cameron, D., Anderson, M., Wotzko, R., Brater, E., & Batty-Taylor, M. (2017). *Drama and Digital Arts Cultures*, London: Bloomsbury Methuen Drama.

Cannon, M. (2018). *Digital Media in Education: Teaching, Learning and Literacy Practices with Young Learners*, London: Palgrave Macmillan.

Cannon, M., Potter, J., & Burn, A. (2018). Dynamic, playful and productive literacies. *Changing English*, **25**(2), 180–197.

Carroll, J. (2002). Digital drama: A snapshot of evolving forms. *Melbourne Studies in Education*, **43**(2), 130–141.

Chance, J. (2002). The structural unity of Beowulf: The problem of Grendel's Mother. In D. Donoghue, ed., *'Beowulf': A Verse Translation. Norton Critical Edition*, London: Norton, pp. 152–166.

Chetty, D. (2017). You can't say that! Stories have to be about white people. In N. Shukla, ed., *The Good Immigrant*, London: Unbound, pp. 96–107.

Clarke, M., Shore, A., Rhoades, K., Abrams, L., Miao, J., & Li, J. (2003). *Perceived Effects of State-Mandated Testing Programs on Teaching and Learning: Findings from Interviews with Educators in Low-, Medium- and High-Stakes States*, Chestnut Hill, Massachusetts: National Board on Educational Testing and Public Policy.

Clarke, S., Dickenson, P., & Westbrooke, J. (eds.). (2010). *The Complete Guide to Becoming an English Teacher*, 2nd edn, London: SAGE.

Coles, J. (1991). *Teaching 'Shakespeare'* (Unpublished MA Dissertation), University of London Institute of Education.

Coles, J. (1996). Will it all end in tiers? Shakespeare in the National Curriculum. In M. Simons, ed., *Where We've Been: Articles from the English & Media Magazine*, London: English & Media Centre, pp. 61–66.

Coles, J. (2009). Testing Shakespeare to the limit: Teaching Macbeth in a Year 9 classroom. *English in Education*, **43**(1), 32–49.

Coles, J. (2013a). *Constructions of Shakespeare in the Secondary Curriculum* (PhD), Kings College, University of London.

Coles, J. (2013b). 'Every child's birthright'? Democratic entitlement and the role of canonical literature in the English National Curriculum. *Curriculum Journal*, **24**(1), 50–66.

Coles, J. (2015). Teaching Shakespeare with film adaptations. In S. Brindley & B. Marshall, eds., *MasterClass in English Education: Transforming Teaching and Learning*, London and New York: Bloomsbury Academic.

Coles, J. (2020). Wheeling out the big guns: The literary canon in the English classroom. In J. Davison & C. Daly, eds., *Debates in English Teaching*, 2nd edn, Abingdon: Routledge, pp. 103–117.

Coles, J., & Bryer, T. (2018). Reading as enactment: Transforming Beowulf through drama, film and computer game. *English in Education*, **52**(1), 54–66.

Coles, J., Bryer, T., & Ferreira, D. (2021). Beowulf goes to school: Adaptations and transformations for the secondary classroom. In S. C. Thomson, ed., *Medieval Stories and Storytelling: Multimedia and Multi-Temporal Perspectives*, Turnhout: Brepols, pp. 31–53.

Coles, J., & Pitfield, M. (2006). Routes into English teaching: Beginning teachers' reflections on college-based and school-based Initial Teacher Education programmes. *Changing English*, **13**(3), 283–292.

Coles, J., & Pitfield, M. (2022a). Reading Shakespeare from the inside out. *Teaching English*, **29**, 22–26.

Coles, J., & Pitfield, M. (2022b). *Reading Shakespeare through Drama: Elements in Shakespeare Pedagogy*, Cambridge: Cambridge University Press.

Cox, C. B. (1991a). *Cox on Cox: An English Curriculum for the 1990s*, London: Hodder and Stoughton.

Cox, C. B. (1991b). Editorial. *Critical Quarterly*, **32**(4), 1–6.

Cox, C. B., & Dyson, A. E. (eds.). (1969). *A Black Paper: Fight for Education*, London: Critical Quarterly Society.

Cremin, T., Goouch, K., Blakemore, L., Goff, E., & Macdonald, R. (2006). Connecting drama and writing: Seizing the moment to write. *Research in Drama Education*, **11**(3), 273–291.

Crumpler, T., & Schneider, J. (2002). Writing with their whole being: A cross study analysis of children's writing from five classrooms using process drama. *Research in Drama Education*, **7**(1), 61–79.

Csikszentmihalyi, M. (1997). *Finding Flow: The Psychology of Engagement with Everyday Life*, New York: Basic Books.

Cunningham, P., & Yamasaki, Y. (2018). Space and time in the creative curriculum: Drama and education in two island nations in the early twentieth century. *Espacio, Tiempo y Educación*, **5**(2), 11–33.

Cushing, I. (2022). Word rich or word poor? Deficit discourses, raciolinguistic ideologies and the resurgence of the 'word gap' in England's education policy. *Critical Inquiry in Language Studies*. Retrieved from www.tandfonline.com/doi/epdf/10.1 080/15427587.2022.2102014

Cziboly, A., Lyngstad, M. B., & Zheng, S. (2022). The influence of the 'conventions approach' on the practice of drama in different cultures. In M. McAvoy & P. O'Connor, eds., *The Routledge Companion to Drama in Education*, London: Routledge, pp. 94–109.

Daly, C. (2004). Trainee English teachers and the struggle for subject knowledge. *Changing English*, **11**(1), 189–204.

Daniels, K. (2014). Cultural agents creating texts: A collaborative space adventure. *Literacy*, **48**(2), 103–111.

Davis, D. (1998). An appreciation of Gavin Bolton's 'Acting in Classroom Drama' – by way of a foreword. In G. Bolton, *Acting in Classroom Drama*, Stoke on Trent: Trentham Books, pp. IX–XXI.

Davison, J., & Daly, C. (eds.). (2019). *Learning to Teach English in the Secondary School: A Companion to School Experience*, 5th edn, London and New York: Routledge.

Davison, J., & Daly, C. (eds.). (2020). *Debates in English Teaching*, 2nd edn, London: Routledge.

Day, C., Kington, A., Stobart, G., & Sammons, P. (2006). The personal and professional selves of teachers: Stable and unstable identities. *British Educational Research Journal*, **32**(4), 601–616.

DeMichele, M. (2015). Improv and ink: Increasing individual writing fluency with collaborative improv. *International Journal of Education & the Arts*, **16**(10), 1–25.

DES. (1975). *A Language for Life ('The Bullock Report')*, London: HMSO.

DES. (1986). *English from 5 to 16: Curriculum Matters 1*, London: HMSO.

DES. (1990). *English in the National Curriculum (No. 2)*, London: HMSO.

DES/Welsh Office. (1989). *English for Ages 5–16 ('The Cox Report')*, London: HMSO.

DfE. (2011/2021). *Teachers' Standards*. Retrieved from www.gov.uk/government/publications/teachers-standards

DfE. (2014). *The National Curriculum in England: English Programmes of Study*. Retrieved from www.gov.uk/government/publications/national-curriculum-in-england-english-programmes-of-study

DfEE. (2001). *Key Stage 3 National Strategy Framework for Teaching English: Years 7, 8 and 9*, London: DfEE Publications.

DfEE/QCA. (1999). *The National Curriculum for England: English*, London: DfEE Publications.

DfES. (2003). *Key Stage 3 National Strategy Drama Objectives Bank*, London: DfES Publications.

Doecke, B. (2015). Storytelling and professional learning. *Changing English*, **22**(2), 142–156.

Doecke, B. (2017). What kind of 'knowledge' is English? (Re-reading the Newbolt Report). *Changing English*, **24**(3), 230–245.

Doecke, B., & McClenaghan, D. (2011). *Confronting Practice: Classroom Investigations into Language and Learning*, Putney, NSW: Phoenix Education.

Dunn, J., Harden, A., & Marino, S. (2013). Drama and writing: Overcoming the hurdle of the blank page. In M. Anderson & J. Dunn, eds., *How Drama Activates Learning: Contemporary Research and Practice*, London: Bloomsbury Academic, pp. 245–259.

Dunn, J., & Jones, A. (2022). Dramatic approaches in the English classroom: Embodied, agentic and aesthetic learning. In M. McAvoy & P. O'Connor, eds., *The Routledge Companion to Drama in Education*, Abingdon and New York: Routledge, pp. 310–323.

Dymoke, S. (2002). The dead hand of the exam: The impact of the NEAB Anthology on poetry teaching at GCSE. *Changing English*, **9**(1), 85–93.

Dyson, A. H. (1993). *Social Worlds and Children Learning to Write in an Urban Primary School*, New York: Teachers College Press.

Eaglestone, R. (2020). 'Powerful knowledge', 'cultural literacy', and the study of literature in schools. Retrieved from https://onlinelibrary.wiley.com/doi/10.1111/2048-416X.2020.12006.x

Edmiston, B. (2003). What's my position: Role, frame and positioning when using process drama. *Research in Drama Education*, **8**(2), 221–229.

Edmiston, B., & Enciso, P. (2002). Reflections and refractions of meaning: Dialogic approaches to reading with classroom drama. In J. Flood, D. Lapp, J. R. Squire, & J. M. Jensen, eds., *Handbook of Research on Teaching the English Language Arts*, Mahwah, New Jersey: Lawrence Erlbaum, pp. 868–880.

Elliott, V. (2014). The treasure house of a nation? Literary heritage, curriculum and devolution in Scotland and England in the twenty-first century. *Curriculum Journal*, **25**(2), 282–300.

Elliott, V. (2021). *Knowledge in English: Canon, Curriculum and Cultural Literacy*, Abingdon and New York: Routledge.

Elliott, V., & Olive, S. (2021). Secondary Shakespeare in the UK: What gets taught and why? *English in Education*, **55**(2), 102–115.

Ellis, V. (2007). Taking subject knowledge seriously: From professional knowledge recipes to complex conceptualizations of teacher development. *Curriculum Journal*, **18**(4), 447–462.

The English Association. (1908). *The Teaching of Shakespeare in Schools*, Oxford: The English Association.

The English Centre. (1985). *The Island*, London: ILEA English Centre.

Eriksson, S. (2011). Distancing. In S. Schonmann, ed., *Key Concepts in Theatre/Drama Education*, Rotterdam: Sense Publishers, pp. 65–71.

Evans, M. (1989). *Signifying Nothing: Truth's True Contexts in Shakespeare's Text*, London: Harvester Wheatsheaf.

Fellowes, A. (2001). *Bilingual Shakespeare: A Practical Approach for Teachers*, Stoke on Trent and Sterling: Trentham Books.

Findlay, K. (2006). Context and learning factors in the development of teacher identity: A case study of Newly Qualified Teachers during their induction year. *Journal of In-Service Education*, **32**(4), 511–532.

Finlay-Johnson, H. (1911). *The Dramatic Method of Teaching*, Boston, New York, Chicago and London: The Athenaeum Press/Ginn and Company.

Fleer, M. (2014). *Theorising Play in the Early Years*, Cambridge: Cambridge University Press.

Fleming, M. (2011). Learning in and through the Arts. In J. Sefton-Green, P. Thomson, K. Jones, & L. Bresler, eds., *The Routledge International Handbook of Creative Learning*, London and New York: Routledge, pp. 177–185.

Fleming, M., & Stevens, D. (2015). *English Teaching in the Secondary School: Linking Theory and Practice*, 4th edn, Abingdon: Routledge.

Flower, A. (1931). Making Shakespeare live. *The New Era*, **12**, 81–83.

Franks, A. (1996). Drama education, the body and representation (or, the mystery of the missing bodies). *Research in Drama Education*, **1**(1), 105–119.

Franks, A. (1997). Drama, desire and schooling: Drives to learning in creative and expressive school subjects. *Changing English*, **4**(1), 131–147.

Franks, A. (1999). Where the action is: How drama contributes to the art of teaching and learning in English. *English in Education*, **33**(2), 39–49.

Franks, A. (2014). Drama and the representation of affect: Structures of feeling and signs of learning. *Research in Drama Education*, **19**(2), 1–13.

Franks, A. (2015). How environment affects learning: School teachers engaging with theatre-based pedagogies. In S. Davis, B. Ferholt, H. Grainger Clemson, S. M. Jansson, & A. Marjanovic-Shane, eds., *Dramatic Interactions in Education: Vygotskian and Sociocultural Approaches to Drama, Education and Research*, London: Bloomsbury, pp. 229–244.

Franks, A., & Bryer, T. (2019). Drama in teaching and learning English. In J. Davison & C. Daly, eds., *Learning to Teach English in the Secondary School: A Companion to School Experience*, 5th edn, London and New York: Routledge, pp. 152–165.

Franks, A., Durran, J., & Burn, A. (2006). Stories of the three-legged stool: English, media, drama, from critique to production. *English in Education*, **40**(1), 64–79.

Franks, A., Thomson, P., Hall, C., & Jones, K. (2014). Teachers, arts practice and pedagogy. *Changing English*, **21**(2), 171–181.

Freebody, P., (2020). Foreword: 'Important news about herself' and the drama of what matters. In *Stand Up For Literature: Dramatic Approaches in the Secondary English Classroom*, Sydney, NSW: Currency Press, pp. viii–ix.

Galloway, S., & Strand, S. (2010). *Creating a Community of Practice: Final Report to the Royal Shakespeare Company's Learning and Performance Network*, Coventry: University of Warwick, CEDAR – Centre for Educational Development, Appraisal and Research.

Gibb, N. (2010). Speech to the Reform Conference. Retrieved from www.gov.uk/government/speeches/nick-gibb-to-the-reform-conference

Gibb, N. (2017). The importance of knowledge-based education. Retrieved from www.gov.uk/government/speeches/nick-gibb-the-importance-of-knowledge-based-education

Gibbons, S. (2008). How L.A.T.E. it was, how L.A.T.E. *English in Education*, 42(2), 118–130.

Gibbons, S. (2013). *The London Association for the Teaching of English 1947–67: A History*, London: IOE Press.

Gibbons, S. (2016). W(h)ither the radicals? *English in Education*, 50(1), 35–43.

Gibbons, S. (2017). *English and Its Teachers: A History of Policy, Pedagogy and Practice*, London and New York: Routledge.

Gibson, R. (ed.). (1990). *Secondary School Shakespeare*, Cambridge: Cambridge Institute of Education.

Gibson, R. (1998). *Teaching Shakespeare*, Cambridge: Cambridge University Press.

Gillham, G. (1974). *Report on Condercum School Project (unpublished)*, Newcastle: Newcastle Upon Tyne LEA.

Glover, M. (2018). The dangling conversation: The location and function of author, text and reader in literary texts. *English in Education*, 52(1), 67–78.

Goffman, E. (1959). *The Presentation of Self in Everyday Life*, London: Penguin Books.

Goffman, E. (1974). *Frame Analysis: An Essay on the Organization of Experience*, Cambridge, Massachusetts: Harvard University Press.

Goodwyn, A. (2010). The status of literature in a national curriculum: A case study of England. *English in Australia*, 45(1), 18–27.

Gordon, J. (2015). *Teaching English in Secondary Schools*, London: SAGE.

Gove, M. (2013a). Michael Gove speaks about the importance of teaching. Retrieved from www.gov.uk/government/speeches/michael-gove-speaks-about-the-importance-of-teaching

Gove, M. (2013b). What does it mean to be an educated person? Presented at the Brighton Conference. Retrieved from www.gov.uk/government/speeches/what-does-it-mean-to-be-an-educated-person.

Graff, G. (1992). *Beyond the Culture Wars: How Teaching the Conflicts Can Revitalize American Education*, New York: W.W. Norton.

Grainger, T., Goouch, K., & Lambirth, A. (2005). *Creativity and Writing: Developing Voice and Verve in the Classroom*, London: Routledge.

Green, A. (2006). University to school: Challenging assumptions in subject knowledge development. *Changing English*, 13(1), 111–123.

Green, A. (ed.). (2011). *Becoming a Reflective English Teacher*, Maidenhead: Open University Press.

Guillory, J. (1993). *Cultural Capital: The Problem of Literary Canon Formation*, London: University of Chicago Press.

Haddon, J. (2009). *Teaching Reading Shakespeare*, Abingdon and New York: Routledge.

Haughey, J. (2012). 'What's past is prologue': *English Journal* routes of a performance-based approach to teaching Shakespeare. *English Journal*, 101(3), 60–65.

Haydock, N., & Risden, E. L. (2013). *Beowulf on Film: Adaptations and Variations*, Jefferson, North Carolina and London: McFarland & Company Publishers.

Heaney, S. (ed.). (2000). *Beowulf [A new translation]*, London: Faber and Faber.

Heathcote, D. (1980). *Drama as Context*, Aberdeen: National Association for the Teaching of English.

Heathcote, D. (1984). Improvisation. In L. Johnson and C. O'Neill, eds., *Dorothy Heathcote: Collected Writings on Education and Drama*, London: Hutchinson, pp. 44–48.

Heathcote, D. (2015a). Notes on signs and portents. In C. O'Neill, ed., *Dorothy Heathcote on Education and Drama: Essential Writings*, Abingdon: Routledge, pp. 79–87.

Heathcote, D. (2015b). Signs and portents. In C. O'Neill, ed., *Dorothy Heathcote in Education and Drama: Essential Writings*, Abingdon: Routledge, pp. 70–78.

Heilbronn, R. (2010a). The nature of practice-based knowledge and understanding. In R. Heilbronn & J. Yandell, eds., *Critical Practice in Teacher Education: A Study of Professional Learning*, London: Institute of Education, Bedford Way Papers, pp. 2–14.

Heilbronn, R. (2010b). The reflective practitioner. In R. Heilbronn & J. Yandell, eds., *Critical Practice in Teacher Education: A Study of Professional Learning*, London: Institute of Education, Bedford Way Papers, pp. 29–38.

Hirsch, E. (1987). *Cultural Literacy: What Every American Needs to Know*, Boston, Massachusetts: Houghton Mifflin.

Hirsch, E. D. (2007). *The Knowledge Deficit: Closing the Shocking Educational Gap for American Children*, Boston, Massachusetts: Houghton Mifflin.

Hodge, B., & Kress, G. R. (1988). *Social Semiotics*, Cambridge: Polity Press in association with Basil Blackwell.

Höglund, H. (2022). The heartbeat of poetry: Student videomaking in response to poetry. *Written Communication*, **39**(2), 276–302.

Holzman, L. (2010). Without creating ZPDs there is no creativity. In M. C. Connery, V. John-Steiner, & A. Marjanovic-Shane, eds., *Vygotsky and Creativity: A Cultural-Historical Approach to Play, Meaning Making and the Arts*, New York: Peter Lang, pp. 27–39.

Hornbrook, D. (1989). *Education and Dramatic Art*, 2nd edn, Abingdon and New York: Routledge.

Hornbrook, D. (1998). The teaching and learning of drama: Introduction. In D. Hornbrook, ed., *On the Subject of Drama*, London and New York: Routledge, pp. 3–5.

Hourd, M. (1940). Dramatization. *The New Era*, **21**, 149–152.

Hourd, M. (1949). *The Education of the Poetic Spirit: A Study of Children's Expression in the English Lesson*, Melbourne, London and Toronto: Heinemann Educational Books.

House of Commons. (2008). *Children Schools and Families – Third Report*, London: House of Commons. Retrieved from https://publications.parliament.uk/pa/cm200708/cmselect/cmchilsch/169/16902.htm

House of Commons. (2009). *Children Schools and Families Committee – Fourth Report: National Curriculum*, London: House of Commons. Retrieved from https://publications.parliament.uk/pa/cm200809/cmselect/cmchilsch/344/34402.htm

Hulson, M. (2006). *Schemes for Classroom Drama*, Stoke on Trent and Sterling: Trentham Books.

Hutcheon, L. (2013). *A Theory of Adaptation*, 2nd edn, London: Routledge.

Hutchings, M. (2015). *Exam Factories? The Impact of Accountability Measures on Children and Young People*, London: National Union of Teachers. Retrieved from www.researchgate.net/publication/309771525_Exam_Factories_The_impact_of_accountability_measures_on_children_and_young_people

Inman, E. (1931). Play-making with eight-to-twelve-year-olds. *The New Era*, **12**, 96–97.

Irish, T. (2011). Would you risk it for Shakespeare? A case study of using active approaches in the English classroom. *English in Education*, **45**(1), 6–19.

Iser, W. (1980). Interaction between text and reader. In S. R. Suleiman & I. Crosman, eds., *The Reader in the Text: Essays on Audience and Interpretation*, Princeton, New Jersey: Princeton University Press, pp. 106–119.

Iser, W. (1989). *Prospecting: From Reader Response to Literary Anthropology*, Baltimore, Maryland and London: The Johns Hopkins University Press.

Jackson, A. (2007). *Theatre, Education and the Making of Meanings: Art or Instrument?* Manchester: Manchester University Press.

Jones, B. D., & Egley, R. J. (2004). Voices from the frontlines: Teachers' perceptions of high-stakes testing. *Education Policy Analysis Archives*, **12**(39). Retrieved from https://files.eric.ed.gov/fulltext/EJ853506.pdf

Jones, K. (1983). *Beyond Progressive Education*, London and Basingstoke: MacMillan Press.

Jones, K. (ed.). (1992). *English and the National Curriculum: Cox's Revolution?* London: Kogan Page in association with the Institute of Education, University of London.

Kana, P., & Aitken, V. (2007). 'She didn't ask me about my Grandma': Using process drama to explore issues of cultural exclusion and educational leadership. *Journal of Educational Administration*, **45**(6), 697–710.

Kempe, A. (2001). Drama as a framework for the development of literacy. *National Foundation for Educational Research (NFER)*, **25**, 1–7.

Kempe, A. (2021). Review: Stand Up for Literature. *Teaching English*, **27**(Autumn), 81.

Kempe, A., & Holroyd, J. (2004). *Speaking, Listening and Drama*, London: David Fulton.

Kidd, D. (2011). The mantle of Macbeth. *English in Education*, **45**(1), 72–85.

Kitchen, J. (2018). *Power of Play: Facilitating Ensemble 'Third Space' for Active Citizenship in Shakespeare Education* (PhD), University of Warwick.

Knights, B. (2015). English studies: A very brief history. In S. Brindley & B. Marshall, eds., *Master Class in English Education: Transforming Teaching and Learning*, London: Bloomsbury, pp. 5–15.

Knights, B., & Thurgar-Dawson, C. (2008). *Active Reading: Transformative Writing in Literary Studies*, London and New York: Continuum.

Kress, G. R. (2010). *Multimodality: A Social Semiotic Approach to Contemporary Communication*, London and New York: Routledge.

Kress, G. R., & van Leeuwen, T. (2001). *Multimodal Discourse: The Modes and Media of Contemporary Communication*, London and New York: Oxford University Press.

Kress, G. R., Jewitt, C., Bourne, J., Franks, A., Hardcastle, J., Jones, K., & Reid, E. (2005). *English in Urban Classrooms: A Multimodal Perspective on Teaching and Learning*, London and New York: RoutledgeFalmer.

Lankshear, C., & Knobel, M. (2011). *New Literacies: Everyday Practices and Social Learning*, Maidenhead: Open University Press. Retrieved from http://site.ebrary.com/lib/academiccompletetitles/home.action

Larson, R., Barton, T. L., Eastman, A. M., Hipps, G. M., Dunning, S., Caldwell, M., Green, J., Hollingsworth, A. M., & Farrell, E. (1976). A statement on the preparation of teachers of English: NCTE Standing Committee on teacher preparation and certification. *English Education*, 7(4), 195–210.

Lawlor, S. (ed.). (2004). *Comparing Standards: Teaching the Teachers. The Report of the Politeia Education Commission*, London: Politeia.

Lee, B. K., Enciso, P., & Austin Theatre Alliance. (2017). The Big Glamorous Monster (or Lady Gaga's Adventures at Sea): Improving student writing through dramatic approaches in schools. *Journal of Literacy Research*, **49**(2), 157–180.

Lee, B. K., Enciso, P., & Brown, M. (2020). The effect of drama-based pedagogies on K-12 literacy-related outcomes: A meta-analysis of 30 years of research. *International Journal of Education & the Arts*, **21**(30), 1–30.

Lee, B. K., Patall, E. A., & Steingut, R. R. (2015). The effect of drama-based pedagogy on pre K-16 outcomes: A meta-analysis of research from 1985 to 2012. *Review of Educational Research*, **85**(1), 3–49.

Lester, J. A. (1926). The active English class: A visit to Caldwell Cook's 'Mummery' at the Perse School, in Cambridge, England. *The English Journal*, **15**(6), 443–449.

Mackey, M. (2007). *Literacies across Media: Playing the Text*, 2nd edn, London: Routledge.

Male, D. A. (1973). *Approaches to Drama*, London: Unwin Educational Books.

Mansell, W. (2022). The creeping growth of Oak's curriculum. *Educate: The Magazine of the National Education Union*, November/December, 35.

Manuel, J., Hughes, J., Anderson, M., & Arnold, R. (2008). Drama and English teaching. In M. Anderson, J. Hughes, & J. Manuel, eds., *Drama and English Teaching: Imagination, Action and Engagement*, Sydney, NSW: Oxford University Press, pp. 1–12.

Marenbon, J. (1987). *English Our English*, London: Centre for Policy Studies.

Marshall, B., Gibbons, S., Haywood, L., & Spencer, E. (2019). *Policy, Belief and Practice in the Secondary English Classroom: A Case-Study Approach from Canada, England and Scotland*, London: Bloomsbury Academic.

Maxwell, J. C. (1967). Foreword. In J. Moffett, *Drama: What Is Happening. The Use of Dramatic Activities in the Teaching of English*, Champaign, Illinois: NCTE, pp. v–vi.

McCallum, A. (2012). *Creativity and Learning in Secondary English: Teaching for a Creative Classroom*, Abingdon: Routledge.

McGrane, J., Stiff, J., Baird, J.-A., Lenkeit, J., & Hopfenbeck, T. (2017). *Progress in International Reading Literacy Study (PIRLS): National Report for England*, London: DfE.

McGregor, L., Tate, M., & Robinson, K. (1977). *Learning through Drama: Schools Council Drama Teaching Project (10–16)*, London: Heinemann Educational Books.

McGuinn, N. (2014). *The English Teacher's Drama Handbook*, Abingdon and New York: Routledge.

McLuskie, K. (2009). Dancing and thinking: Teaching 'Shakespeare' in the twenty-first century. In G. B. Shand, ed., *Teaching Shakespeare: Passing It On*, Chichester: Blackwell, pp. 123–141.

McNaughton, M. J. (1997). Drama and children's writing: A study of the influence of drama on the imaginative writing of primary school children. *Research in Drama Education*, 2(1), 55–86.

Medina, C. L., Perry, M., Lee, B. K., & Deliman, A. (2021). Reading with drama: Relations between texts, readers and experiences. *Literacy*, 55(2), 136–144.

Medway, P., Hardcastle, J., Brewis, G., & Crook, D. (2014). *English Teachers in a Postwar Democracy: Emerging Choice in London Schools, 1945–1965*, Basingstoke: Palgrave Macmillan.

Mills, K. (2016). *Literacy Theories for the Digital Age: Social, Critical, Multimodal, Spatial, Material and Sensory Lenses*, Bristol: Multilingual Matters.

Mills, K., Comber, B., & Kelly, P. (2013). Sensing place: Embodiment, sensoriality, kinesis, and children behind the camera. *English Teaching: Practice and Critique*, 12(2), 11–27.

Moffett, J. (1967). *Drama: What Is Happening. The Use of Dramatic Activities in the Teaching of English*, Champaign, Illinois: NCTE.

Moll, L. C., Amanti, C., Neff, D., & Gonzalez, N. (1992). Funds of knowledge for teaching: Using a qualitative approach to connect homes and classrooms. *Theory into Practice*, 31(2), 132–141.

Montgomerie, D., & Ferguson, J. (1999). Bears don't need phonics: An examination of the role of drama in laying the foundations for critical thinking in the reading process. *Research in Drama Education*, 4(1), 11–20.

Moore, A. (2004). *The Good Teacher: Dominant Discourses in Teaching and Teacher Education*, London: Routledge.

Naidoo, B. (1992). *Through Whose Eyes? Exploring Racism, Reader, Text and Context*, Stoke-on-Trent: Trentham Books.

NASBTT. (2020). *Subject Knowledge for Teaching (SKfT) Framework: A Fresh Look at the Subject Knowledge for Teaching Framework*, 3rd edn, National Association of School-Based Teacher Trainers. Retrieved from www.nasbtt.org.uk/wp-con tent/uploads/2020/03/Subject-Knowledge-for-Teaching-SKfT-Framework-March-2020.pdf

Nash, A., Hewing, W., & Hemming, J. (1979). *School Under Siege (How to Survive 21 Days at School)*, London: ILEA English Centre.

Neelands, J. (1984). *Making Sense of Drama: A Guide to Classroom Practice*, Oxford: Heinemann Educational Books.

Neelands, J. (2004). Remember we are human! Literacy for a pro-human society. *English Drama Media*, 2, 11–17.

Neelands, J. (2008). Common culture: Diversity and power in English/Drama/Media classrooms. *English Drama Media*, 11, 9–15.

Neelands, J. (2010a). Prologue. In P. O'Connor, ed., *Creating Democratic Citizenship through Drama Education: The Writings of Jonothan Neelands*, London: Trentham Books, pp. xiii–xxi.

Neelands, J. (2010b). The meaning of drama. In P. O'Connor, ed., *Creating Democratic Citizenship through Drama Education: The Writings of Jonothan Neelands*, London: Trentham Books, pp. 67–77.

Neelands, J. (2011). Drama as creative learning. In J. Sefton-Green, P. Thomson, K. Jones, & L. Bresler, eds., *The Routledge International Handbook of Creative Learning*, Abingdon: Routledge, pp. 168–176.

Neelands, J., & Goode, T. (2015). *Structuring Drama Work: 100 Key Conventions for Theatre and Drama (Cambridge International Examinations)*, 3rd edn, Cambridge: Cambridge University Press.

Neelands, J., & O'Hanlon, J. (2011). There is some soul of good: An action-centred approach to teaching Shakespeare in schools. In P. Holland, ed., *Shakespeare Survey 64*, Cambridge: Cambridge University Press, pp. 240–250.

Neelands, J., Booth, D., & Ziegler, S. (1993). *Writing in Imagined Contexts: Research into Drama-Influenced Writing*, Toronto: Toronto Board of Education (Ontario) Research Department.

Nelmes, J. (ed.). (2003). *An Introduction to Film Studies*, 3rd edn, London and New York: Routledge.

Nelson-Addy, L. (2020). A journey of discovery: Breaking away from the single story. *Teaching English*, **23**, 35–36.

Newbolt, H. (1921). *The Teaching of English in England ('The Newbolt Report')*, London: HMSO.

Nicholson, H. (2005). *Applied Drama: The Gift of Theatre*, Basingstoke: Palgrave Macmillan.

Nicholson, H. (2011). *Theatre, Education and Performance: The Map and the Story*, Basingstoke and New York: Palgrave Macmillan.

Ntelioglou, B. Y. (2011). 'But why do I have to take this class?' The mandatory drama-ESL class and multiliteracies pedagogy. *Research in Drama Education*, **16**(4), 595–616.

O'Brien, P. (ed.). (1993). *Shakespeare Set Free: Teaching Romeo and Juliet, Macbeth, A Midsummer Night's Dream*, New York: Washington Square Press.

O'Connor, P. (2010). Section one: Making sense of drama. In P. O'Connor, ed., *Creating Democratic Citizenship through Drama Education: The Writings of Jonothan Neelands*, London: Trentham Books, pp. 1–5.

O'Connor, P. (2016). New Zealand vignette. *Research in Drama Education*, **21**(1), 76–77.

OECD. (2018). *PISA: 2018 Results*. Retrieved from www.oecd.org/pisa/publica tions/pisa-2018-results.htm

Ofsted. (2011). *Excellence in English*. Retrieved from www.gov.uk/government/ publications/excellence-in-english

Ofsted. (2012). *Moving English Forward*. Retrieved from www.gov.uk/government/ publications/moving-english-forward

Ofsted. (2022). Research review series: English (23 May). Retrieved from www.gov. uk/government/publications/curriculum-research-review-series-english/curricu lum-research-review-series-english

O'Hanlon, J. (2008). Shakespeare for all? Accessing Shakespeare in English. *English Drama Media*, **10**, 9–14.

Olive, S. (2015). *Shakespeare Valued: Education Policy and Pedagogy 1989–2009*, Bristol: Intellect.

O'Neill, C. (1983). Role-play and text. *The English Magazine*, **11**, 19–21.

O'Neill, C. (1995). *Drama Worlds: A Framework for Process Drama*, Portsmouth, New Hampshire: Heinemann.

O'Neill, C. (2006). Alienation and empowerment. In P. Taylor & C. D. Warner, eds., *Structure and Spontaneity: The Process Drama of Cecily O'Neill*, Stoke on Trent: Trentham Books, pp. 141–149.

O'Neill, C. (2015a). Part I Teachers and teaching: Thresholds of security. In C. O'Neill, ed., *Dorothy Heathcote on Education and Drama: Essential Writings*, Abingdon: Routledge, pp. 18–19.

O'Neill, C. (2015b). Part II Drama in practice: Introduction. In C. O'Neill, ed., *Dorothy Heathcote on Education and Drama: Essential Writings*, Abingdon: Routledge, pp. 37–41.

O'Neill, C., & Lambert, A. (1982). *Drama Structures: A Practical Handbook for Teachers*, London: Hutchinson Education.

O'Neill, C., Lambert, A., Linnell, R., & Warr-Wood, J. (1976). *Drama Guidelines*, London: Heinemann Educational Books/London Drama.

O'Neill, C., & Rogers, T. (1994). Drama and literary response: Prying open the text. *English in Australia*, **108**, 47–51.

O'Toole, J., & Dunn, J. (2020). *Stand Up for Literature: Dramatic Approaches in the Secondary English Classroom*, Sydney, NSW: Currency Press.

Parry, C. (1969). Drama. In D. Thompson, ed., *Directions in the Teaching of English*, London: Cambridge University Press, pp. 138–152.

Parry, C. (1972). *English through Drama: A Way of Teaching*, Cambridge: Cambridge University Press.

Pedulla, J. J., Abrams, L. M., Madaus, G. F., Russell, M. K., Ramos, M. A., & Miao, J. (2003). *Perceived Effects of State-Mandated Testing Programs on Teaching and Learning: Findings from a National Survey of Teachers*, Chestnut Hill, Massachusetts: National Board on Educational Testing and Public Policy.

Perryman, J., Ball, S., Maguire, M., & Braun, A. (2011). Life in the pressure cooker: School league tables and English and Mathematics teachers' responses to accountability in a results-driven era. *British Journal of Educational Studies*, **59**(2), 179–195.

Piazzoli, E. (2011). Process drama: The use of affective space to reduce language anxiety in the additional language learning classroom. *Research in Drama Education*, **16**, 557–574.

Pike, M. (2004). *Teaching Secondary English*, London: SAGE.

Pillay, A. (2021). Talking back to Shakespeare in a South African lecture-room: Engaging in critical conversations about resistance. *Changing English*, **28**(3), 286–295.

Pitfield, M. (2006). Making a crisis out of a drama: The relationship between English and Drama within the English curriculum for ages 11–14. *Changing English*, **13**(1), 97–109.

Pitfield, M. (2011). Re-constructing the relationship between Drama and English: Student-teachers' perspectives at the end of an initial teacher education year. *English in Education*, **45**(1), 52–71.

Pitfield, M. (2020). *Reading through Drama: The Contribution that Drama makes to Teaching and Learning in English* (PhD), University of Nottingham.

Pitfield, M., & Coles, J. (2013). Shaping teachers of Shakespeare: Transformative moments in beginning teachers' practice, Presented at the NATE Annual Conference, Stratford-Upon-Avon.

Pitfield, M., Gilbert, F., Asamoah Boateng, C., & Stanger, C. (2021). Selective amnesia and the political act of remembering English teaching. *Pedagogy, Culture and Society*. https://doi-org.libproxy.ucl.ac.uk/10.1080/14681366.2021.1990988

Potter, J. (2010). Embodied memory and curatorship in children's digital video production. *English Teaching: Practice and Critique*, 9(1), 22–35.

Potter, J., & Bryer, T. (2017). 'Finger flowment' and moving image language: Learning filmmaking with tablet devices. In B. Parry, C. Burnett, & G. Merchant, eds., *Literacy, Media, Technology: Past, Present and Future*, London: Bloomsbury, pp. 111–127.

Prescott, P. (2013). Open-space Shakespeare: Teaching 'Measure for Measure' in three dimensions. *Teaching English*, 1, 63–67.

Protherough, R., & Atkinson, J. (1991). *The Making of English Teachers*, Buckingham: Open University Press.

QCA. (2007). *The National Curriculum 2007*, Coventry: Qualifications and Curriculum Authority.

Quigley, A. (2018). *Closing the Vocabulary Gap*, London: Routledge.

Rajendran, C. (2014). Acting as agency: Re-connecting selves and others in multicultural Singapore. *Theatre, Dance and Performance Training*, 5, 169–180.

Rawson, W. (1931). Outlook tower. *The New Era*, 12, 75–77.

Reynolds, K. (2011). *Children's Literature: A Very Short Introduction*, Oxford: Oxford University Press.

Rosen, H. (2017a). The dramatic mode. In J. Richmond, ed., *Harold Rosen: Writings on Life, Language and Learning, 1958–2008*, London: UCL IOE Press, pp. 314–329.

Rosen, H. (2017b). Neither Bleak House nor Liberty Hall: English in the curriculum. In J. Richmond, ed., *Harold Rosen: Writings on Life, Language and Learning, 1958–2008*, London: UCL IOE Press, pp. 73–89.

Rosen, H. (2017c). The Walworth School English Syllabus. In J. Richmond, ed., *Harold Rosen: Writings on Life, Language and Learning, 1958–2008*, London: UCL IOE Press, pp. 207–219.

Rosenblatt, L. (1994). *The Reader, the Text, the Poem: The Transactional Theory of the Literary Work*, Carbondale, Illinois: Southern Illinois University Press.

Rothstein, R., Jacobsen, R., & Wilder, T. (2008). *Grading Education: Getting Accountability Right*, New York: Teachers' College Press.

RSC. (2016). *The Learning and Performance Network: Final Impact Report 2016*, Stratford: RSC. Retrieved from https://cdn2.rsc.org.uk/sitefinity/education-pdfs/lpn-10-years-of-transforming-experiences-of-shakespeare/the-learning-and-performance-network-final-impact-evaluation-report-2016.pdf?sfvrsn=e3b42921_2

Saunders, J. N., & Ewing, R. A. (2022). 'It lifts up your imagination'. Drama-rich pedagogy, literature and literacy: The School Drama Programme. In M. McAvoy & P. O'Connor, eds., *The Routledge Companion to Drama in Education*, Abingdon and New York: Routledge, pp. 433–449.

Schechner, R. (1988). Playing. *Play and Culture*, 1, 3–9.

Scholes, R. (1985). *Textual Power: Literary Theory and the Teaching of English*, London and New Haven, Connecticut: Yale University Press.

Seely, J. (1976). *In Context: Language and Drama in the Secondary School*, London: Oxford University Press.

Sefton-Green, J. (1995). Neither 'reading' nor 'writing': The history of practical work in media education. *Changing English*, **2**(2), 77–96.

Shapiro, J. (2020). *Shakespeare in a Divided America*, London: Faber & Faber.

Shelton, N. R., & McDermott, M. (2010). Using literature and drama to understand social justice. *Teacher Development: An International Journal of Professional Development*, **14**(1), 123–135.

Shulman, L. S. (1987). Knowledge and teaching: Foundations of the New Reform. *Harvard Educational Review*, **57**(1), 1–22.

Simons, M. (ed.). (1996). *Where We've Been: Articles from the English and Media Magazine*, London: English & Media Centre.

Sinfield, A. (1985). Give an account of Shakespeare and education, showing why you think they are effective and what you have appreciated about them. Support your comments with precise references. In J. Dollimore & A. Sinfield, eds., *Political Shakespeare: New Essays in Cultural Materialism*, Manchester: Manchester University Press, pp. 134–157.

Smith, L. (2023). Top ten texts: A survey of commonly-taught KS3 class readers. *Teaching English*, **23**, 30–33.

Steadman, S. (2020). *The Making of Teachers: A Study of Trainee Teachers' Experiences of Learning to Teach in Different Postgraduate Routes in England* (PhD), King's College London.

Stevens, D., Cliff Hodges, G., Gibbons, S., Hunt, P., & Turvey, A. (2006). Transformations in learning and teaching through Initial Teacher Education. *Literacy*, **40**(2), 97–105.

Stewart, T. T. (2012). English teachers, administrators and dialogue: Transcending the asymmetry of power in the discourse of educational policy. *English Education*, **44**(4), 375–393.

Stinson, M. (2008). Process drama and teaching English to speakers of other languages. In M. Anderson, J. Hughes, & J. Manuel, eds., *Drama and English Teaching: Imagination, Action and Engagement*, Melbourne, VIC: Oxford University Press, pp. 193–212.

Stinson, M., & Piazzoli, E. (2013). Drama for additional language learning: Drama contexts and pedagogical possibilities. In M. Anderson & J. Dunn, eds., *How Drama Activates Learning: Contemporary Research and Practice*, London and New York: Bloomsbury, pp. 208–225.

Stinson, M., & Saunders, N. (2016). Drama in the Australian National Curriculum: Decisions, tensions and uncertainties. *Research in Drama Education*, **21**(1), 93–104.

Stone, B. (1965). Spoken English in the College of Education. *NATE Bulletin: Some Aspects of Oracy*, **II**(2), 34–36.

Stredder, J. (2009). *The North Face of Shakespeare: Activities for Teaching the Plays*, Cambridge: Cambridge University Press.

Taylor, G. (1990). *Reinventing Shakespeare: A Cultural History from the Restoration to the Present*, London: Hogarth Press.

Taylor, R. (2016). The multimodal texture of engagement: Prosodic language, gaze and posture in engaged, creative classroom interaction. *Thinking Skills and Creativity*, **20**, 83–96.

Thew, N. (2006). *Teaching Shakespeare: A Survey of the Undergraduate Level in Higher Education*, London: The Higher Education Academy English Subject Centre.

Thomas, P. (2022). English: Some misconceptions. Reflections on Ofsted's Research Review for English. *Teaching English*, **30**, 64–69.

Thomas, P., & NATE. (2020). Creativity in English: A NATE position paper. *Teaching English*, **23**, 15–17.

Thomson, P., & Hall, C. (2022). Cultural Capitals matter, differentially: A Bourdicusian reading of perspectives from senior secondary students in England. *British Journal of Sociology of Education*, **43**(6), 1–18.

Thomson, P., Hall, C., Jones, K., & Sefton-Green, J. (2012). *The Signature Pedagogies Project: Final Report*, Creativity, Culture and Education. Retrieved from www. creativitycultureeducation.org//wp-content/uploads/2018/10/Signature_Pedagogies_Final_Report_April_2012.pdf

Thomson, P., Hall, C., Thomas, D., Jones, K., & Franks, A. (2010). *A Study of the Learning and Performance Network: An Education Programme of the Royal Shakespeare Company*, Newcastle: Creativity, Culture and Education.

Tolkien, J. R. R. (2002). 'Beowulf': The monsters and the critics. In D. Donoghue, ed., *'Beowulf': A Verse Translation*, London: Norton, pp. 103–130.

Trivedi, P. (2011). 'You taught me language': Shakespeare in India. In P. Holland, ed., *Shakespeare Survey: Volume 64: Shakespeare as Cultural Catalyst*, Cambridge: Cambridge University Press, pp. 231–239.

Turvey, A. (2005). Who'd be an English teacher? *Changing English*, **12**(1), 3–18.

Turvey, A., & Lloyd, J. (2014). Great expectations and the complexities of teacher development. *English in Education*, **48**(1), 76–92.

Vygotsky, L. S. (1931). Imagination and creativity of the adolescent. Retrieved from www.marxists.org/archive/vygotsky/works/1931/adolescent/ch12.htm

Vygotsky, L. S. (1971). *The Psychology of Art*, Cambridge, Massachusetts: MIT Press.

Vygotsky, L. S. (1978). *Mind in Society: The Development of Higher Psychological Processes*, Cambridge, Massachusetts: Harvard University Press.

Vygotsky, L. S. (1986). *Thought and Language*, Cambridge, Massachusetts: MIT Press.

Vygotsky, L. S. (2004). Imagination and creativity in childhood. *Journal of Russian and East European Psychology*, **42**(1), 7–97.

Vygotsky, L. S. (2016). Play and its role in the mental development of the child. *International Research in Early Childhood Education*, 7(2), 3–25.

Wade, B., & Sheppard, J. (1994). How teachers teach Shakespeare. *Educational Review*, **46**(1), 21–28.

Wagner, B. J. (1999). *Dorothy Heathcote: Drama as a Learning Medium*, Revised, Portsmouth, New Hampshire: Heinemann.

Wenger, E. (1999). *Communities of Practice: Learning, Meaning and Identity*, Cambridge: Cambridge University Press.

West, A. (1996). How we live now: LINC, politics and the language police in Toytown LEA. In M. Simons, ed., *Where We've Been: Articles from the English & Media Magazine*, London: The English & Media Centre, pp. 67–81.

Wheale, S. (2022). UK's 'strictest headmistress' fears schools will stop teaching Shakespeare. *The Guardian*, 22 May. Retrieved from https://amp.theguardian.com/education/2022/may/22/uks-strictest-headmistress-fears-schools-will-stop-teaching-shakespeare

Williams, R. (1977). *Marxism and Literature*, Oxford: Oxford University Press.

Williams, R. (1983). Drama in a dramatized society. In *Writing in Society*, London: Verso, pp. 11–21.

Wilson, R. (1997). NATO'S pharmacy: Shakespeare by prescription. In J. Joughin, ed., *Shakespeare and National Culture*, Manchester: Manchester University Press, pp. 58–80.

Winston, J. (2015). *Transforming the teaching of Shakespeare with the Royal Shakespeare Company*, London: Bloomsbury Arden Shakespeare.

Witkin, R. W. (1974). *The Intelligence of Feeling*, London: Heinemann Educational Books.

Wood, D. J., Bruner, J. S., & Ross, G. (1976). The role of tutoring in problem solving. *Journal of Child Psychology and Psychiatry*, **17**(2), 89–100.

Wright, T. (2012). *How to Be a Brilliant English Teacher*, Abingdon: Routledge.

Yandell, J. (1997). Reading Shakespeare, or ways with Will. *Changing English*, **4**(2), 277–294.

Yandell, J. (2014). *The Social Construction of Meaning: Reading Literature in Urban English Classrooms*, London: Routledge.

Yandell, J. (2017). Knowledge, English and the formation of teachers. *Pedagogy, Culture and Society*, **25**(4), 583–599.

Yandell, J., & Brady, M. (2016). English and the politics of knowledge. *English in Education*, **50**(1), 44–59.

Yandell, J., Coles, J., & Bryer, T. (2020). Shakespeare for all? Some reflections on the Globe Theatre's Playing Shakespeare with Deutsche Bank project. *Changing English*, **27**(2), 208–228.

Young, M. (2008). *Bringing Knowledge Back In: From Social Constructivism to Social Realism in the Sociology of Education*, London and New York: Routledge.

INDEX